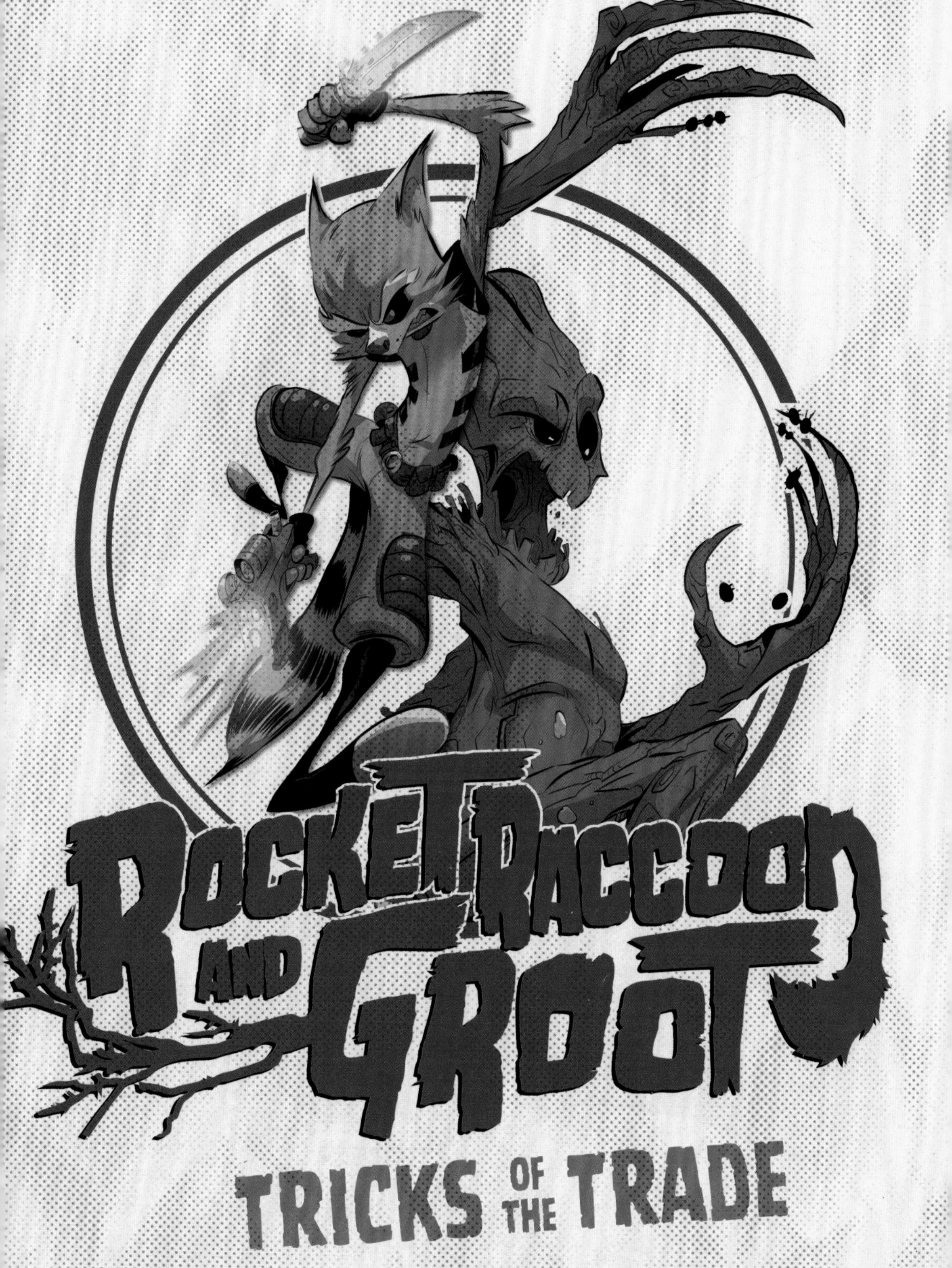

Rocket Raccoon and Groot

Tricks of the Trade

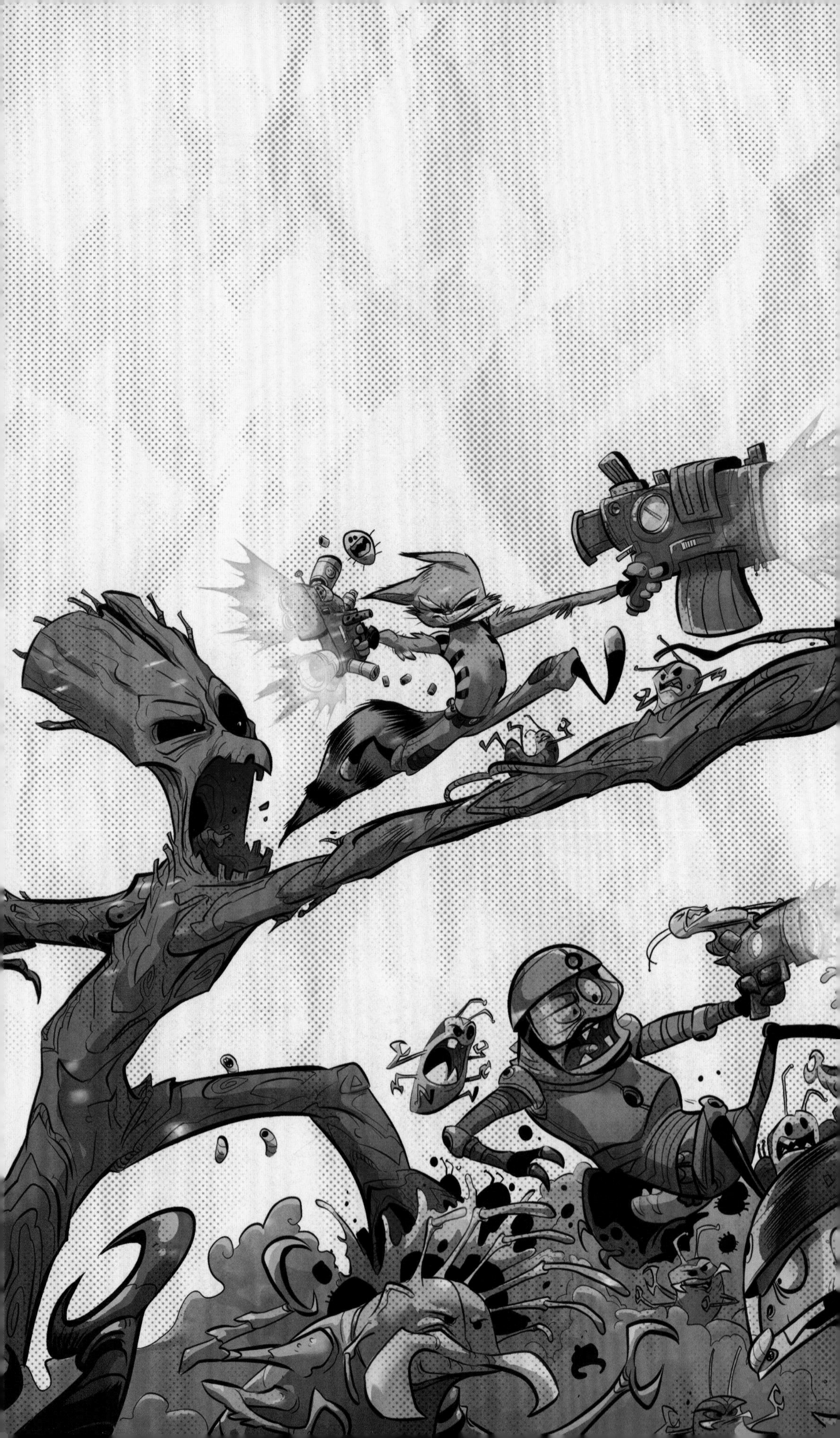

ROCKET RACCOON AND GROOT
TRICKS OF THE TRADE

SKOTTIE YOUNG
WRITER

FILIPE ANDRADE (#1-3), **AARON CONLEY** (#4),
JAY FOSGITT (#5) & **BRETT BEAN** (#6)
ARTISTS

JEAN-FRANCOIS BEAULIEU
COLOR ARTIST

JEFF ECKLEBERRY
LETTERER

SKOTTIE YOUNG
COVER ARTIST

KATHLEEN WISNESKI
ASSISTANT EDITOR

JAKE THOMAS
EDITOR

GROOT CREATED BY STAN LEE, LARRY LIEBER & JACK KIRBY
ROCKET RACCOON CREATED BY BILL MANTLO & KEITH GIFFEN

OLLECTION EDITOR: JENNIFER GRÜNWALD
ASSOCIATE EDITOR: SARAH BRUNSTAD
OCIATE MANAGING EDITOR: ALEX STARBUCK
TOR, SPECIAL PROJECTS: MARK D. BEAZLEY

VP, PRODUCTION & SPECIAL PROJECTS: JEFF YOUNGQUIST
SVP PRINT, SALES & MARKETING: DAVID GABRIEL
BOOK DESIGNER: ADAM DEL RE

EDITOR IN CHIEF: AXEL ALONSO
CHIEF CREATIVE OFFICER: JOE QUESADA
PUBLISHER: DAN BUCKLEY
EXECUTIVE PRODUCER: ALAN FINE

RACCOON & GROOT VOL. 1: TRICKS OF THE TRADE. Contains material originally published in magazine form as ROCKET RACCOON & GROOT #1-6. First printing 2016. ISBN# 978-0-7851-9973-1. Published by MARVEL WORLDWIDE, bsidiary of MARVEL ENTERTAINMENT, LLC. OFFICE OF PUBLICATION: 135 West 50th Street, New York, NY 10020. Copyright © 2016 MARVEL No similarity between any of the names, characters, persons, and/or institutions in this with those of any living or dead person or institution is intended, and any such similarity which may exist is purely coincidental. **Printed in Canada.** ALAN FINE, President, Marvel Entertainment; DAN BUCKLEY, President, TV, Publishing Management; JOE QUESADA, Chief Creative Officer; TOM BREVOORT, SVP of Publishing; DAVID BOGART, SVP of Business Affairs & Operations, Publishing & Partnership; C.B. CEBULSKI, VP of Brand Management & Development, D GABRIEL, SVP of Sales & Marketing, Publishing; JEFF YOUNGQUIST, VP of Production & Special Projects; DAN CARR, Executive Director of Publishing Technology; ALEX MORALES, Director of Publishing Operations; SUSAN CRESPI, n Manager; STAN LEE, Chairman Emeritus. For information regarding advertising in Marvel Comics or on Marvel.com, please contact Vit DeBellis, Integrated Sales Manager, at vdebellis@marvel.com. For Marvel subscription inquiries, l 888-511-5480. **Manufactured between 5/27/2016 and 7/4/2016 by SOLISCO PRINTERS, SCOTT, QC, CANADA.**

654321

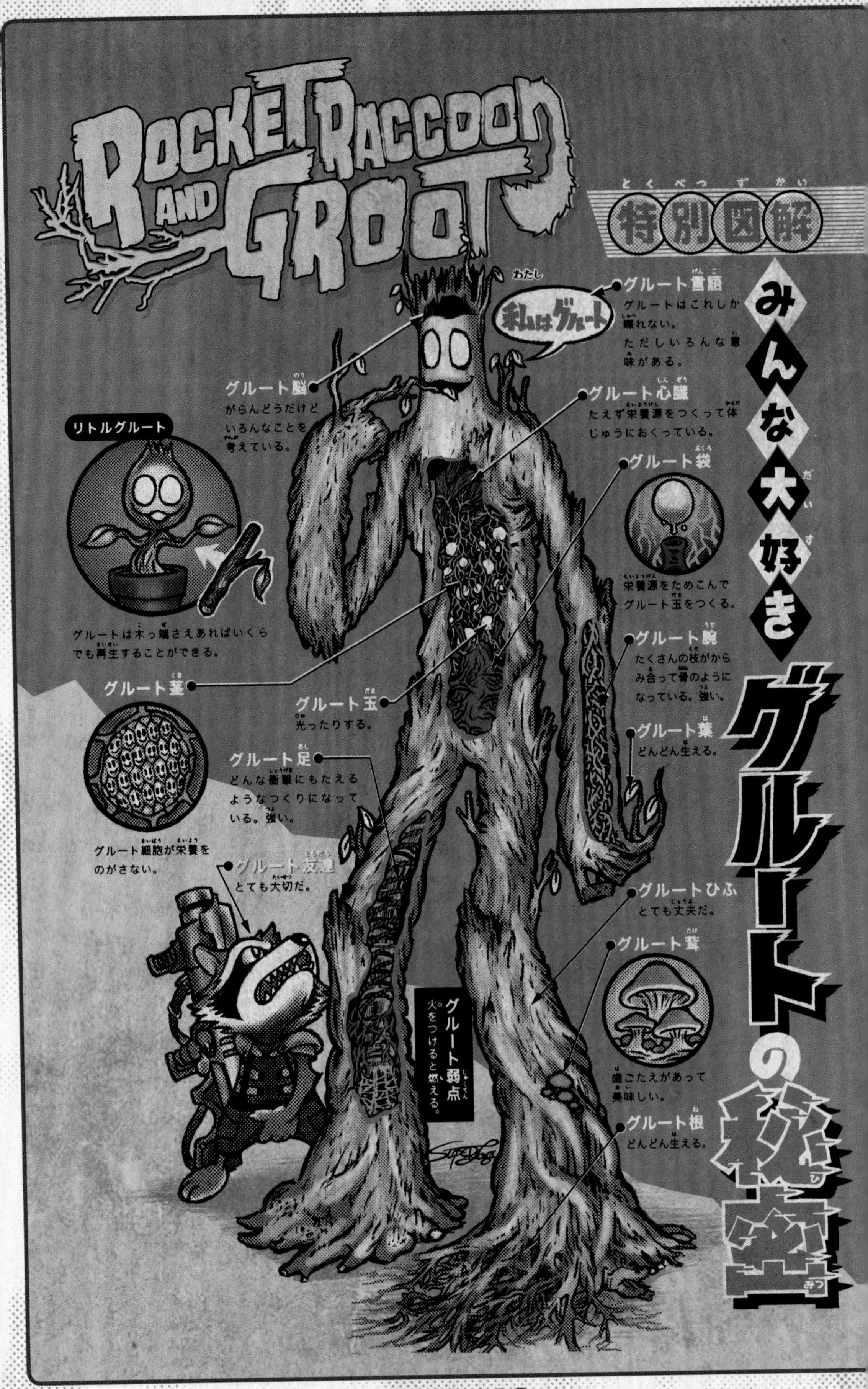
ROCKET RACCOON AND GROOT
特別図解
みんな大好き グルートの秘密
私はグルート
グルート言語
グルートはこれしか喋れない。
ただしいろんな意味がある。
グルート脳
がらんどうだけどいろんなことを考えている。
グルート心臓
たえず栄養源をつくって体じゅうにおくっている。
リトルグルート
グルートは木っ端さえあればいくらでも再生することができる。
グルート袋
栄養源をためこんでグルート玉をつくる。
グルート腕
たくさんの枝がからみ合って骨のようになっている。強い。
グルート茎
グルート細胞が栄養をのがさない。
グルート玉
光ったりする。
グルート葉
どんどん生える。
グルート足
どんな衝撃にもたえるようなつくりになっている。強い。
グルート友達
とても大切だ。
グルートひふ
とても丈夫だ。
グルート茸
歯ごたえがあって美味しい。
グルート弱点
火をつけると燃える。
グルート根
どんどん生える。

SUPERLOG
1 VARIANT

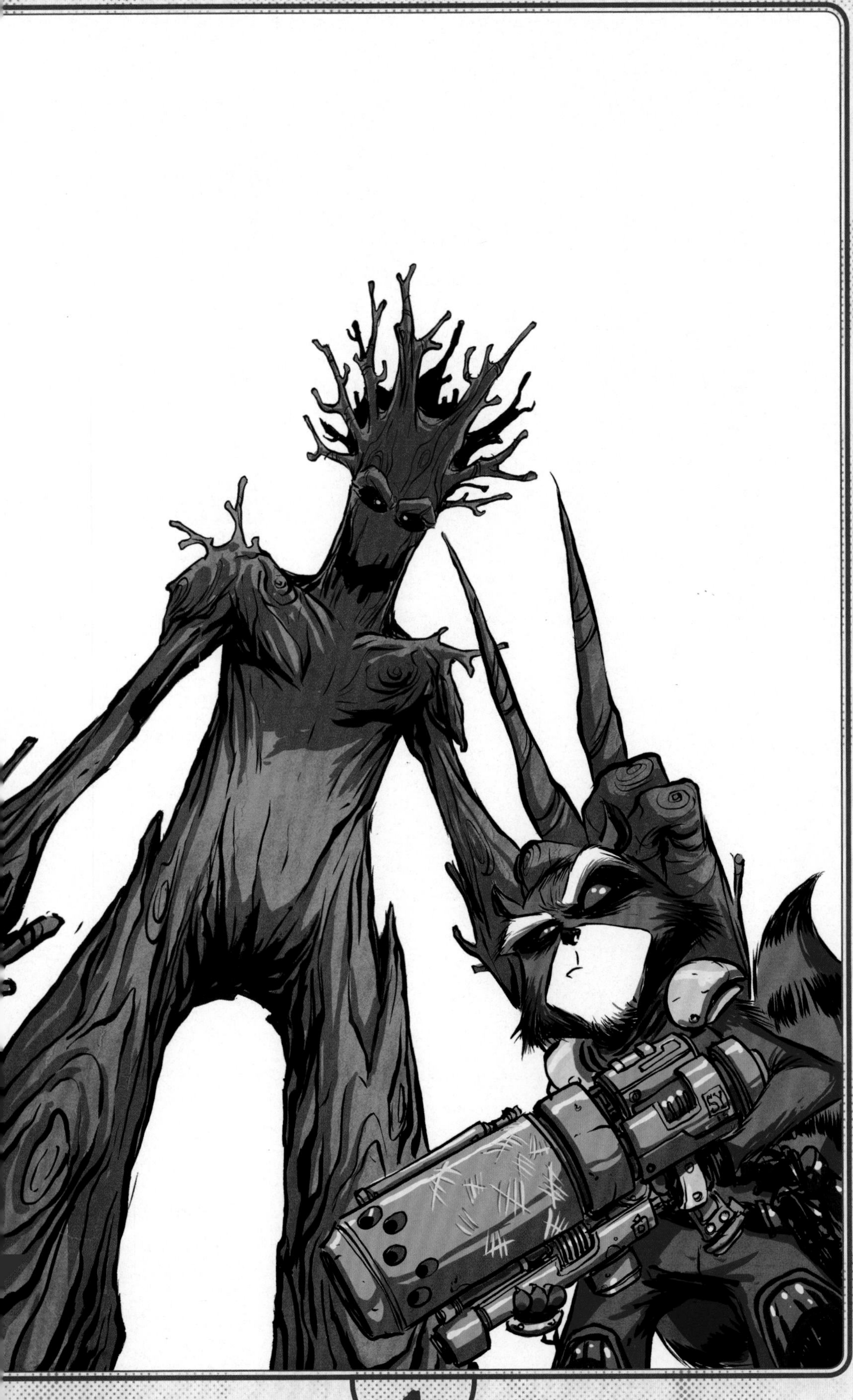

1

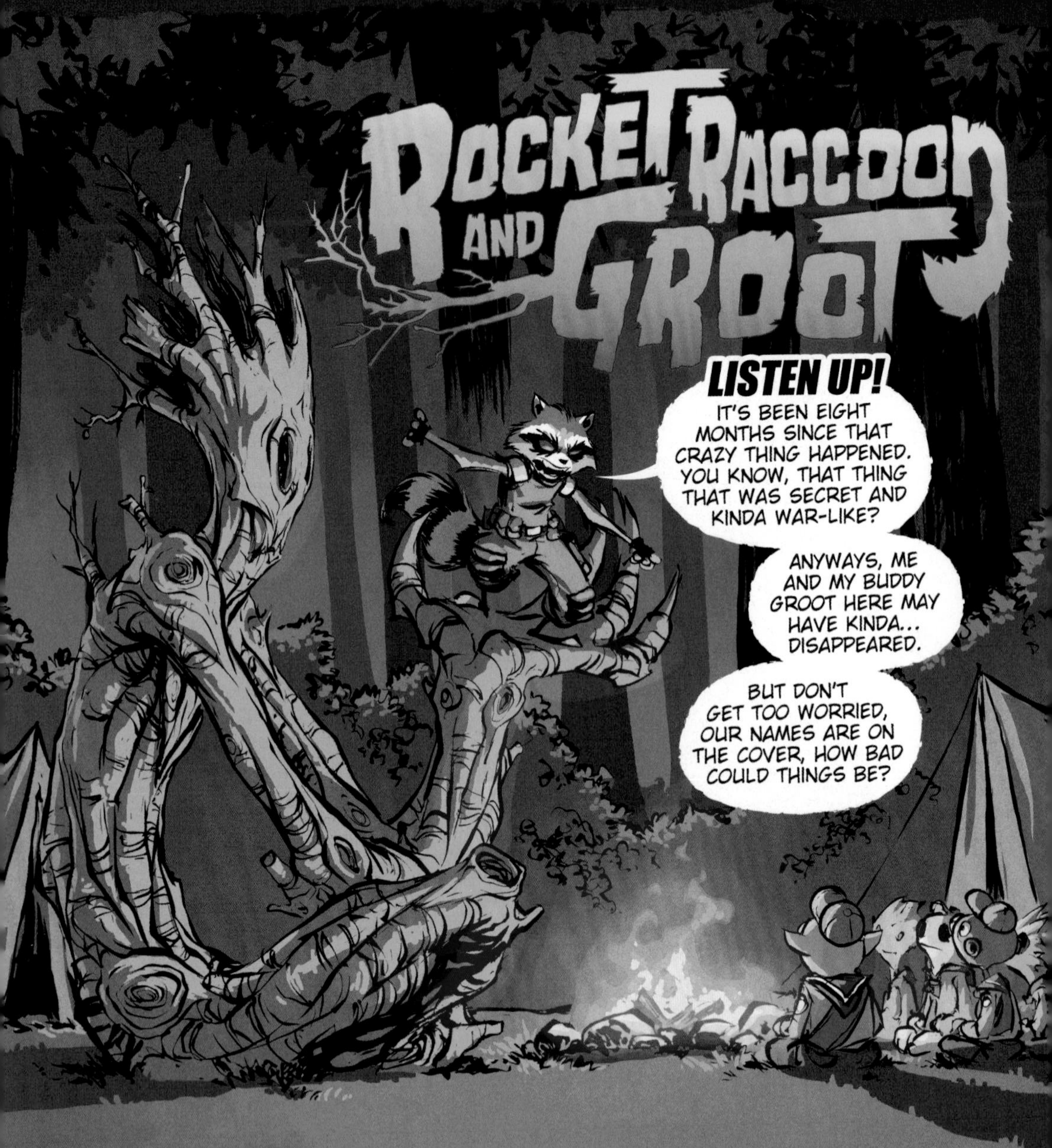
ROCKET RACCOON AND GROOT
LISTEN UP! IT'S BEEN EIGHT MONTHS SINCE THAT CRAZY THING HAPPENED. YOU KNOW, THAT THING THAT WAS SECRET AND KINDA WAR-LIKE?
ANYWAYS, ME AND MY BUDDY GROOT HERE MAY HAVE KINDA... DISAPPEARED.
BUT DON'T GET TOO WORRIED, OUR NAMES ARE ON THE COVER, HOW BAD COULD THINGS BE?

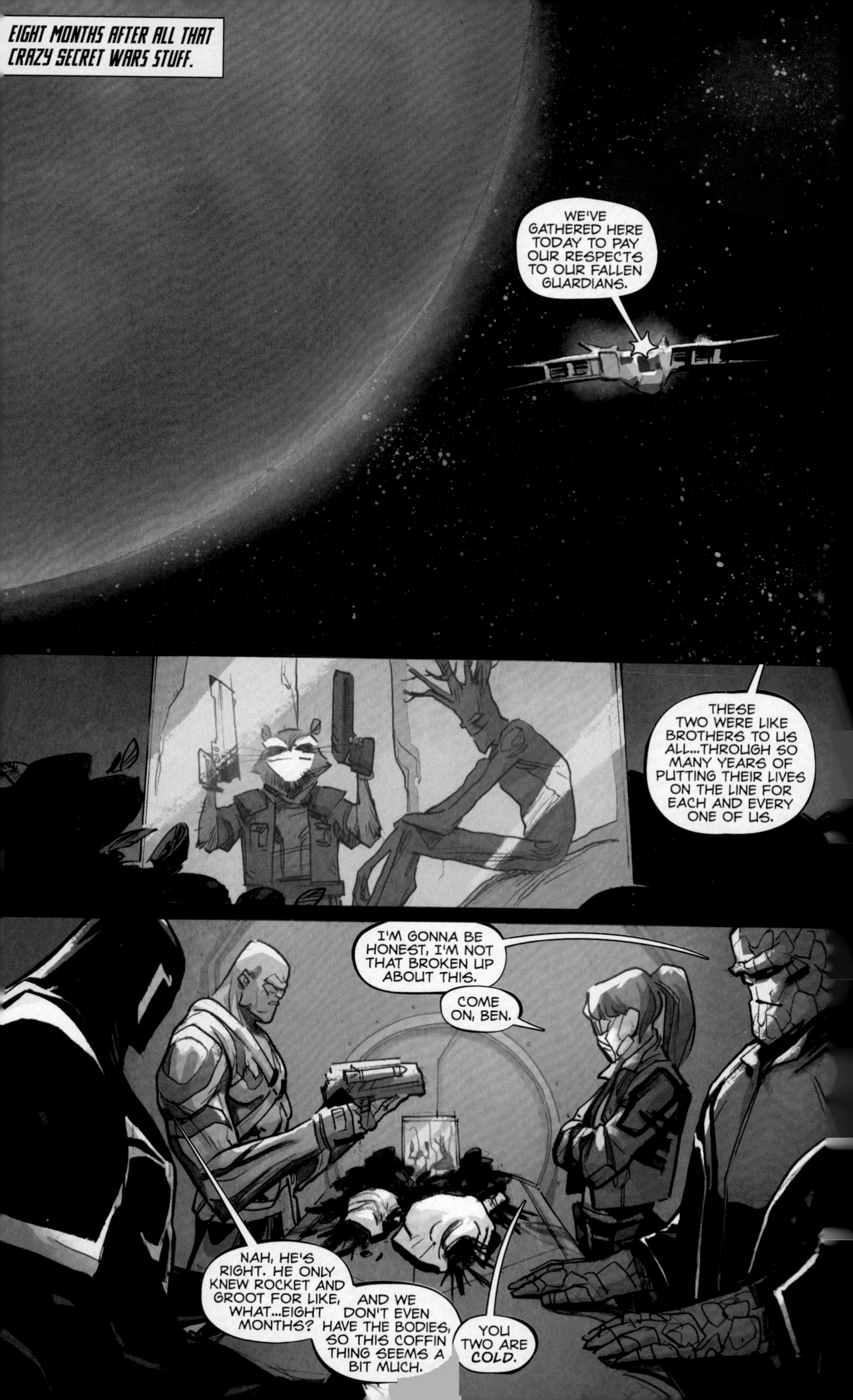
EIGHT MONTHS AFTER ALL THAT CRAZY SECRET WARS STUFF.
WE'VE GATHERED HERE TODAY TO PAY OUR RESPECTS TO OUR FALLEN GUARDIANS.
THESE TWO WERE LIKE BROTHERS TO US ALL...THROUGH SO MANY YEARS OF PUTTING THEIR LIVES ON THE LINE FOR EACH AND EVERY ONE OF US.
I'M GONNA BE HONEST, I'M NOT THAT BROKEN UP ABOUT THIS.
COME ON, BEN.
NAH, HE'S RIGHT. HE ONLY KNEW ROCKET AND GROOT FOR LIKE, WHAT...EIGHT MONTHS?
AND WE DON'T EVEN HAVE THE BODIES, SO THIS COFFIN THING SEEMS A BIT MUCH.
YOU TWO ARE COLD.

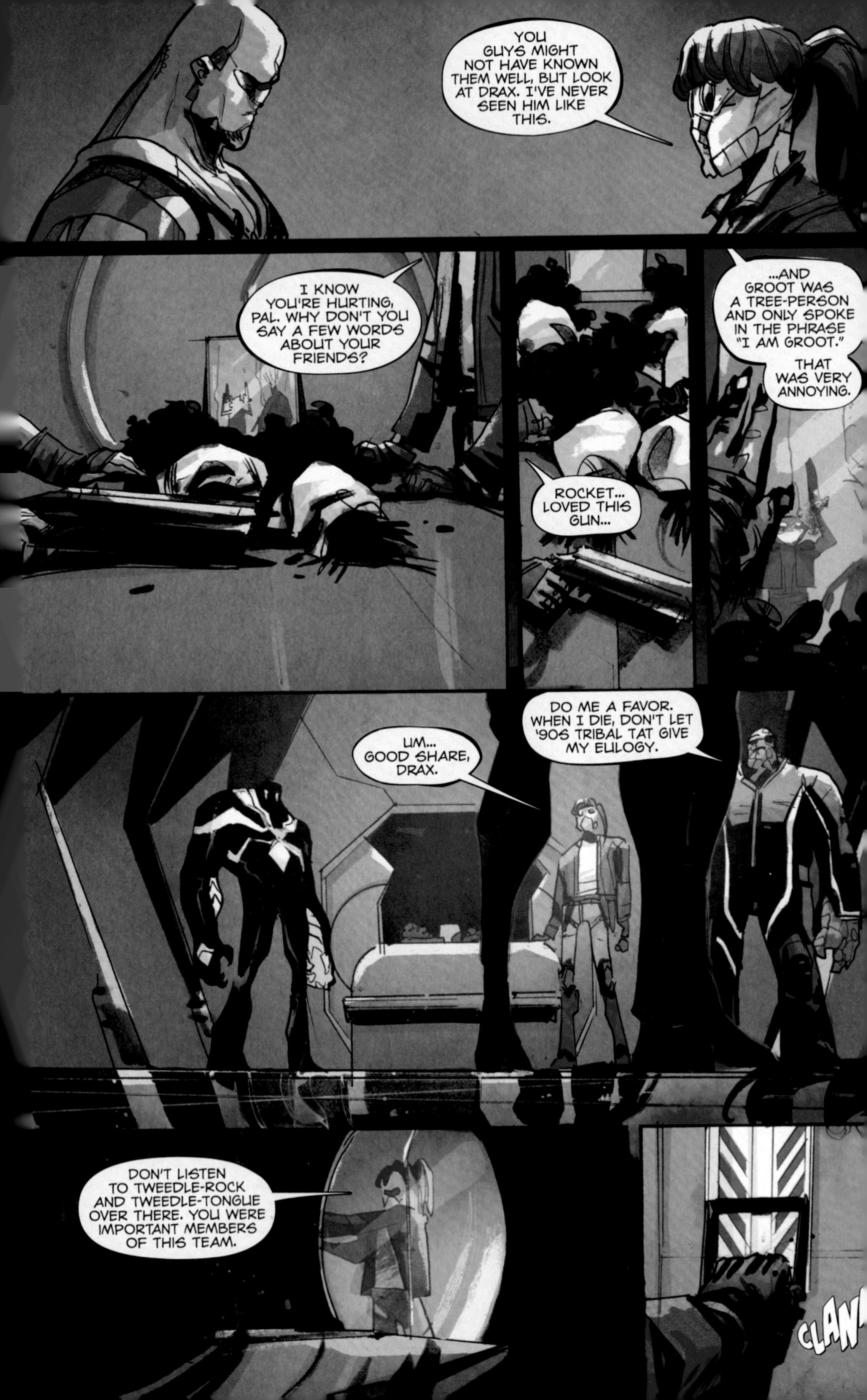
YOU GUYS MIGHT NOT HAVE KNOWN THEM WELL, BUT LOOK AT DRAX. I'VE NEVER SEEN HIM LIKE THIS.
I KNOW YOU'RE HURTING, PAL. WHY DON'T YOU SAY A FEW WORDS ABOUT YOUR FRIENDS?
ROCKET... LOVED THIS GUN...
...AND GROOT WAS A TREE-PERSON AND ONLY SPOKE IN THE PHRASE "I AM GROOT."
THAT WAS VERY ANNOYING.
UM... GOOD SHARE, DRAX.
DO ME A FAVOR. WHEN I DIE, DON'T LET '90S TRIBAL TAT GIVE MY EULOGY.
DON'T LISTEN TO TWEEDLE-ROCK AND TWEEDLE-TONGUE OVER THERE. YOU WERE IMPORTANT MEMBERS OF THIS TEAM.

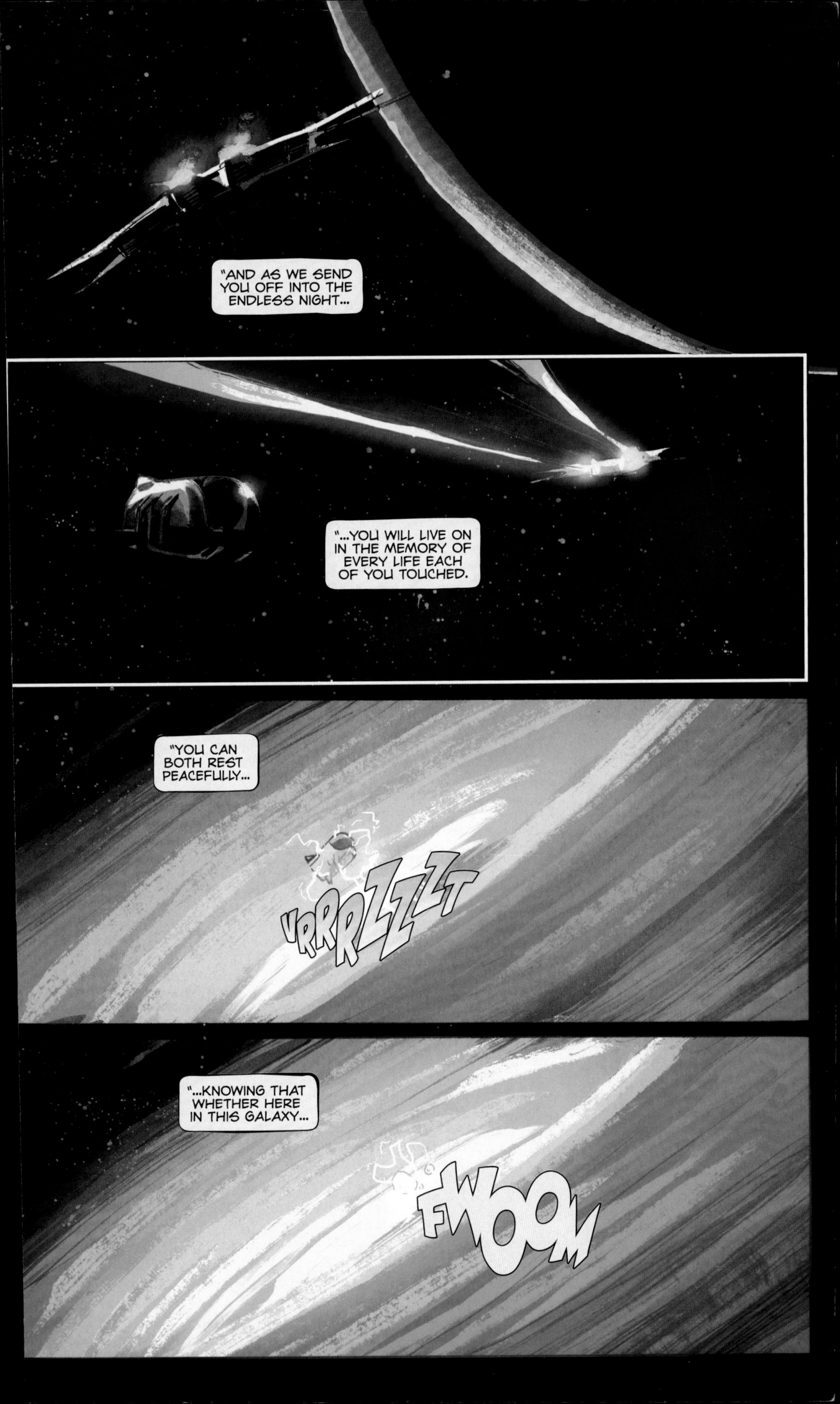
"AND AS WE SEND YOU OFF INTO THE ENDLESS NIGHT...
"...YOU WILL LIVE ON IN THE MEMORY OF EVERY LIFE EACH OF YOU TOUCHED.
"YOU CAN BOTH REST PEACEFULLY...
VRRRZZZZT
"...KNOWING THAT WHETHER HERE IN THIS GALAXY...
FWOOM

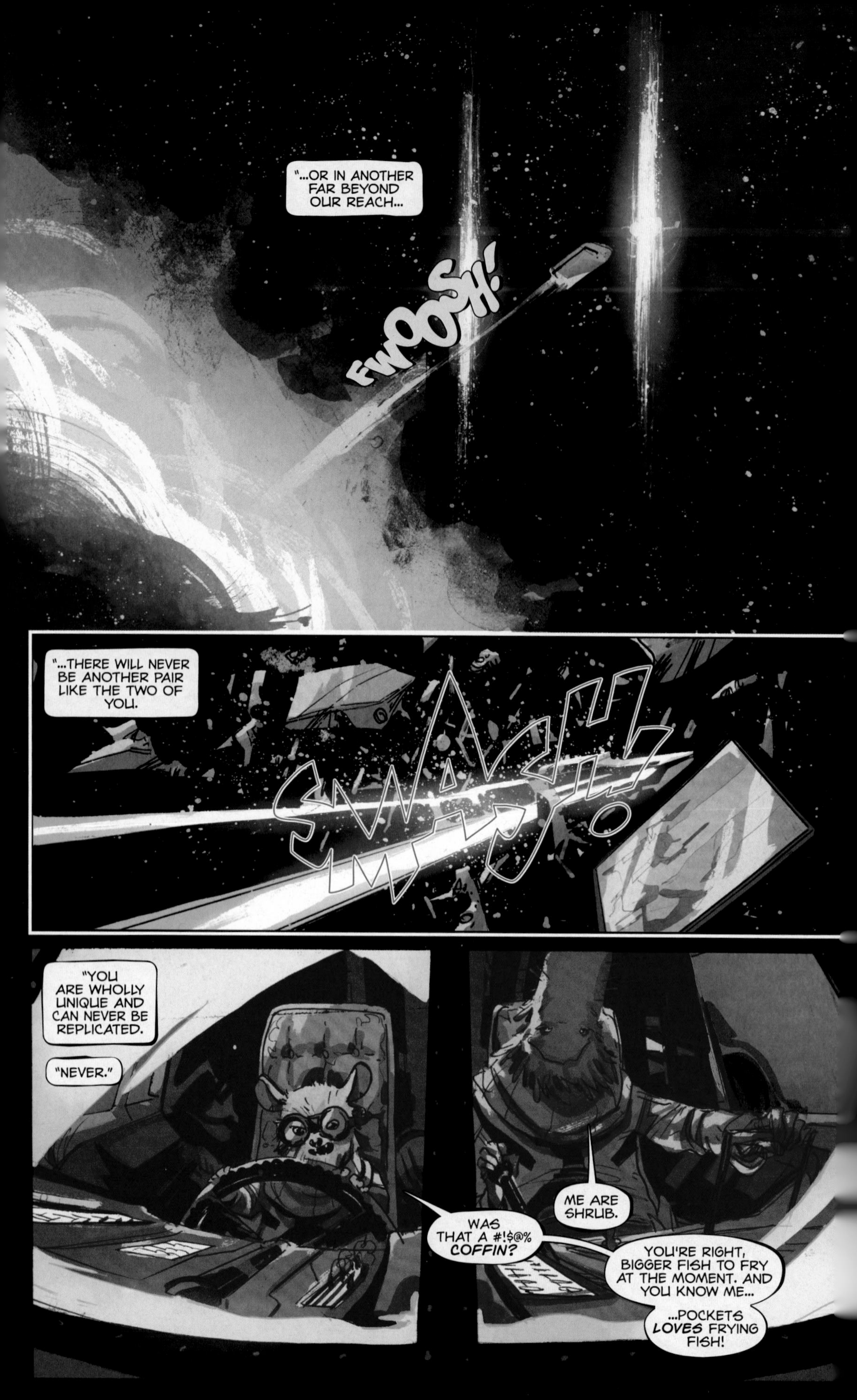
"...OR IN ANOTHER FAR BEYOND OUR REACH...
FWOOSH!
"...THERE WILL NEVER BE ANOTHER PAIR LIKE THE TWO OF YOU.
SWASH!
"YOU ARE WHOLLY UNIQUE AND CAN NEVER BE REPLICATED.
"NEVER."
WAS THAT A #!$@% COFFIN?
ME ARE SHRUB.
YOU'RE RIGHT, BIGGER FISH TO FRY AT THE MOMENT. AND YOU KNOW ME...
...POCKETS LOVES FRYING FISH!

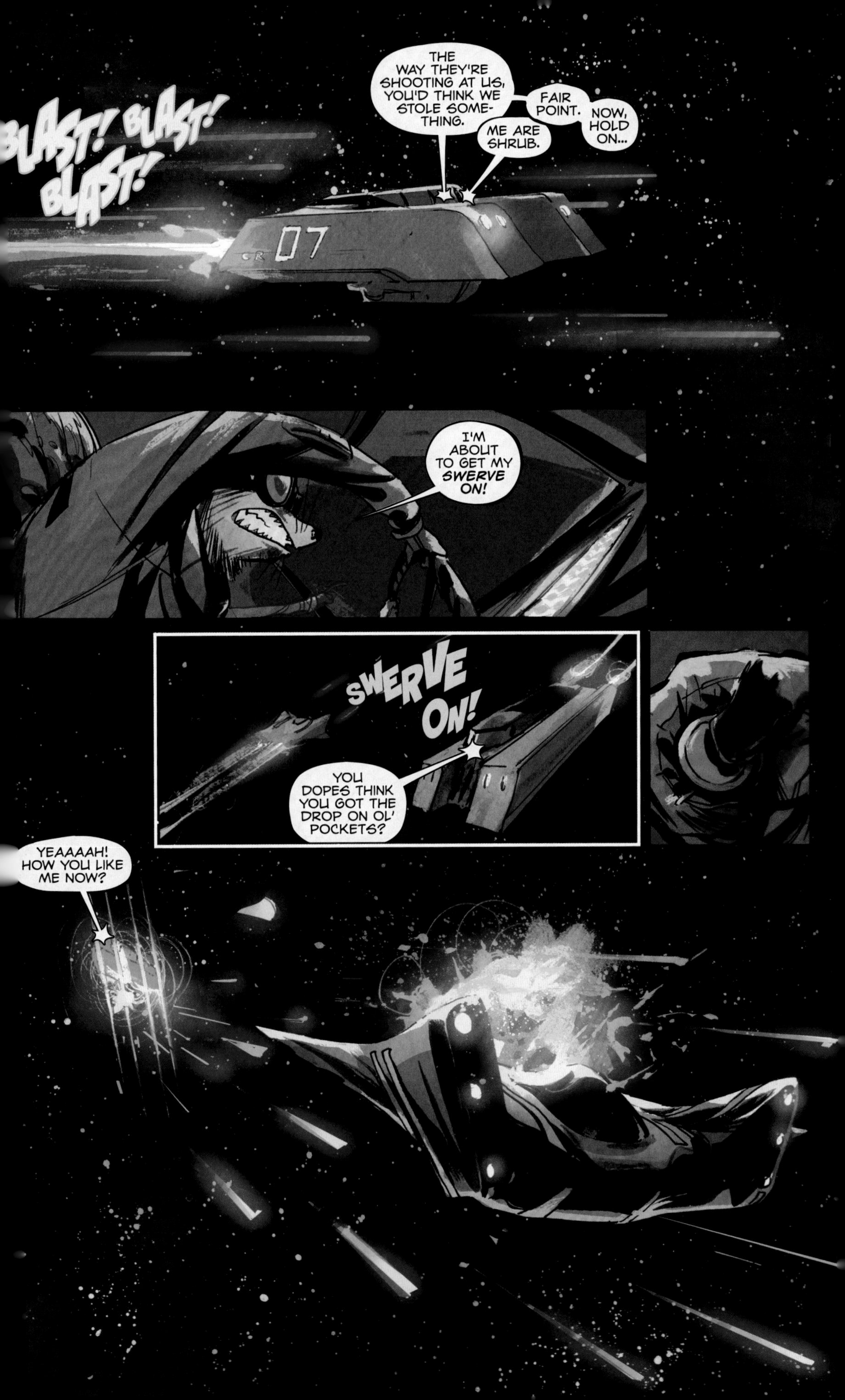
BLAST! BLAST! BLAST!
THE WAY THEY'RE SHOOTING AT US, YOU'D THINK WE STOLE SOME-THING.
FAIR POINT.
ME ARE SHRUB.
NOW, HOLD ON...
I'M ABOUT TO GET MY *SWERVE ON!*
SWERVE ON!
YOU DOPES THINK YOU GOT THE DROP ON OL' POCKETS?
YEAAAAH! HOW YOU LIKE ME NOW?

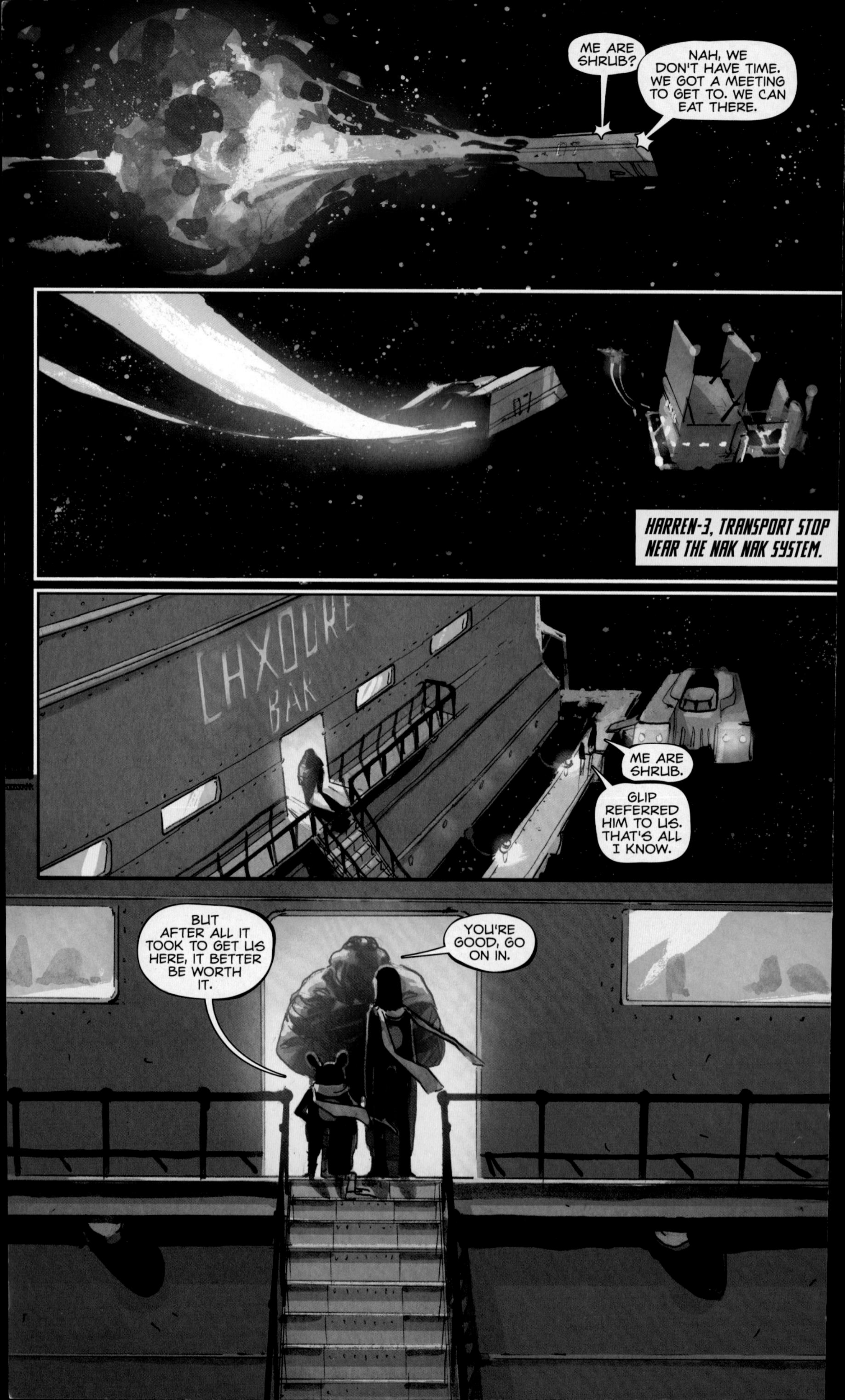
ME ARE SHRUB?
NAH, WE DON'T HAVE TIME. WE GOT A MEETING TO GET TO. WE CAN EAT THERE.
HARREN-3, TRANSPORT STOP NEAR THE NAK NAK SYSTEM.
CAXOORE BAR
ME ARE SHRUB.
GLIP REFERRED HIM TO US. THAT'S ALL I KNOW.
BUT AFTER ALL IT TOOK TO GET US HERE, IT BETTER BE WORTH IT.
YOU'RE GOOD, GO ON IN.

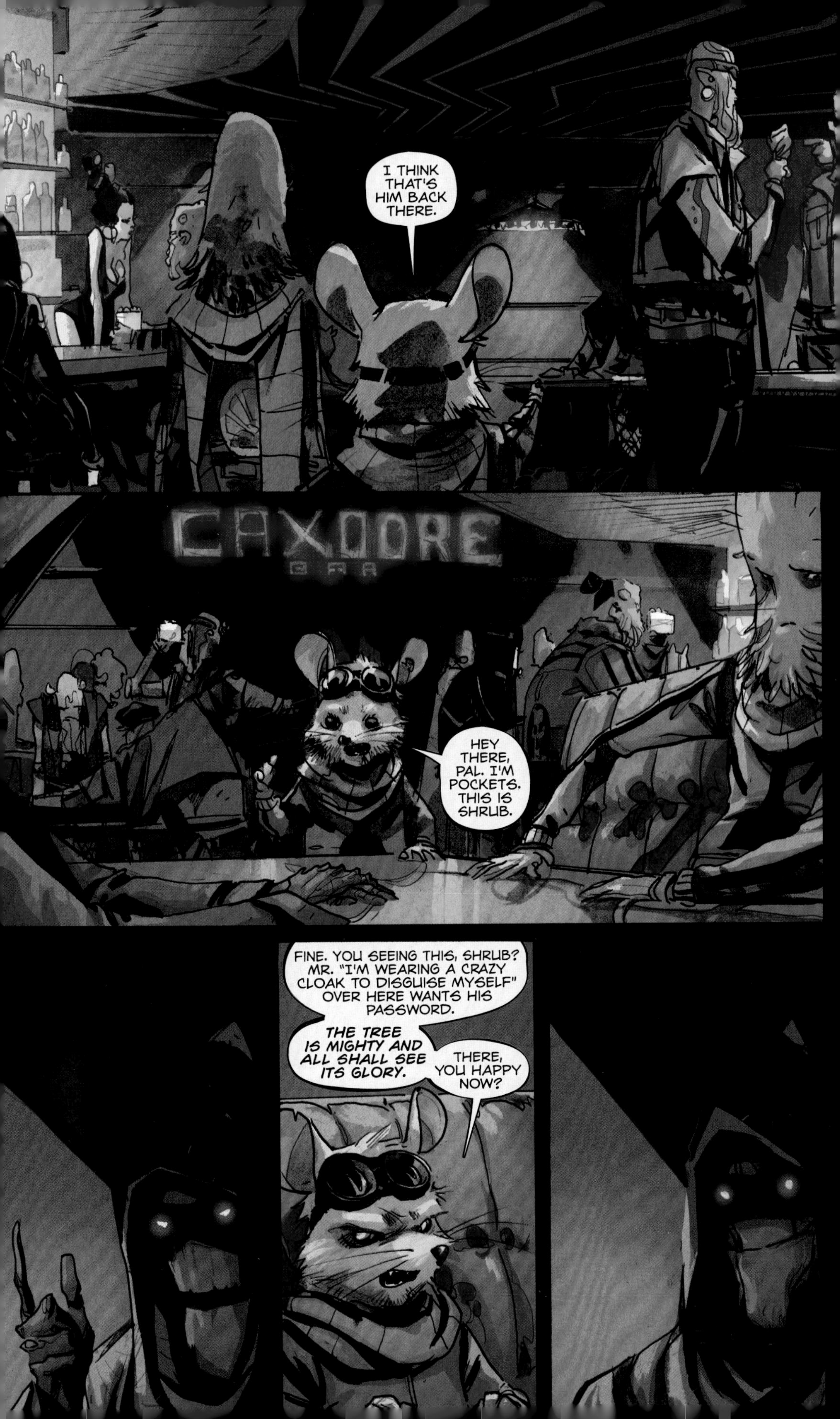
I THINK THAT'S HIM BACK THERE.
CAXOORE
HEY THERE, PAL. I'M POCKETS. THIS IS SHRUB.
FINE. YOU SEEING THIS, SHRUB? MR. "I'M WEARING A CRAZY CLOAK TO DISGUISE MYSELF" OVER HERE WANTS HIS PASSWORD.
THE TREE IS MIGHTY AND ALL SHALL SEE ITS GLORY.
THERE, YOU HAPPY NOW?

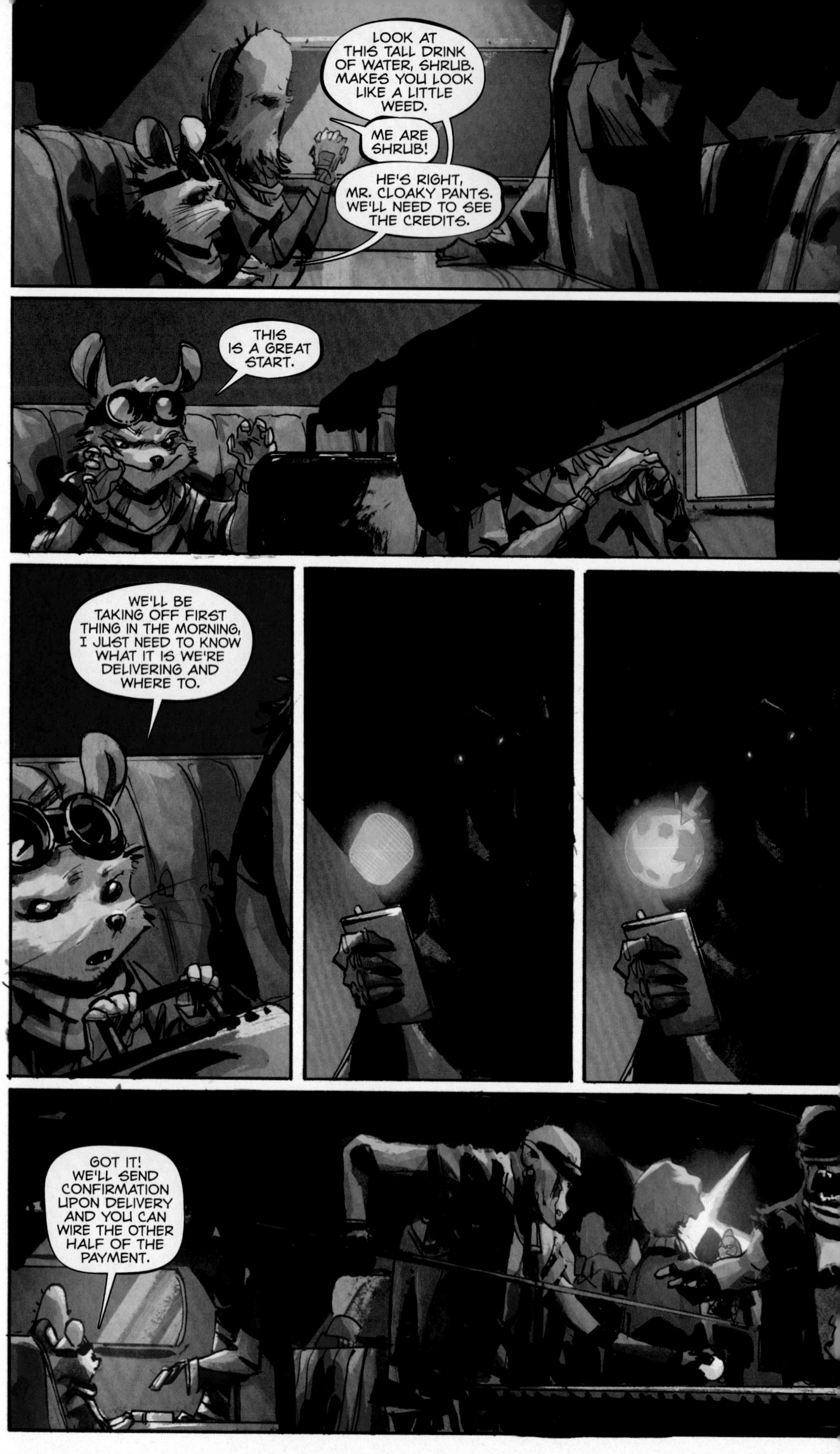
LOOK AT THIS TALL DRINK OF WATER, SHRUB. MAKES YOU LOOK LIKE A LITTLE WEED.
ME ARE SHRUB!
HE'S RIGHT, MR. CLOAKY PANTS. WE'LL NEED TO SEE THE CREDITS.
THIS IS A GREAT START.
WE'LL BE TAKING OFF FIRST THING IN THE MORNING, I JUST NEED TO KNOW WHAT IT IS WE'RE DELIVERING AND WHERE TO.
GOT IT! WE'LL SEND CONFIRMATION UPON DELIVERY AND YOU CAN WIRE THE OTHER HALF OF THE PAYMENT.

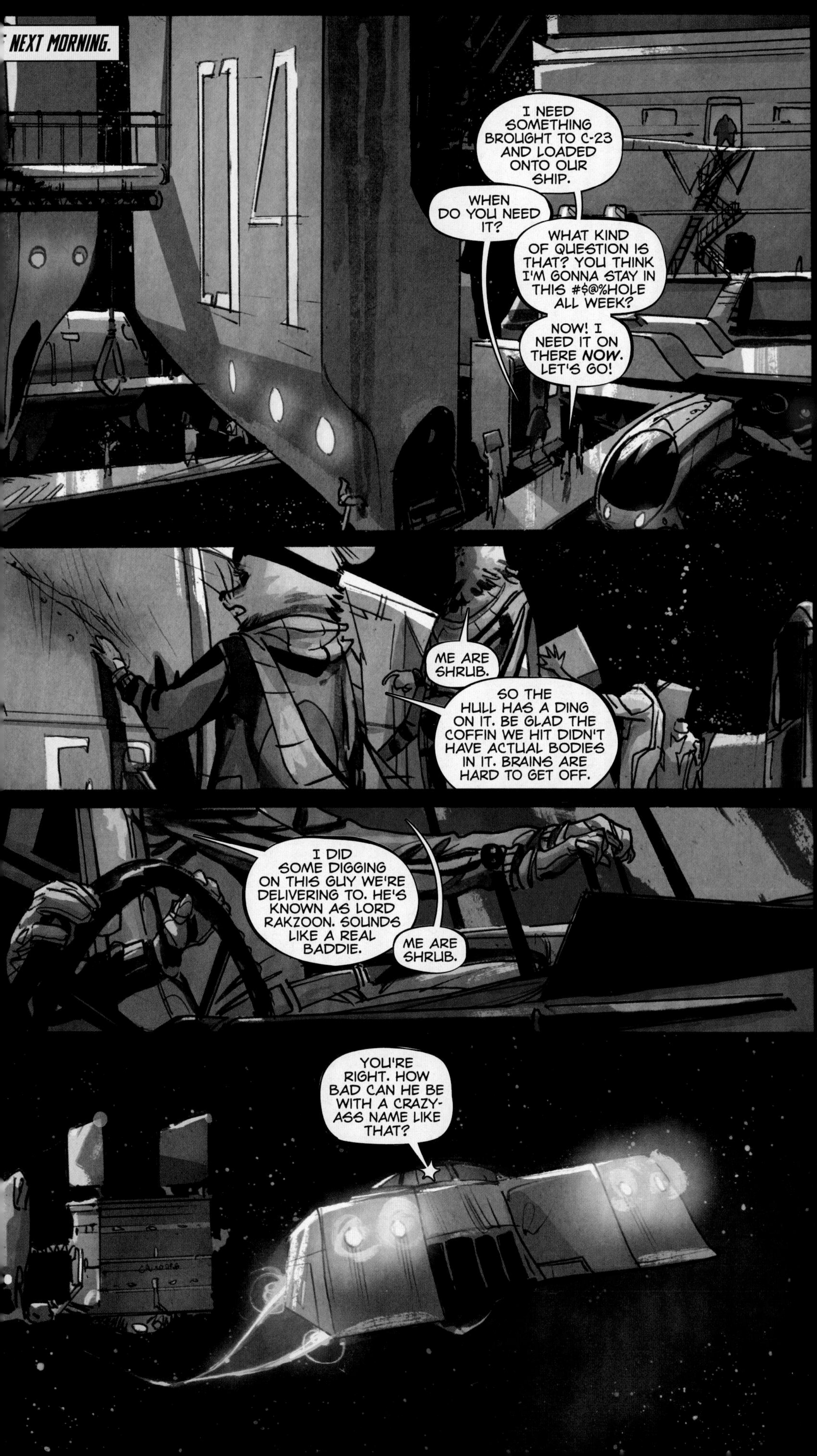
NEXT MORNING.
I NEED SOMETHING BROUGHT TO C-23 AND LOADED ONTO OUR SHIP.
WHEN DO YOU NEED IT?
WHAT KIND OF QUESTION IS THAT? YOU THINK I'M GONNA STAY IN THIS #$@%HOLE ALL WEEK?
NOW! I NEED IT ON THERE NOW. LET'S GO!
ME ARE SHRUB.
SO THE HULL HAS A DING ON IT. BE GLAD THE COFFIN WE HIT DIDN'T HAVE ACTUAL BODIES IN IT. BRAINS ARE HARD TO GET OFF.
I DID SOME DIGGING ON THIS GUY WE'RE DELIVERING TO. HE'S KNOWN AS LORD RAKZOON. SOUNDS LIKE A REAL BADDIE.
ME ARE SHRUB.
YOU'RE RIGHT. HOW BAD CAN HE BE WITH A CRAZY-ASS NAME LIKE THAT?

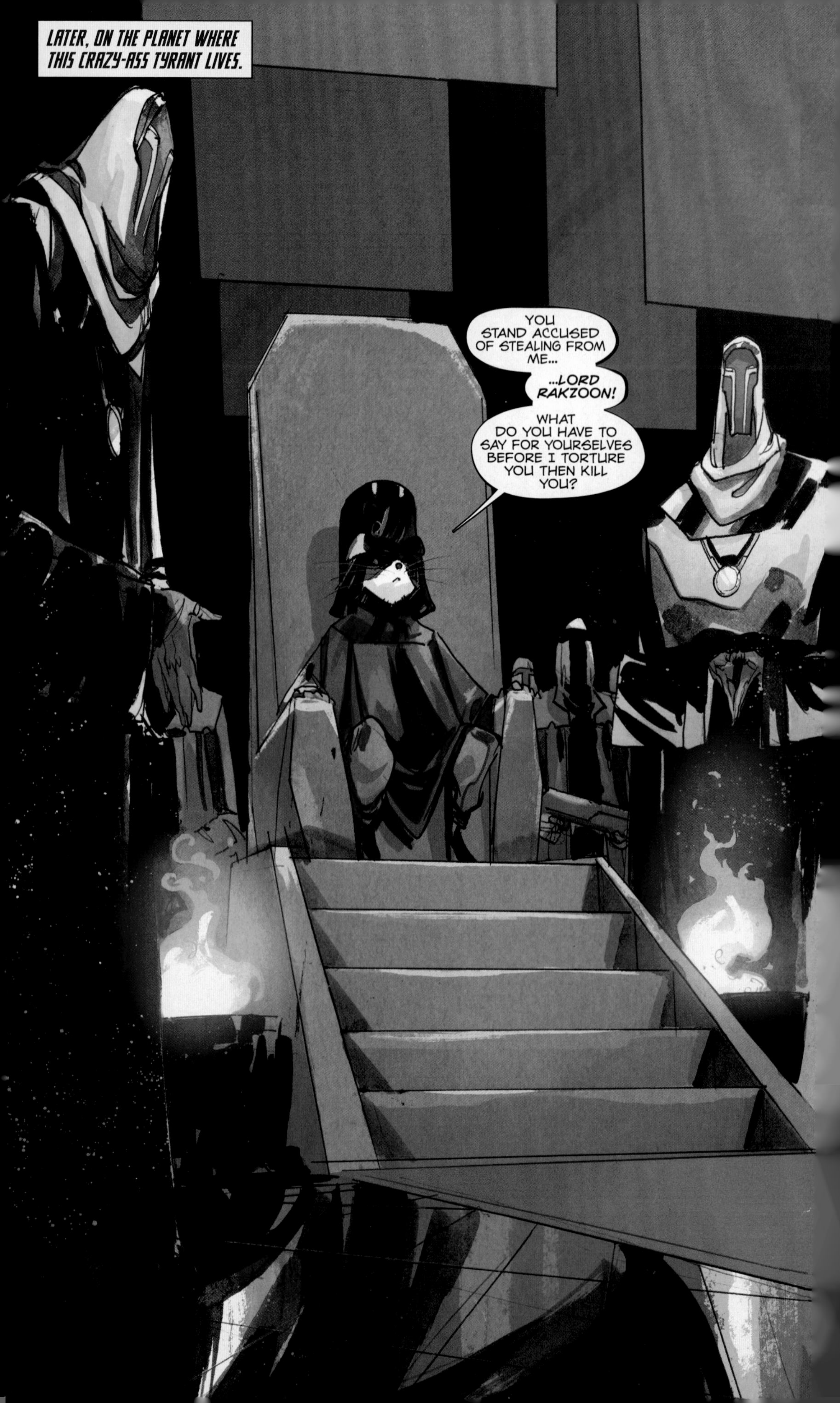
LATER, ON THE PLANET WHERE THIS CRAZY-ASS TYRANT LIVES.
YOU STAND ACCUSED OF STEALING FROM ME...
...LORD RAKZOON!
WHAT DO YOU HAVE TO SAY FOR YOURSELVES BEFORE I TORTURE YOU THEN KILL YOU?

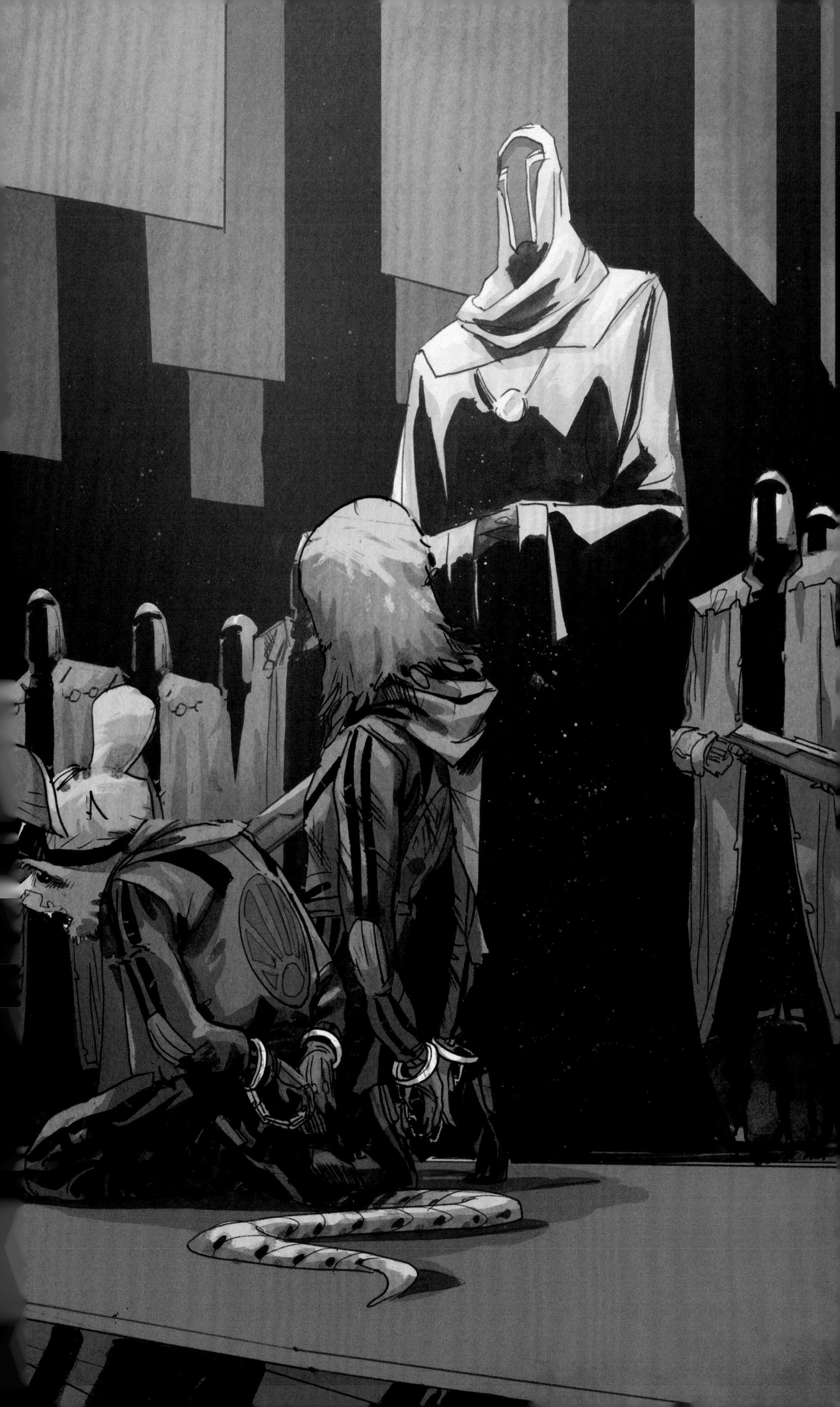

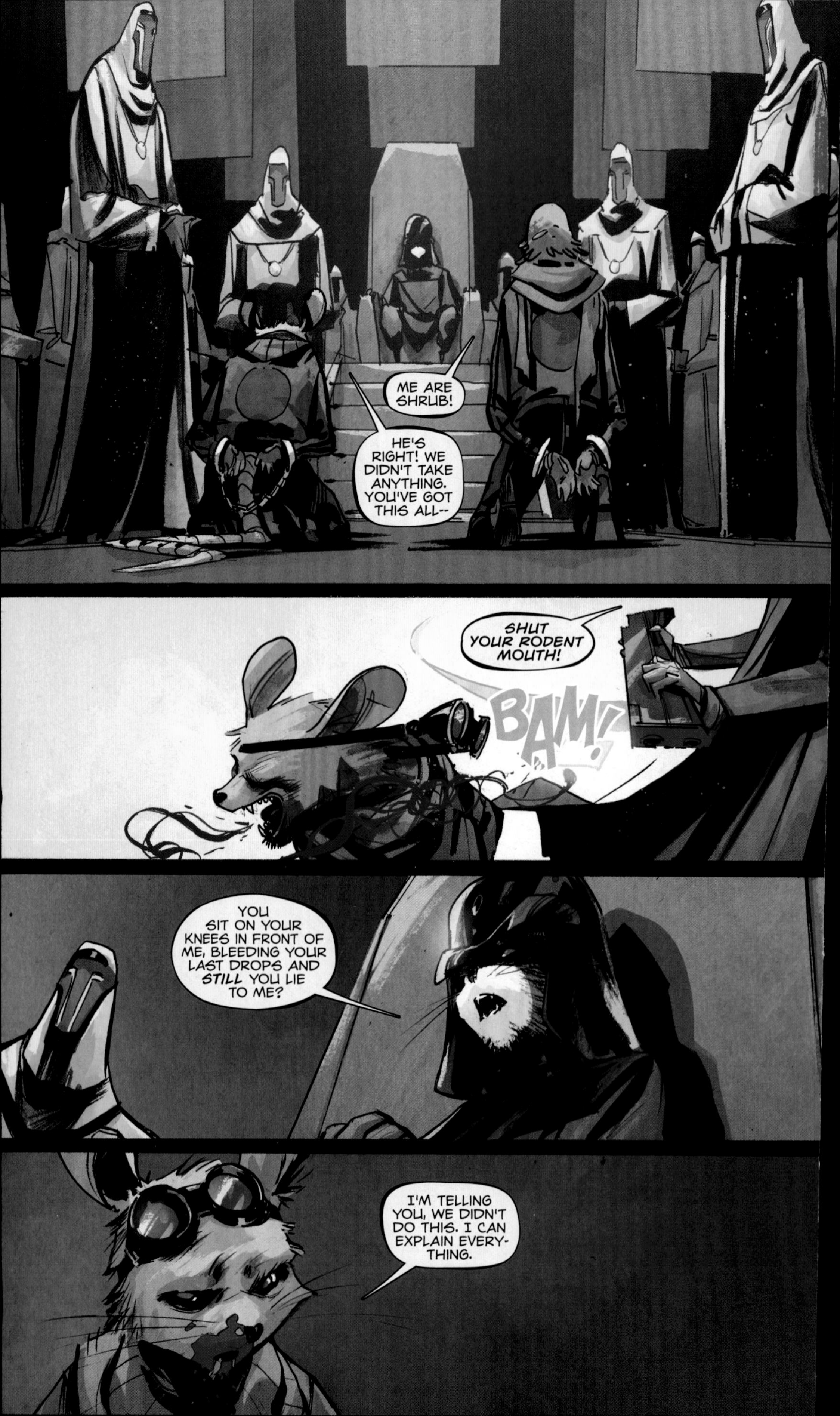
ME ARE SHRUB!
HE'S RIGHT! WE DIDN'T TAKE ANYTHING. YOU'VE GOT THIS ALL--
SHUT YOUR RODENT MOUTH!
BAM!
YOU SIT ON YOUR KNEES IN FRONT OF ME, BLEEDING YOUR LAST DROPS AND STILL YOU LIE TO ME?
I'M TELLING YOU, WE DIDN'T DO THIS. I CAN EXPLAIN EVERY-THING.

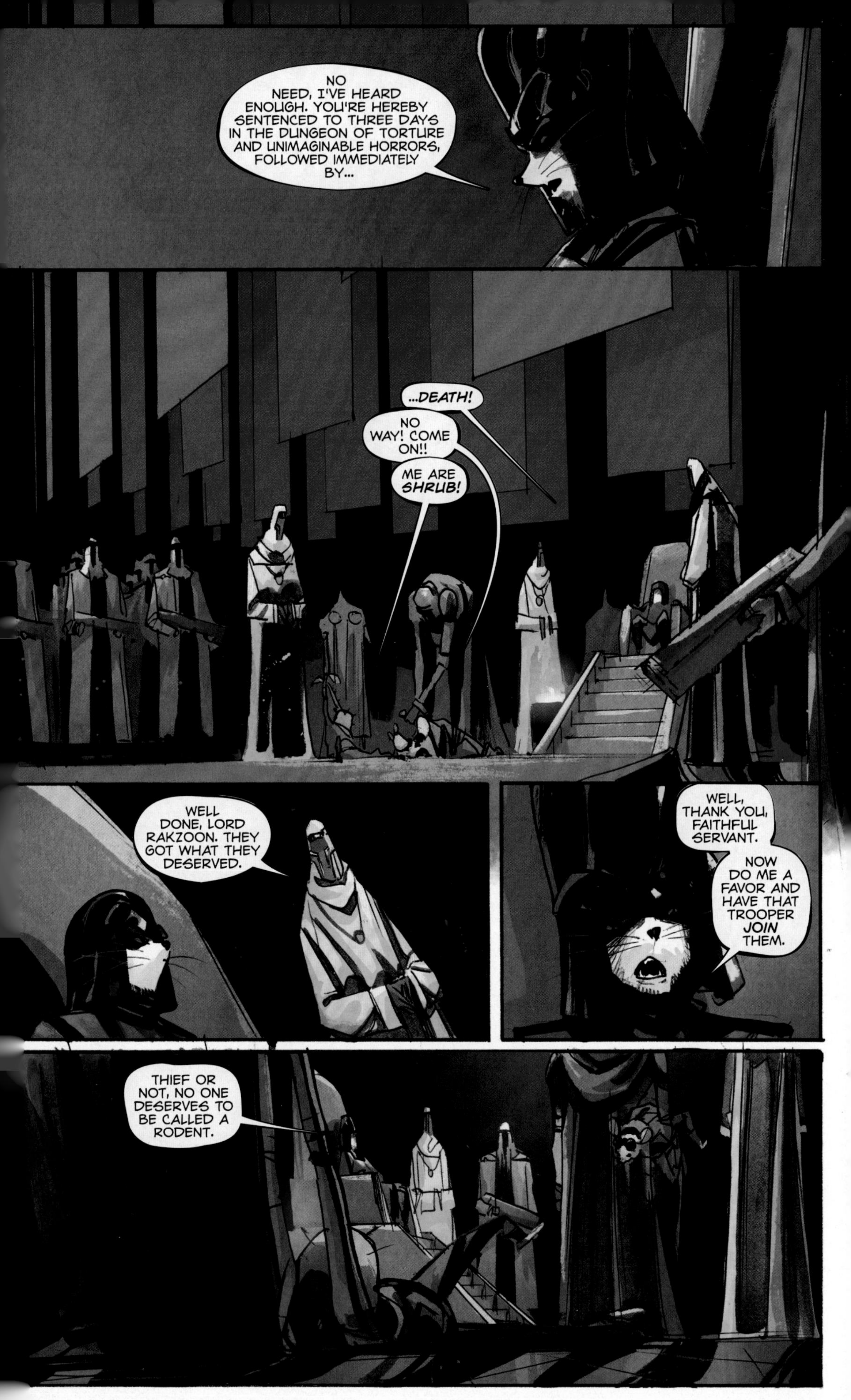
NO NEED, I'VE HEARD ENOUGH. YOU'RE HEREBY SENTENCED TO THREE DAYS IN THE DUNGEON OF TORTURE AND UNIMAGINABLE HORRORS, FOLLOWED IMMEDIATELY BY...
...DEATH!
NO WAY! COME ON!!
ME ARE SHRUB!
WELL DONE, LORD RAKZOON. THEY GOT WHAT THEY DESERVED.
WELL, THANK YOU, FAITHFUL SERVANT.
NOW DO ME A FAVOR AND HAVE THAT TROOPER JOIN THEM.
THIEF OR NOT, NO ONE DESERVES TO BE CALLED A RODENT.

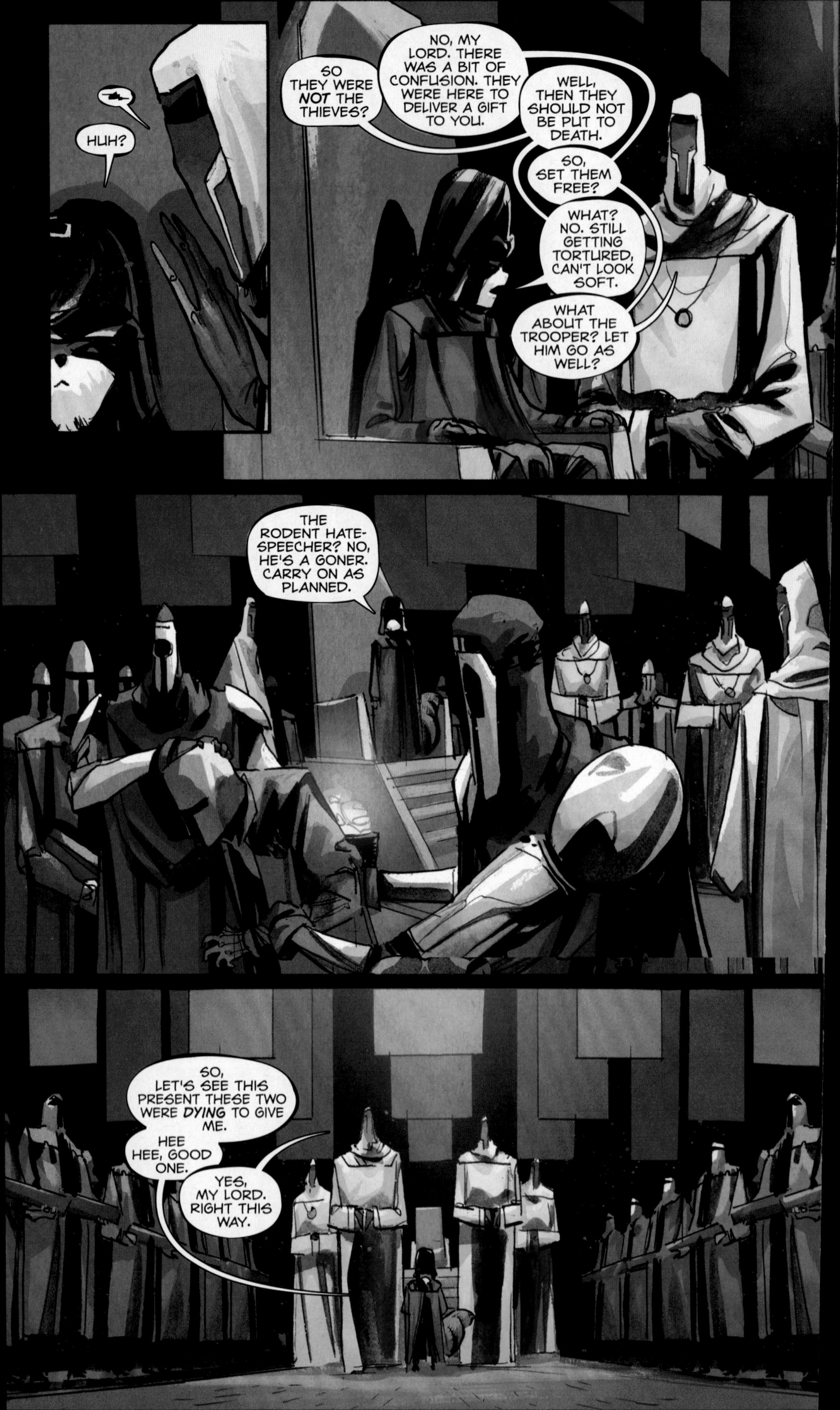
HUH?
SO THEY WERE NOT THE THIEVES?
NO, MY LORD. THERE WAS A BIT OF CONFUSION. THEY WERE HERE TO DELIVER A GIFT TO YOU.
WELL, THEN THEY SHOULD NOT BE PUT TO DEATH.
SO, SET THEM FREE?
WHAT? NO. STILL GETTING TORTURED, CAN'T LOOK SOFT.
WHAT ABOUT THE TROOPER? LET HIM GO AS WELL?
THE RODENT HATE-SPEECHER? NO, HE'S A GONER. CARRY ON AS PLANNED.
SO, LET'S SEE THIS PRESENT THESE TWO WERE DYING TO GIVE ME.
HEE HEE, GOOD ONE.
YES, MY LORD. RIGHT THIS WAY.

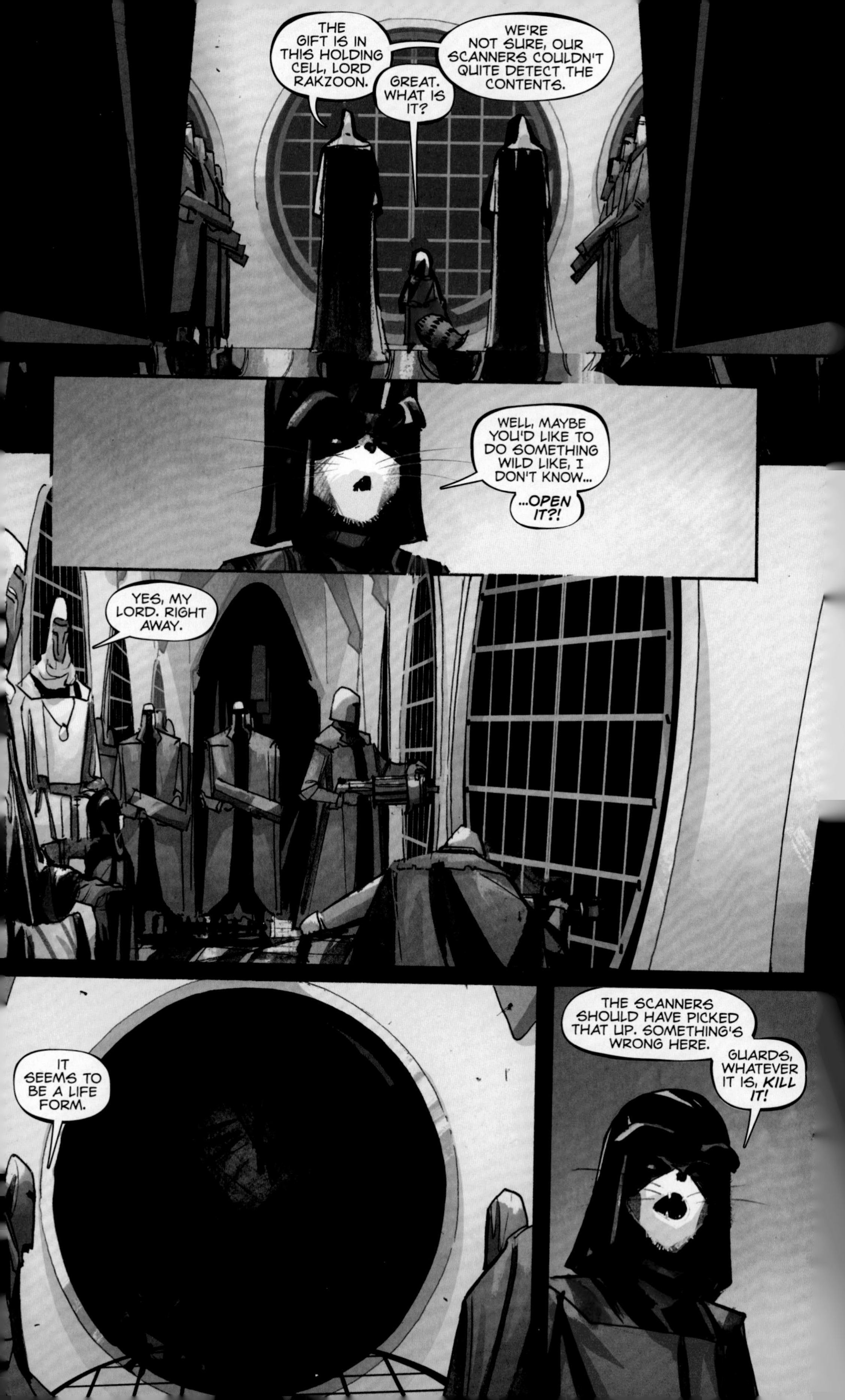
THE GIFT IS IN THIS HOLDING CELL, LORD RAKZOON.
GREAT. WHAT IS IT?
WE'RE NOT SURE, OUR SCANNERS COULDN'T QUITE DETECT THE CONTENTS.
WELL, MAYBE YOU'D LIKE TO DO SOMETHING WILD LIKE, I DON'T KNOW...
...OPEN IT?!
YES, MY LORD. RIGHT AWAY.
IT SEEMS TO BE A LIFE FORM.
THE SCANNERS SHOULD HAVE PICKED THAT UP. SOMETHING'S WRONG HERE.
GUARDS, WHATEVER IT IS, KILL IT!

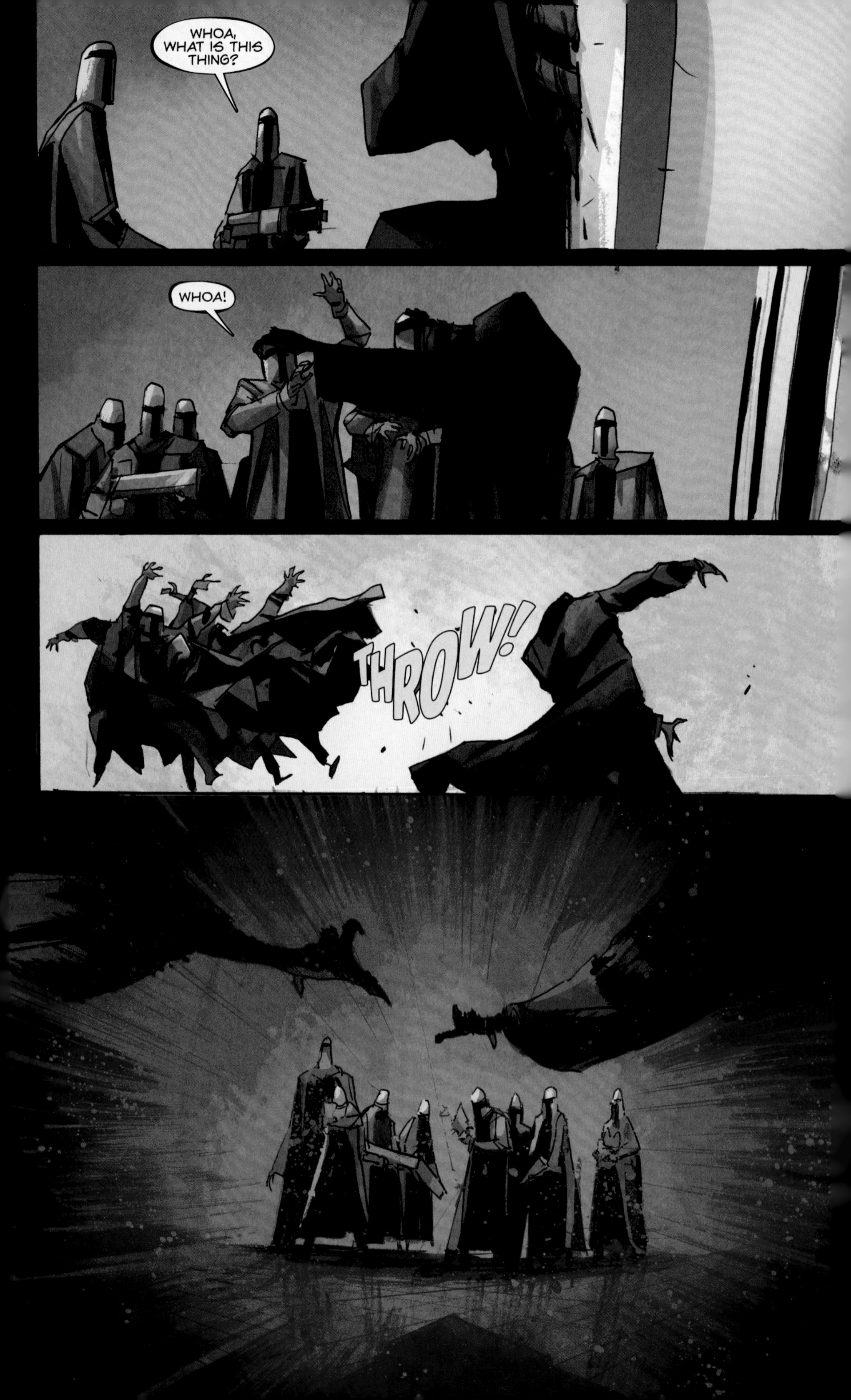
WHOA, WHAT IS THIS THING?
WHOA!
THROW!

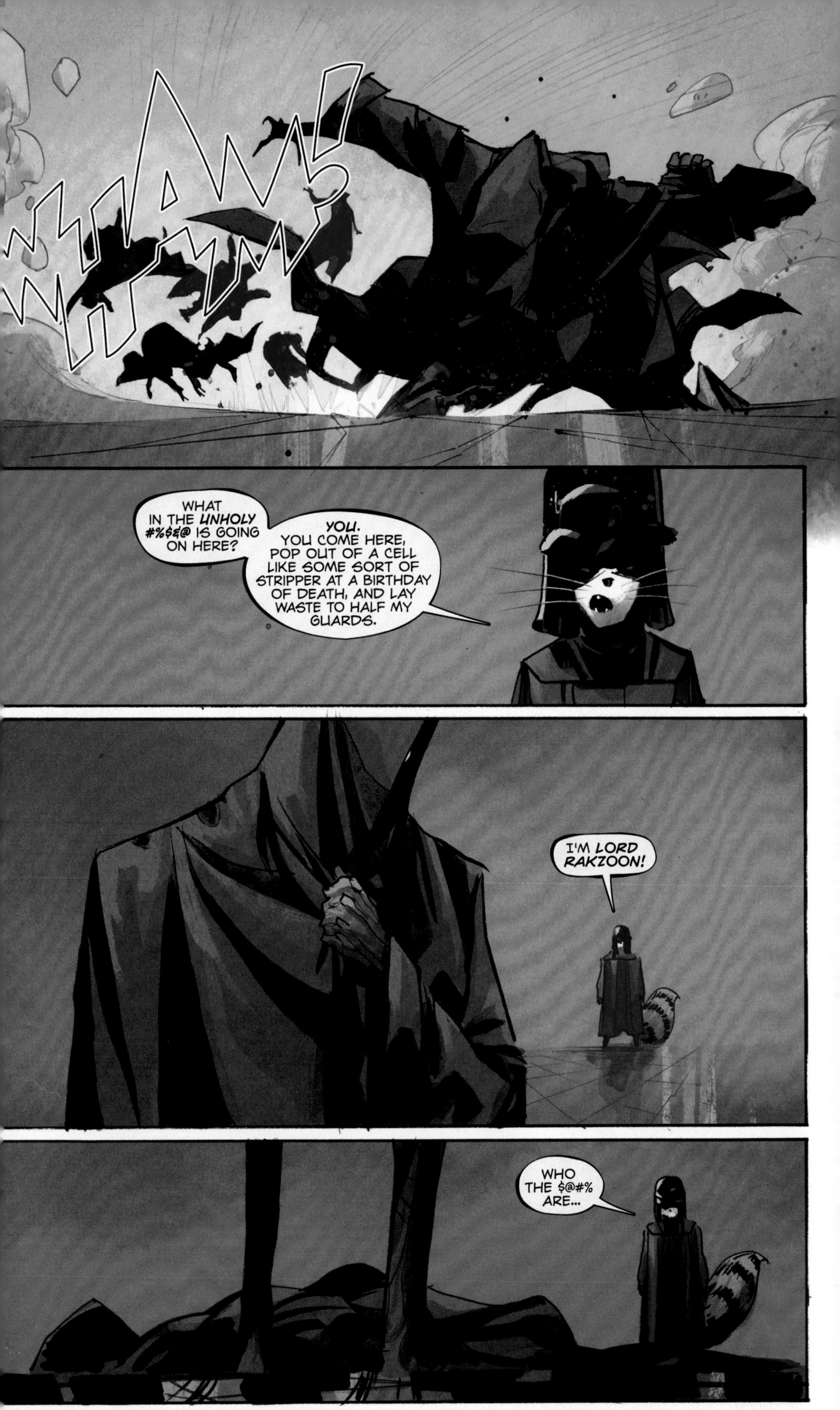
WHAM!
WHAM!
WHAT IN THE UNHOLY #%$&@ IS GOING ON HERE?
YOU. YOU COME HERE, POP OUT OF A CELL LIKE SOME SORT OF STRIPPER AT A BIRTHDAY OF DEATH, AND LAY WASTE TO HALF MY GUARDS.
I'M LORD RAKZOON!
WHO THE $@#% ARE...

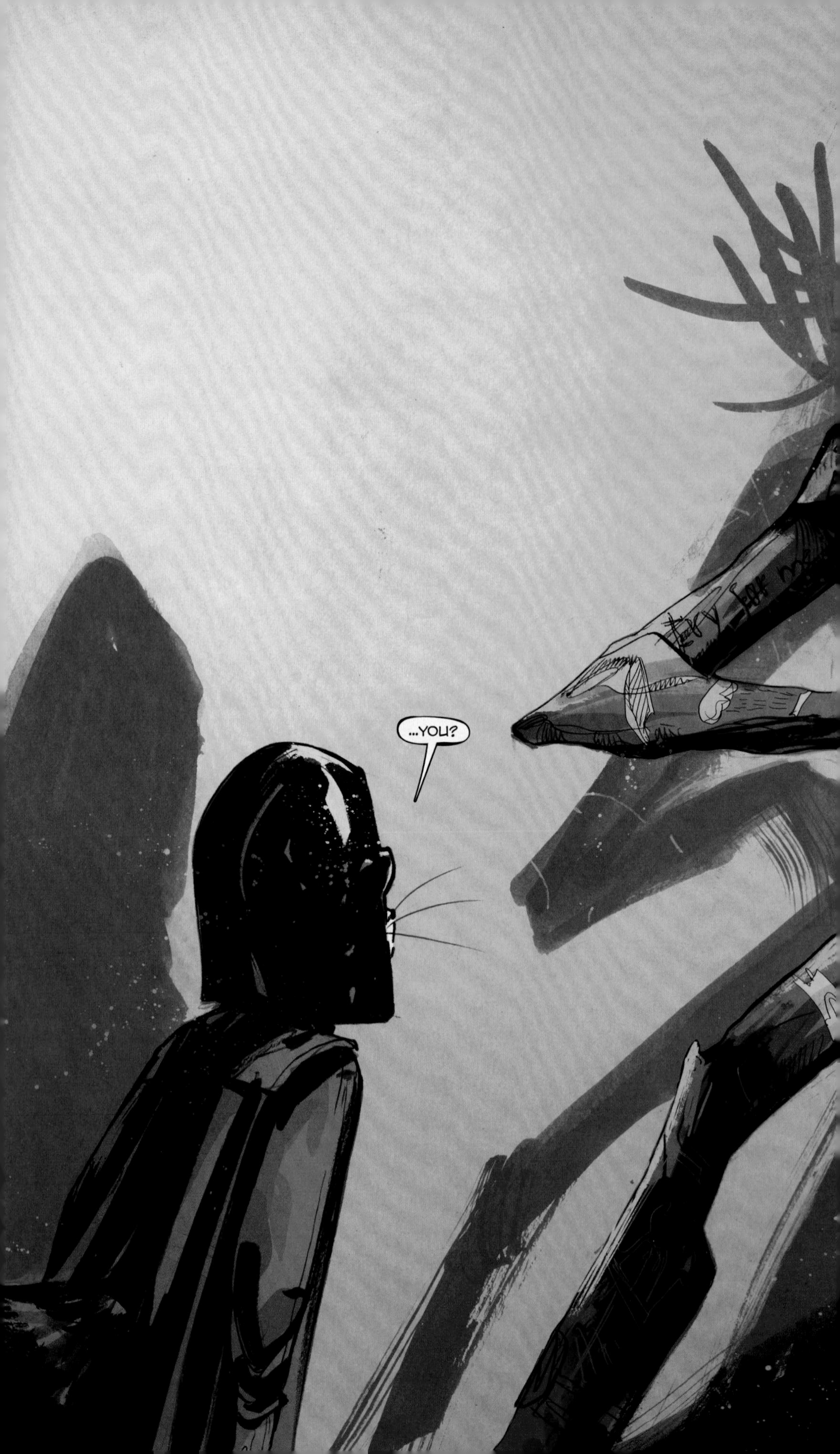
...YOU?

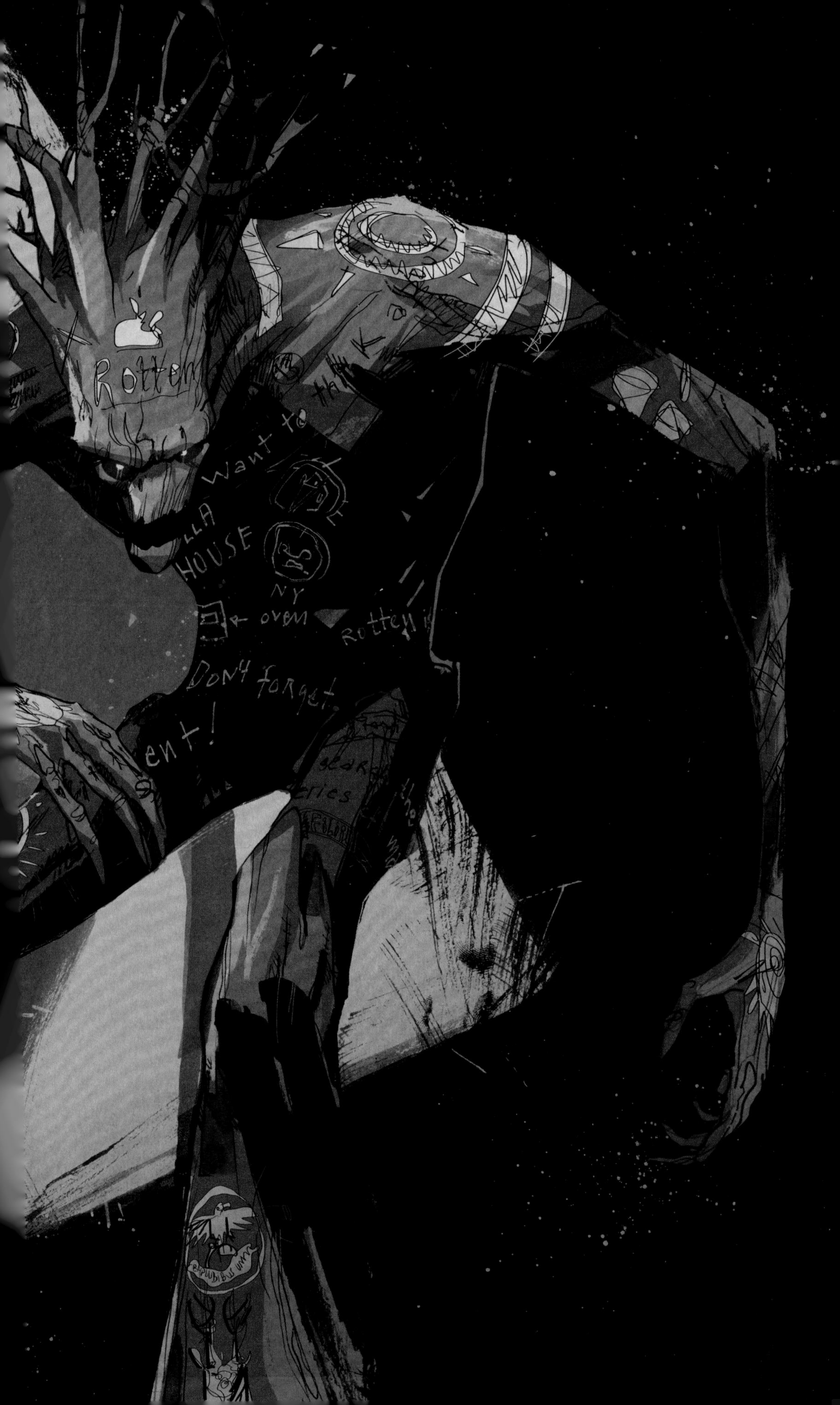

Rotten
Want to
HOUSE
NY
oven
Rotten
Don't forget.
ent!

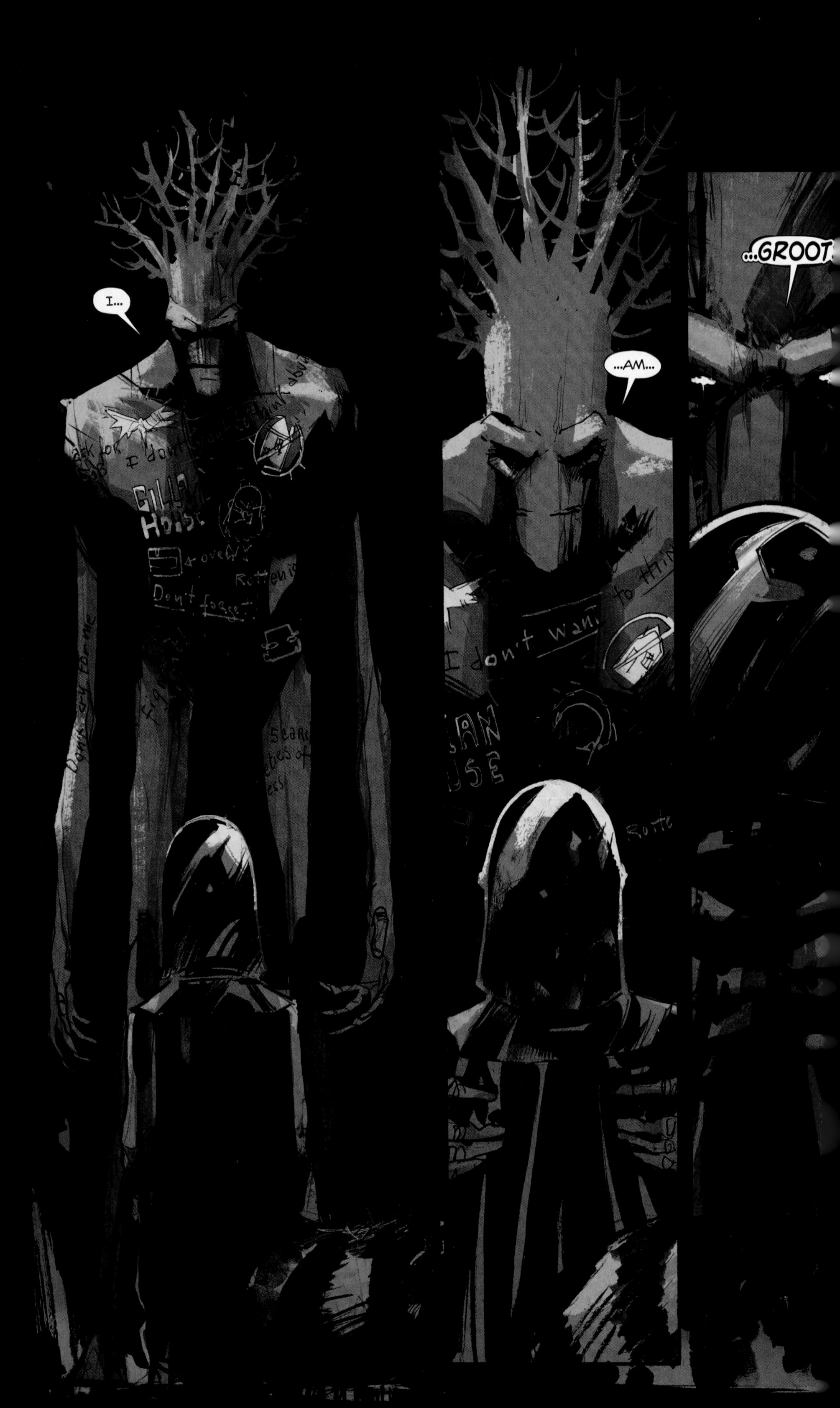
I...
...AM...
...GROOT

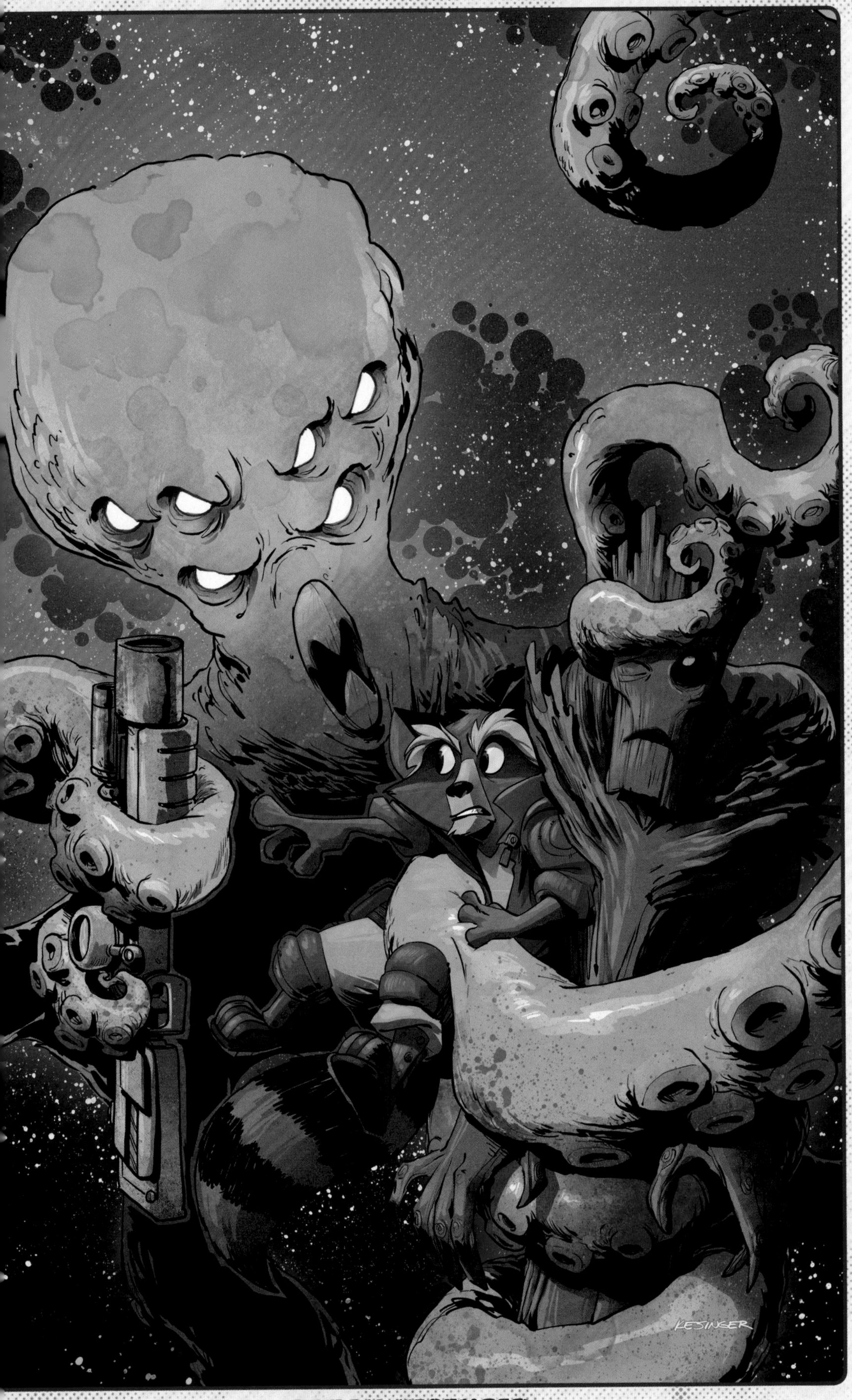
KESINGER

BRIAN KESINGER

2 VARIANT

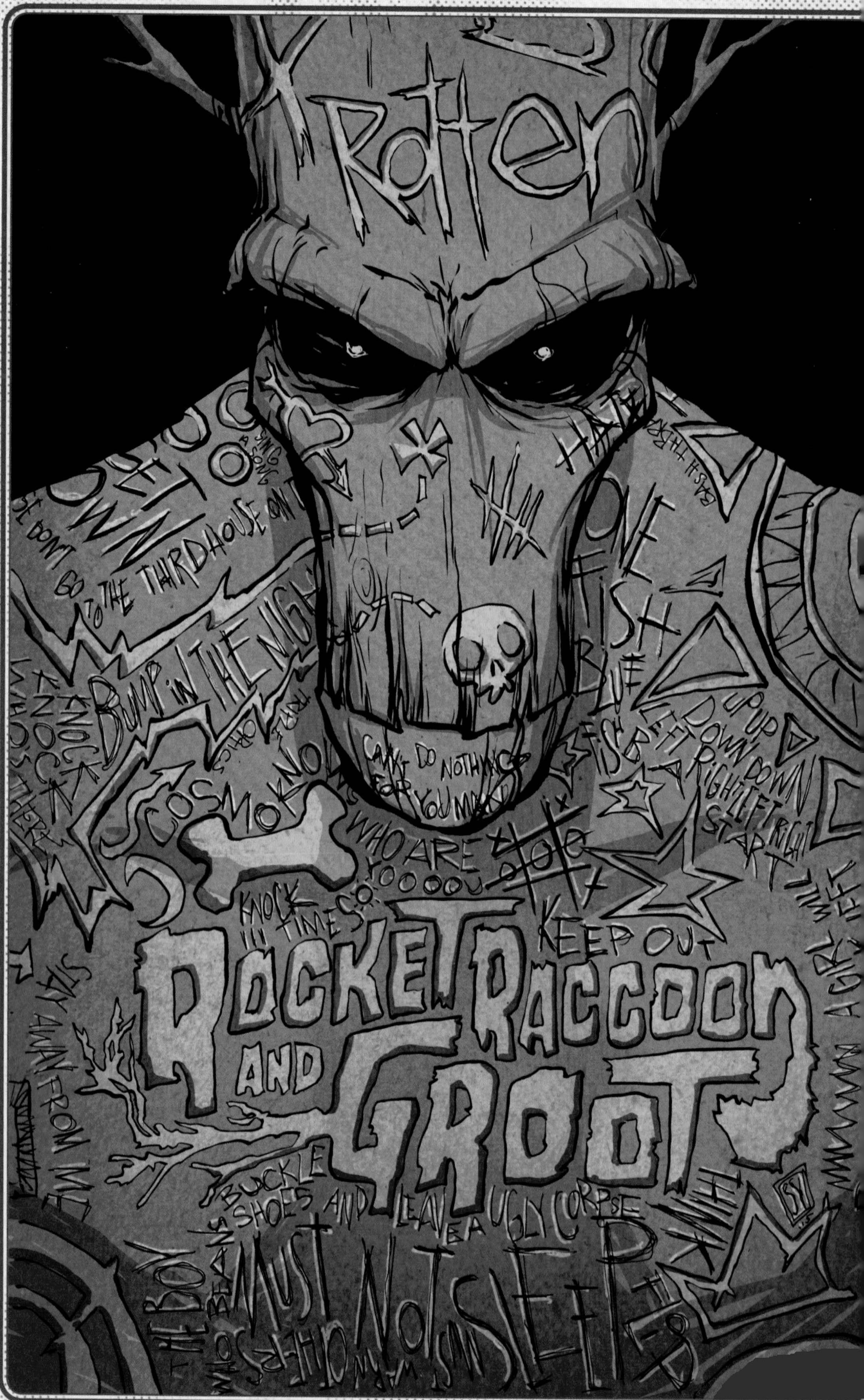
Rotten
BUMP IN THE NIGHT
TO THE THIRD HOUSE ON
KNOCK KNOCK
WHO ARE YOOOOOU
KEEP OUT
UP UP DOWN DOWN LEFT RIGHT LEFT RIGHT B A START
ROCKET RACCOON AND GROOT
BUCKLE SHOES AND LEAVE A UGLY CORPSE
STAY AWAY FROM ME

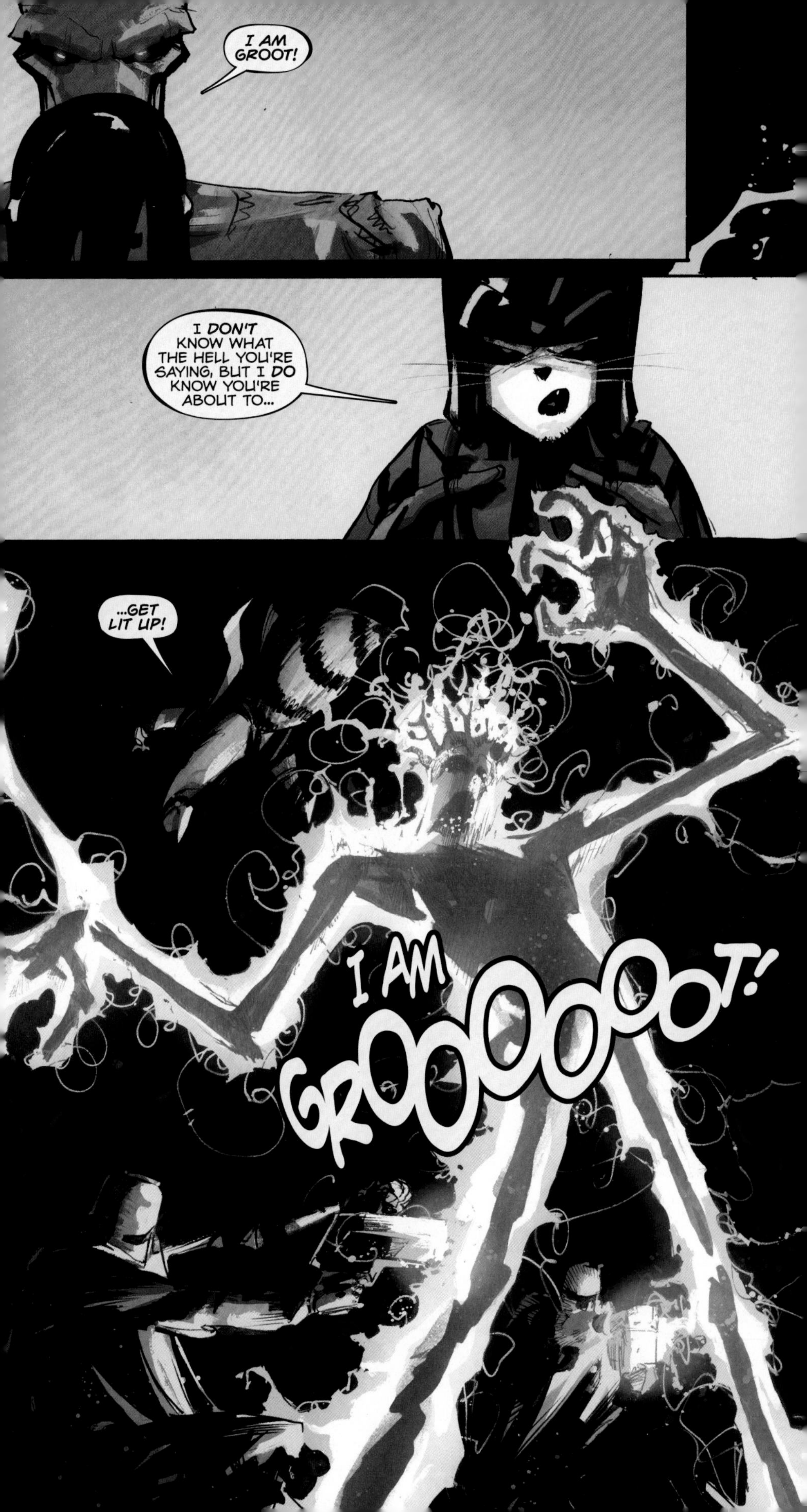
I AM GROOT!
I DON'T KNOW WHAT THE HELL YOU'RE SAYING, BUT I DO KNOW YOU'RE ABOUT TO...
...GET LIT UP!
I AM GROOOOOOOT!

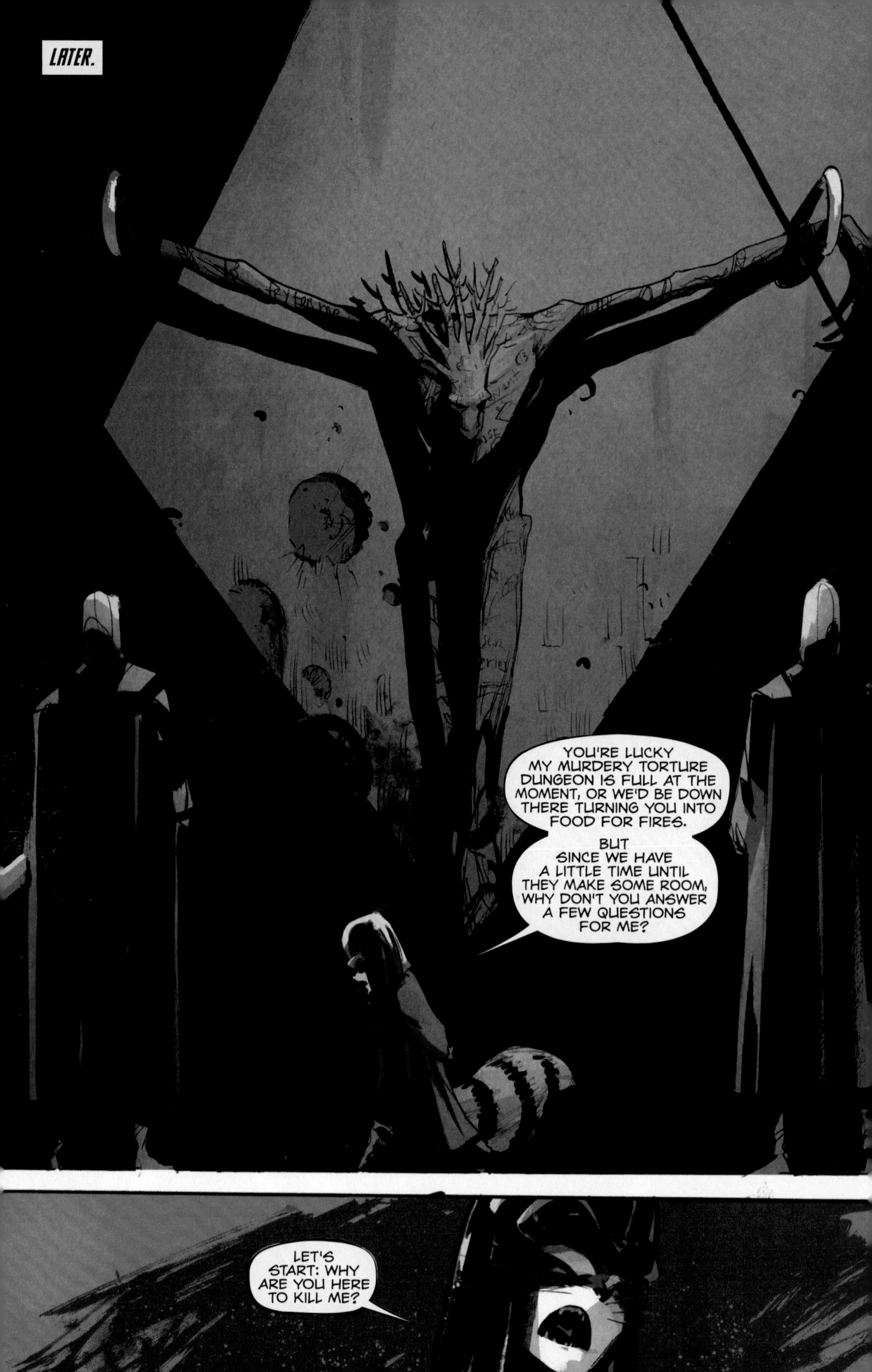
LATER.
YOU'RE LUCKY MY MURDERY TORTURE DUNGEON IS FULL AT THE MOMENT, OR WE'D BE DOWN THERE TURNING YOU INTO FOOD FOR FIRES.
BUT SINCE WE HAVE A LITTLE TIME UNTIL THEY MAKE SOME ROOM, WHY DON'T YOU ANSWER A FEW QUESTIONS FOR ME?

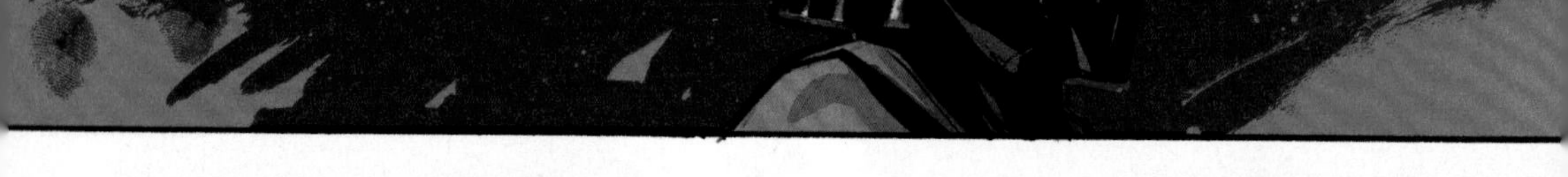
LET'S START: WHY ARE YOU HERE TO KILL ME?

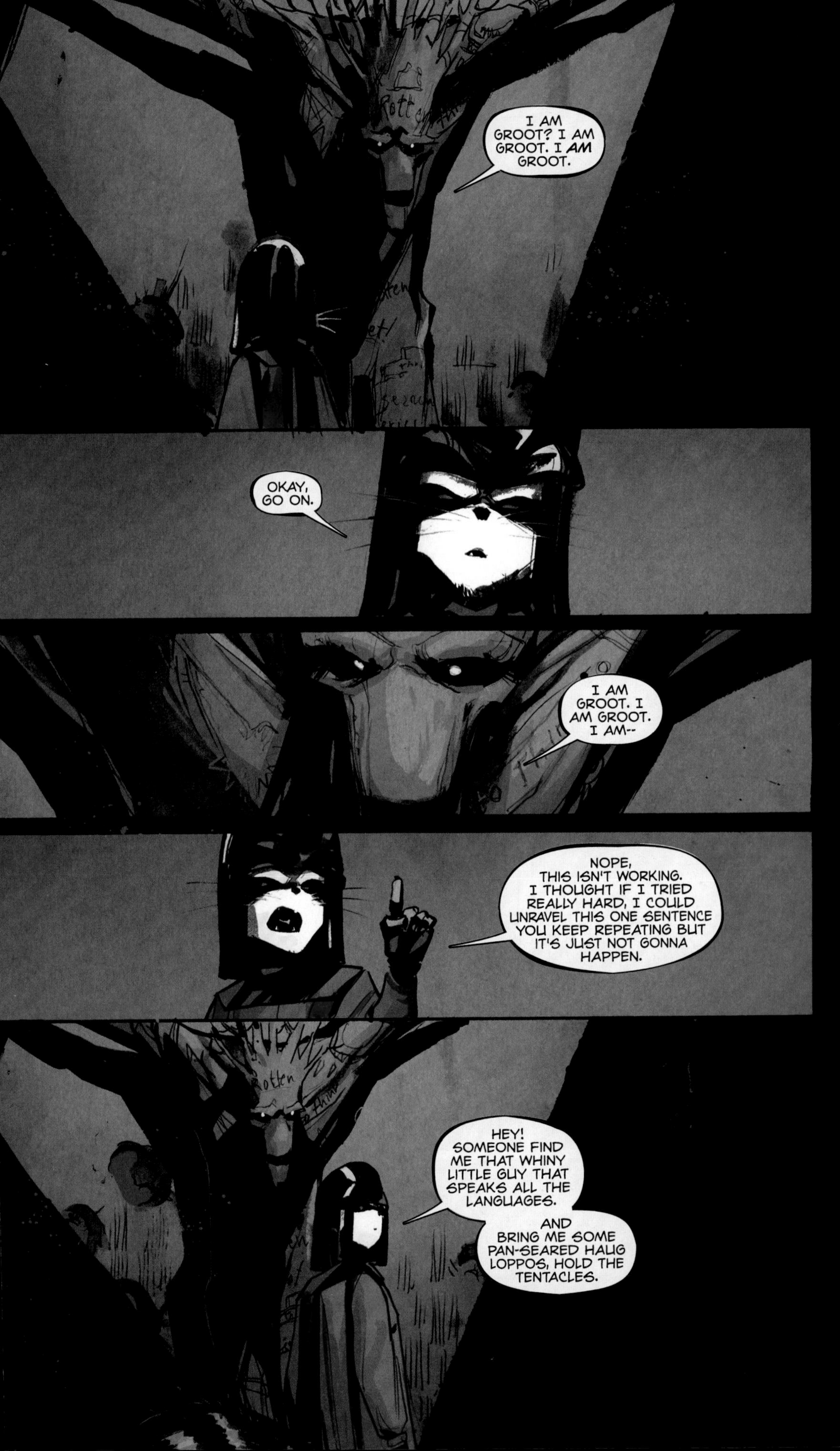
I AM GROOT? I AM GROOT. I *AM* GROOT.
OKAY, GO ON.
I AM GROOT. I AM GROOT. I AM--
NOPE, THIS ISN'T WORKING. I THOUGHT IF I TRIED REALLY HARD, I COULD UNRAVEL THIS ONE SENTENCE YOU KEEP REPEATING BUT IT'S JUST NOT GONNA HAPPEN.
HEY! SOMEONE FIND ME THAT WHINY LITTLE GUY THAT SPEAKS ALL THE LANGUAGES.
AND BRING ME SOME PAN-SEARED HAUG LOPPOS, HOLD THE TENTACLES.

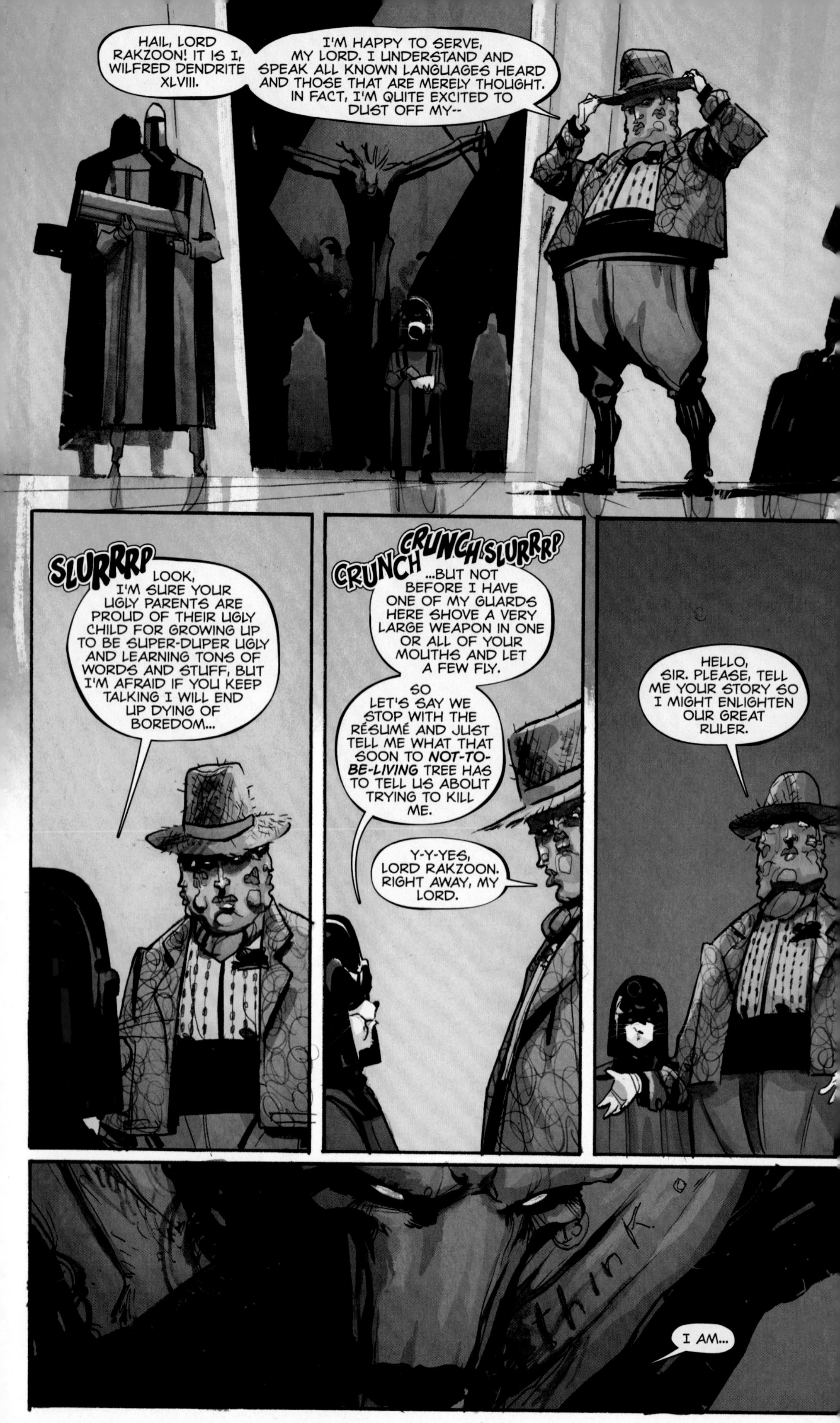
HAIL, LORD RAKZOON! IT IS I, WILFRED DENDRITE XLVIII.
I'M HAPPY TO SERVE, MY LORD. I UNDERSTAND AND SPEAK ALL KNOWN LANGUAGES HEARD AND THOSE THAT ARE MERELY THOUGHT. IN FACT, I'M QUITE EXCITED TO DUST OFF MY--
SLURRRP
LOOK, I'M SURE YOUR UGLY PARENTS ARE PROUD OF THEIR UGLY CHILD FOR GROWING UP TO BE SUPER-DUPER UGLY AND LEARNING TONS OF WORDS AND STUFF, BUT I'M AFRAID IF YOU KEEP TALKING I WILL END UP DYING OF BOREDOM...
CRUNCH CRUNCH SLURRRP
...BUT NOT BEFORE I HAVE ONE OF MY GUARDS HERE SHOVE A VERY LARGE WEAPON IN ONE OR ALL OF YOUR MOUTHS AND LET A FEW FLY.
SO LET'S SAY WE STOP WITH THE RÉSUMÉ AND JUST TELL ME WHAT THAT SOON TO NOT-TO-BE-LIVING TREE HAS TO TELL US ABOUT TRYING TO KILL ME.
Y-Y-YES, LORD RAKZOON. RIGHT AWAY, MY LORD.
HELLO, SIR. PLEASE, TELL ME YOUR STORY SO I MIGHT ENLIGHTEN OUR GREAT RULER.
think
I AM...

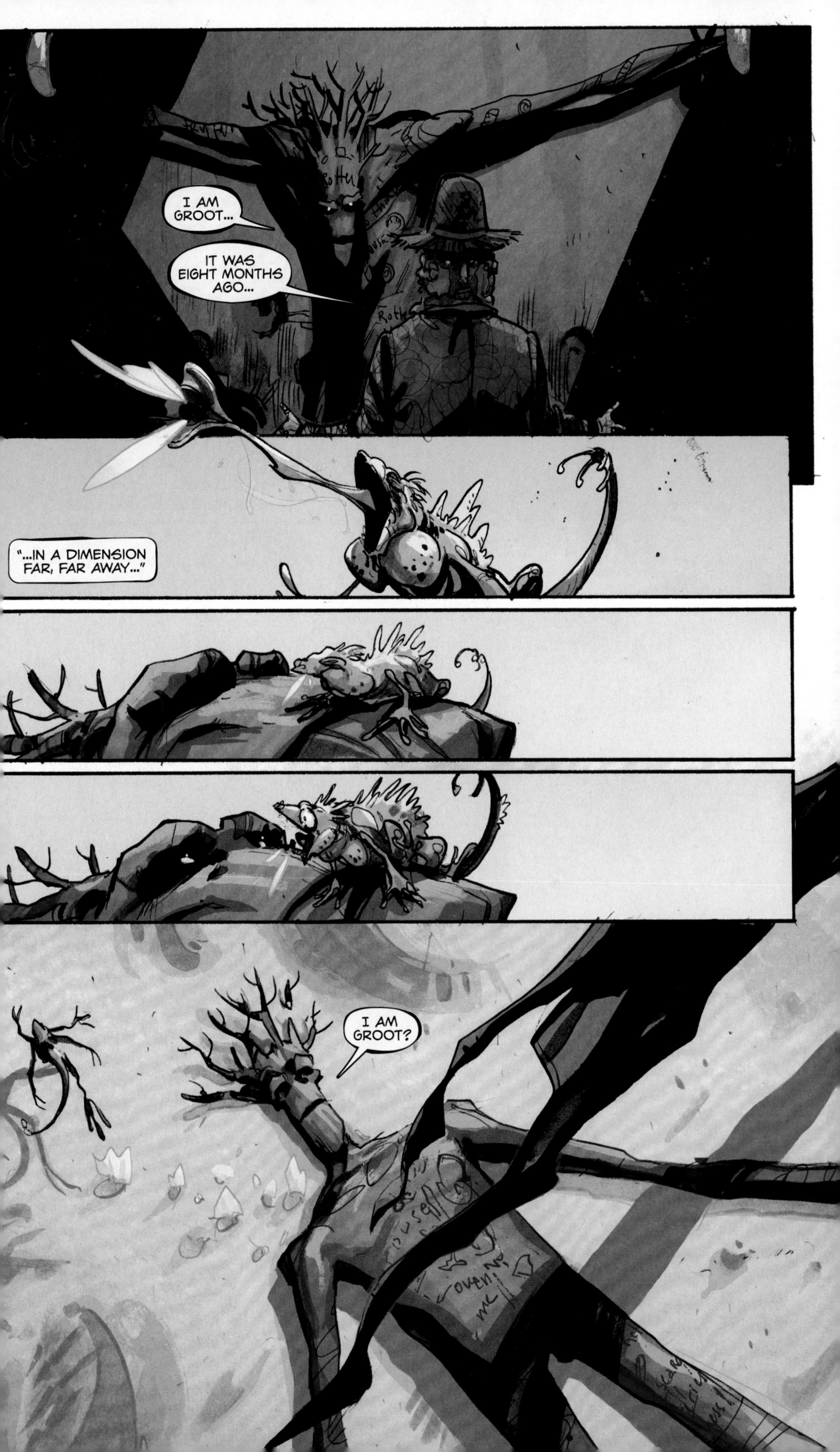
I AM GROOT...
IT WAS EIGHT MONTHS AGO...
"...IN A DIMENSION FAR, FAR AWAY..."
I AM GROOT?

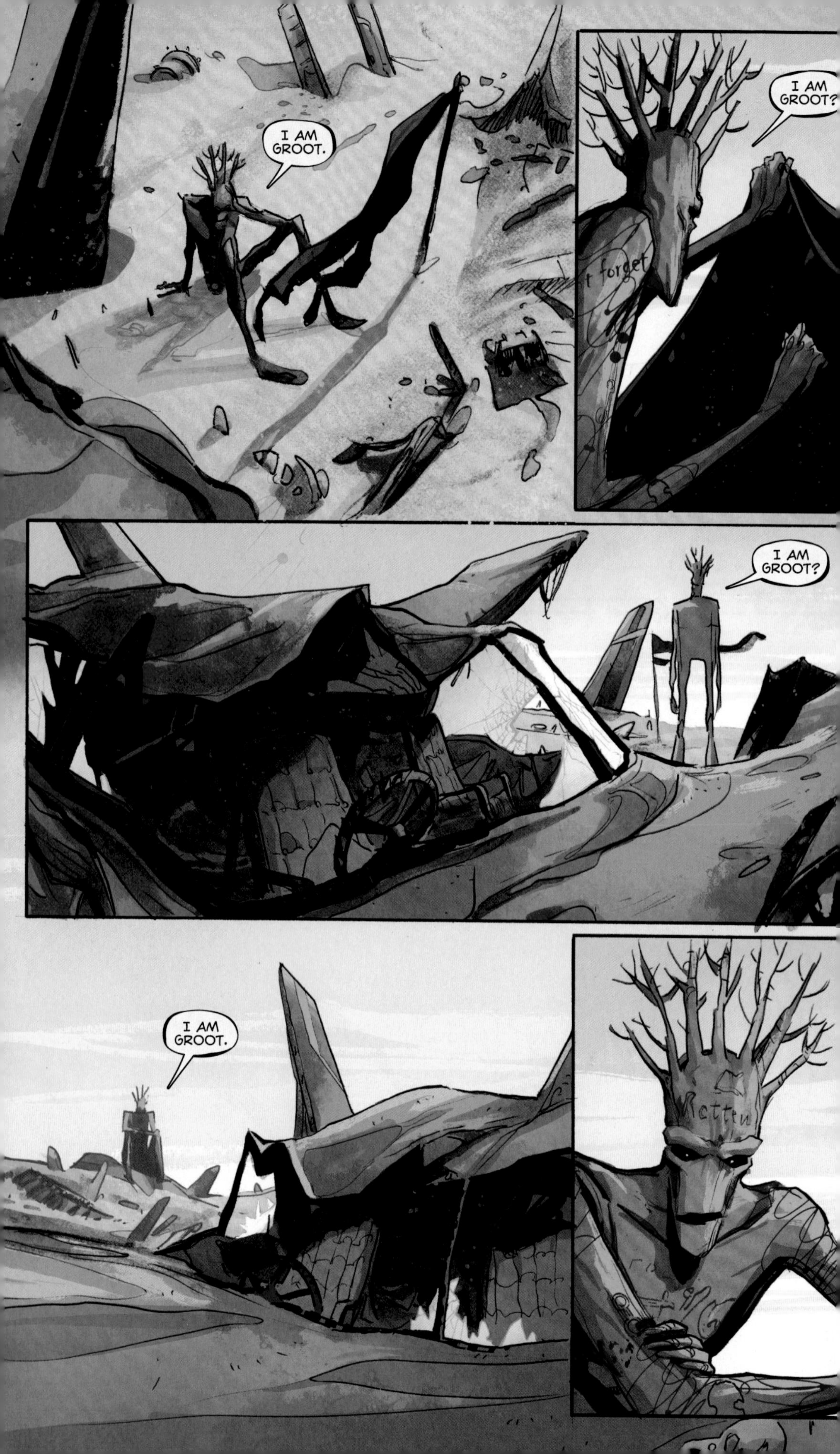
I AM GROOT.
I AM GROOT?
I AM GROOT?
I AM GROOT.

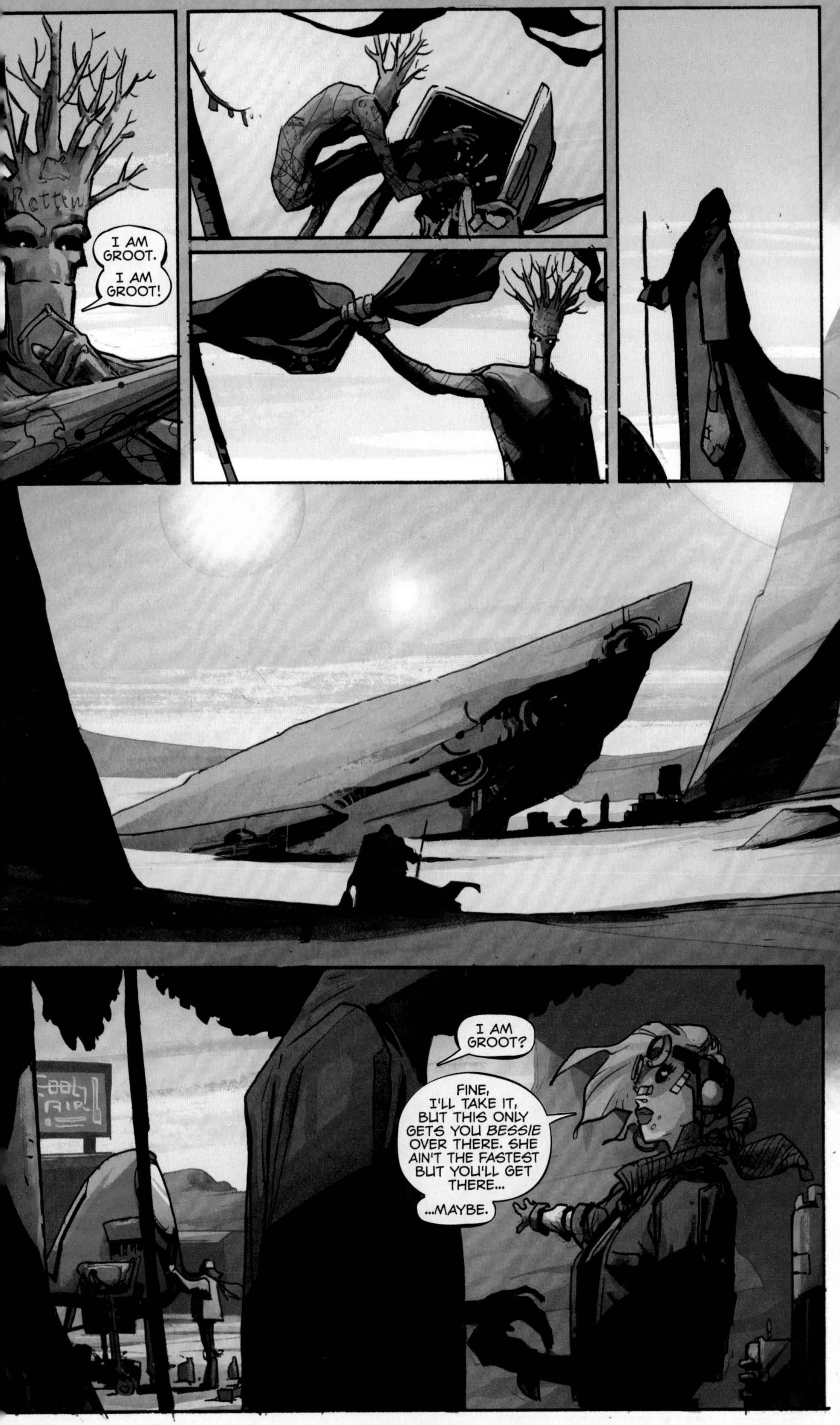
I AM GROOT. I AM GROOT!
I AM GROOT?
FINE, I'LL TAKE IT, BUT THIS ONLY GETS YOU *BESSIE* OVER THERE. SHE AIN'T THE FASTEST BUT YOU'LL GET THERE...
...MAYBE.

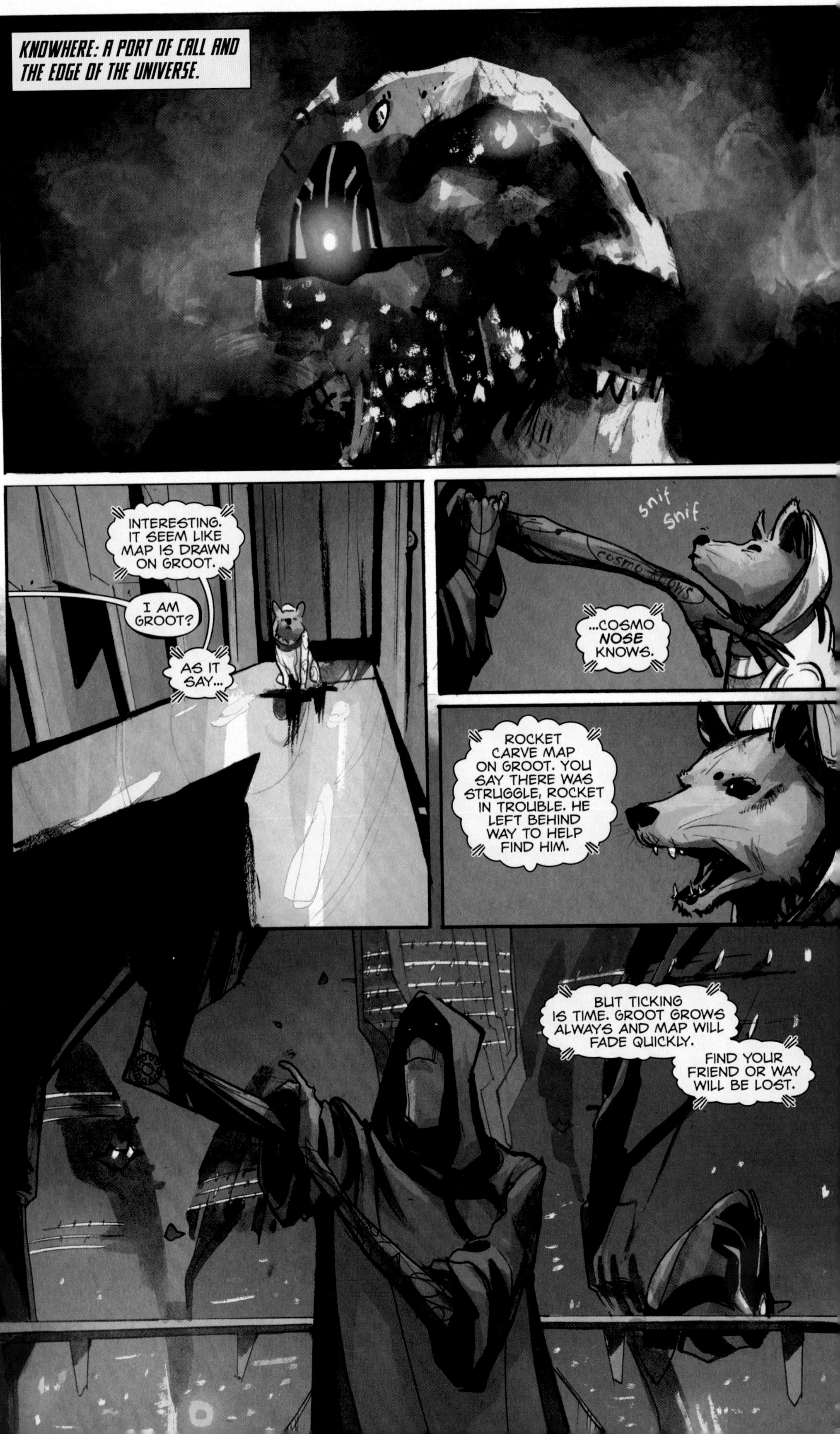
KNOWHERE: A PORT OF CALL AND THE EDGE OF THE UNIVERSE.
INTERESTING. IT SEEM LIKE MAP IS DRAWN ON GROOT.
I AM GROOT?
AS IT SAY...
snif snif
cosmo KNOWS
...COSMO NOSE KNOWS.
ROCKET CARVE MAP ON GROOT. YOU SAY THERE WAS STRUGGLE, ROCKET IN TROUBLE. HE LEFT BEHIND WAY TO HELP FIND HIM.
BUT TICKING IS TIME. GROOT GROWS ALWAYS AND MAP WILL FADE QUICKLY.
FIND YOUR FRIEND OR WAY WILL BE LOST.

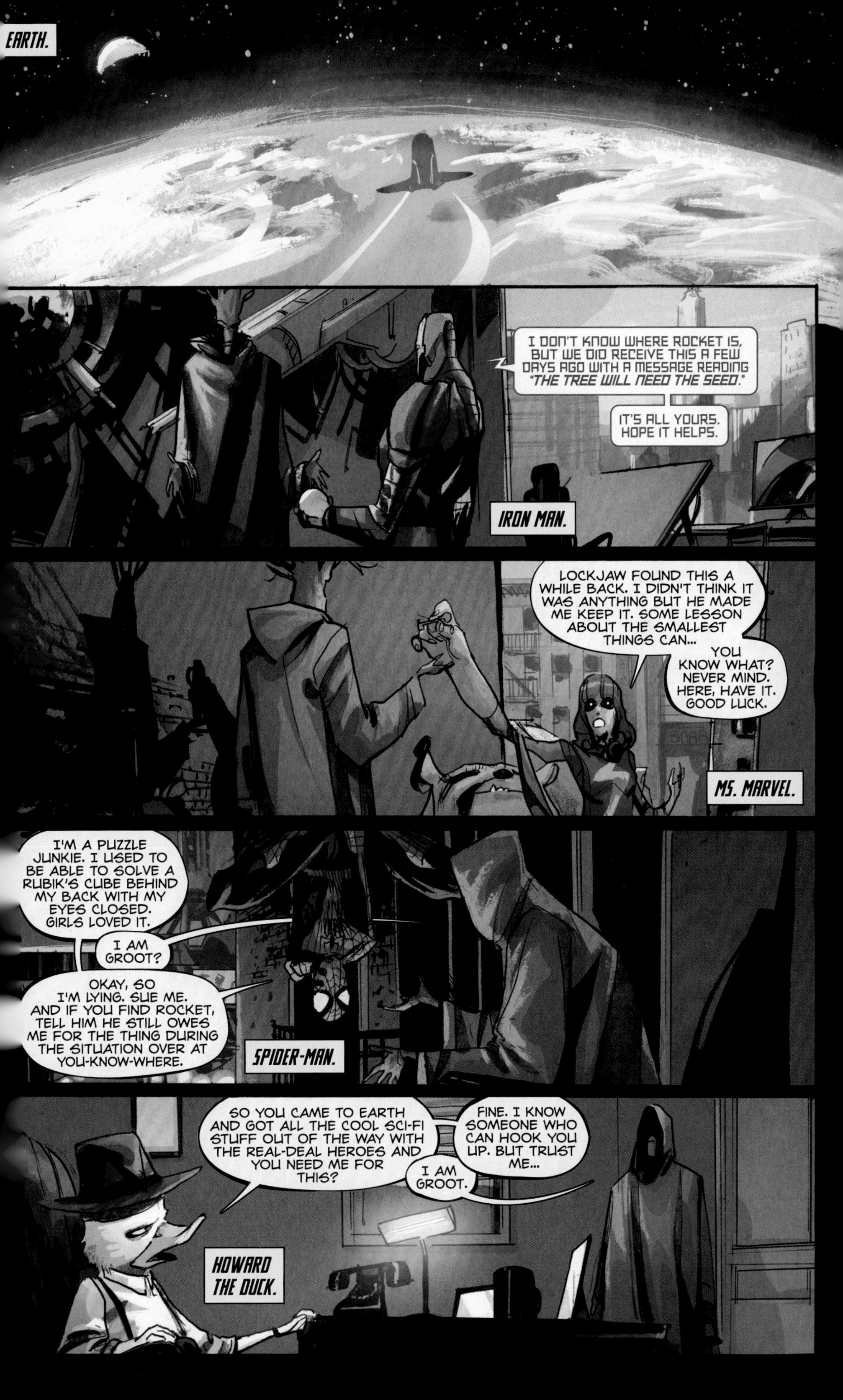
EARTH.
I DON'T KNOW WHERE ROCKET IS, BUT WE DID RECEIVE THIS A FEW DAYS AGO WITH A MESSAGE READING "THE TREE WILL NEED THE SEED."
IT'S ALL YOURS. HOPE IT HELPS.
IRON MAN.
LOCKJAW FOUND THIS A WHILE BACK. I DIDN'T THINK IT WAS ANYTHING BUT HE MADE ME KEEP IT. SOME LESSON ABOUT THE SMALLEST THINGS CAN...
YOU KNOW WHAT? NEVER MIND. HERE, HAVE IT. GOOD LUCK.
MS. MARVEL.
I'M A PUZZLE JUNKIE. I USED TO BE ABLE TO SOLVE A RUBIK'S CUBE BEHIND MY BACK WITH MY EYES CLOSED. GIRLS LOVED IT.
I AM GROOT?
OKAY, SO I'M LYING. SUE ME. AND IF YOU FIND ROCKET, TELL HIM HE STILL OWES ME FOR THE THING DURING THE SITUATION OVER AT YOU-KNOW-WHERE.
SPIDER-MAN.
SO YOU CAME TO EARTH AND GOT ALL THE COOL SCI-FI STUFF OUT OF THE WAY WITH THE REAL-DEAL HEROES AND YOU NEED ME FOR THIS?
I AM GROOT.
FINE. I KNOW SOMEONE WHO CAN HOOK YOU UP. BUT TRUST ME...
HOWARD THE DUCK.

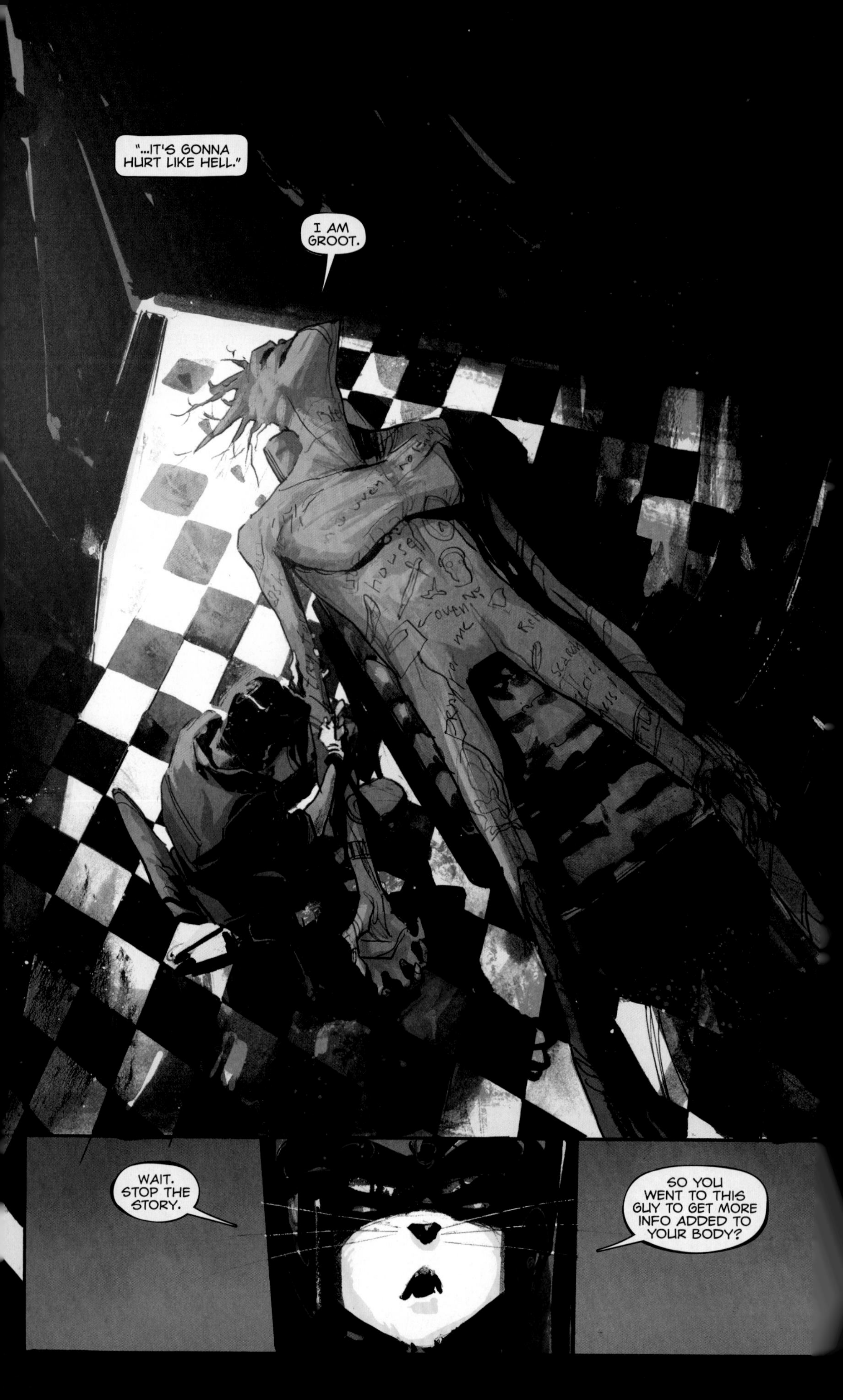
"...IT'S GONNA HURT LIKE HELL."
I AM GROOT.
WAIT. STOP THE STORY.
SO YOU WENT TO THIS GUY TO GET MORE INFO ADDED TO YOUR BODY?

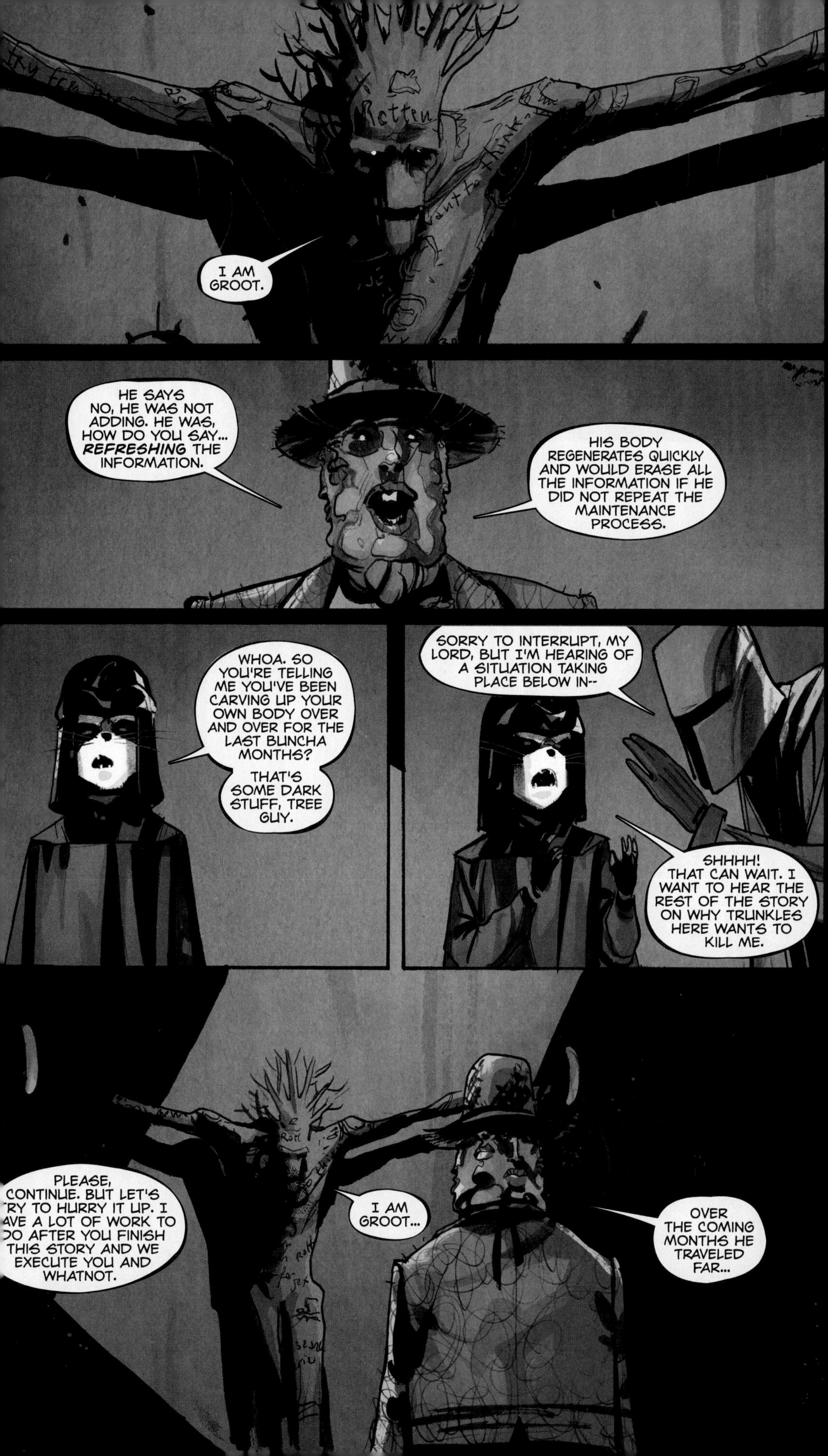
I AM GROOT.
HE SAYS NO, HE WAS NOT ADDING. HE WAS, HOW DO YOU SAY... ***REFRESHING*** THE INFORMATION.
HIS BODY REGENERATES QUICKLY AND WOULD ERASE ALL THE INFORMATION IF HE DID NOT REPEAT THE MAINTENANCE PROCESS.
WHOA. SO YOU'RE TELLING ME YOU'VE BEEN CARVING UP YOUR OWN BODY OVER AND OVER FOR THE LAST BUNCHA MONTHS?
THAT'S SOME DARK STUFF, TREE GUY.
SORRY TO INTERRUPT, MY LORD, BUT I'M HEARING OF A SITUATION TAKING PLACE BELOW IN--
SHHHH! THAT CAN WAIT. I WANT TO HEAR THE REST OF THE STORY ON WHY TRUNKLES HERE WANTS TO KILL ME.
PLEASE, CONTINUE. BUT LET'S RY TO HURRY IT UP. I AVE A LOT OF WORK TO DO AFTER YOU FINISH THIS STORY AND WE EXECUTE YOU AND WHATNOT.
I AM GROOT...
OVER THE COMING MONTHS HE TRAVELED FAR...

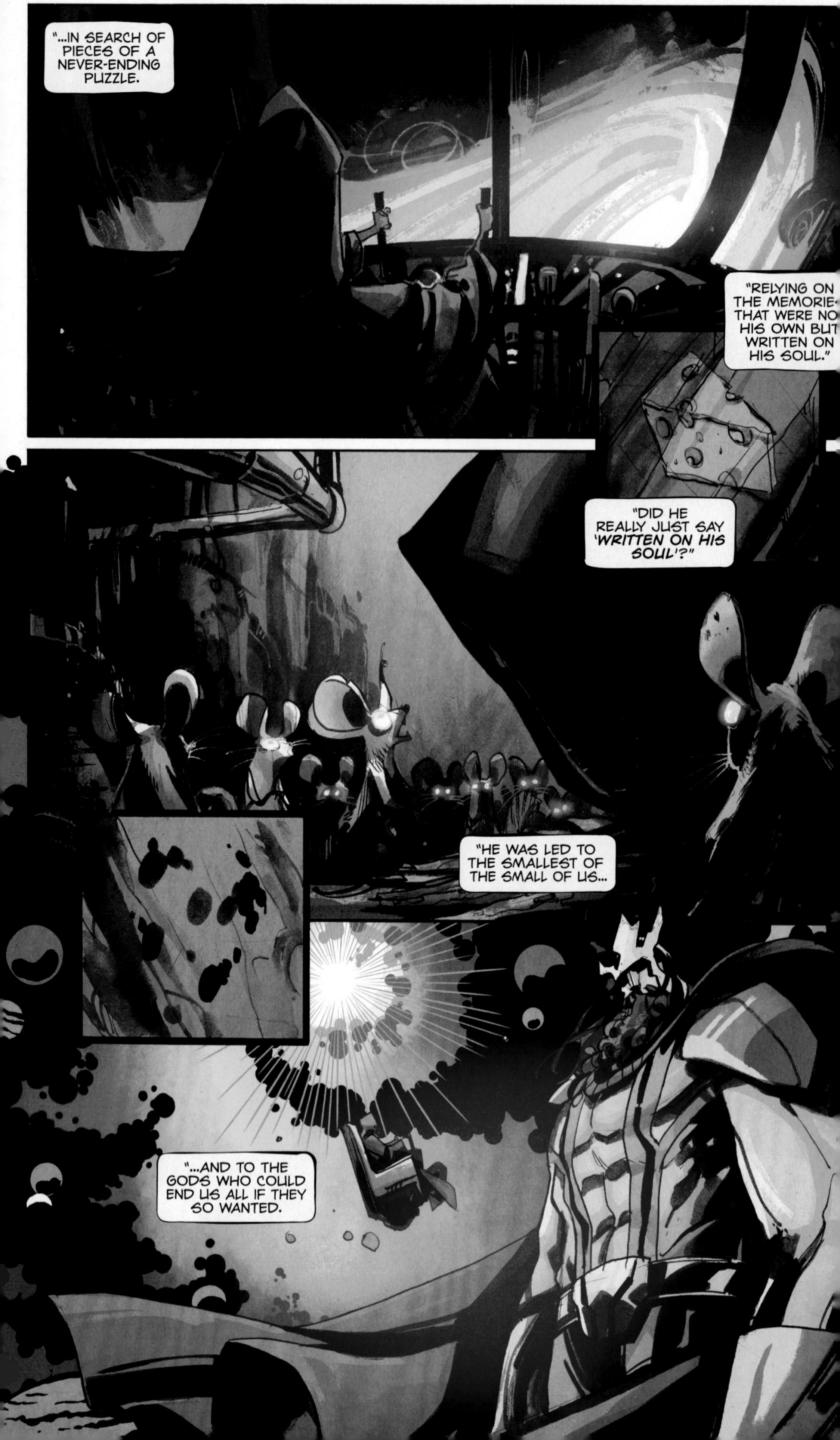
"...IN SEARCH OF PIECES OF A NEVER-ENDING PUZZLE.
"RELYING ON THE MEMORIE THAT WERE NO HIS OWN BUT WRITTEN ON HIS SOUL."
"DID HE REALLY JUST SAY '*WRITTEN ON HIS SOUL*'?"
"HE WAS LED TO THE SMALLEST OF THE SMALL OF US...
"...AND TO THE GODS WHO COULD END US ALL IF THEY SO WANTED.

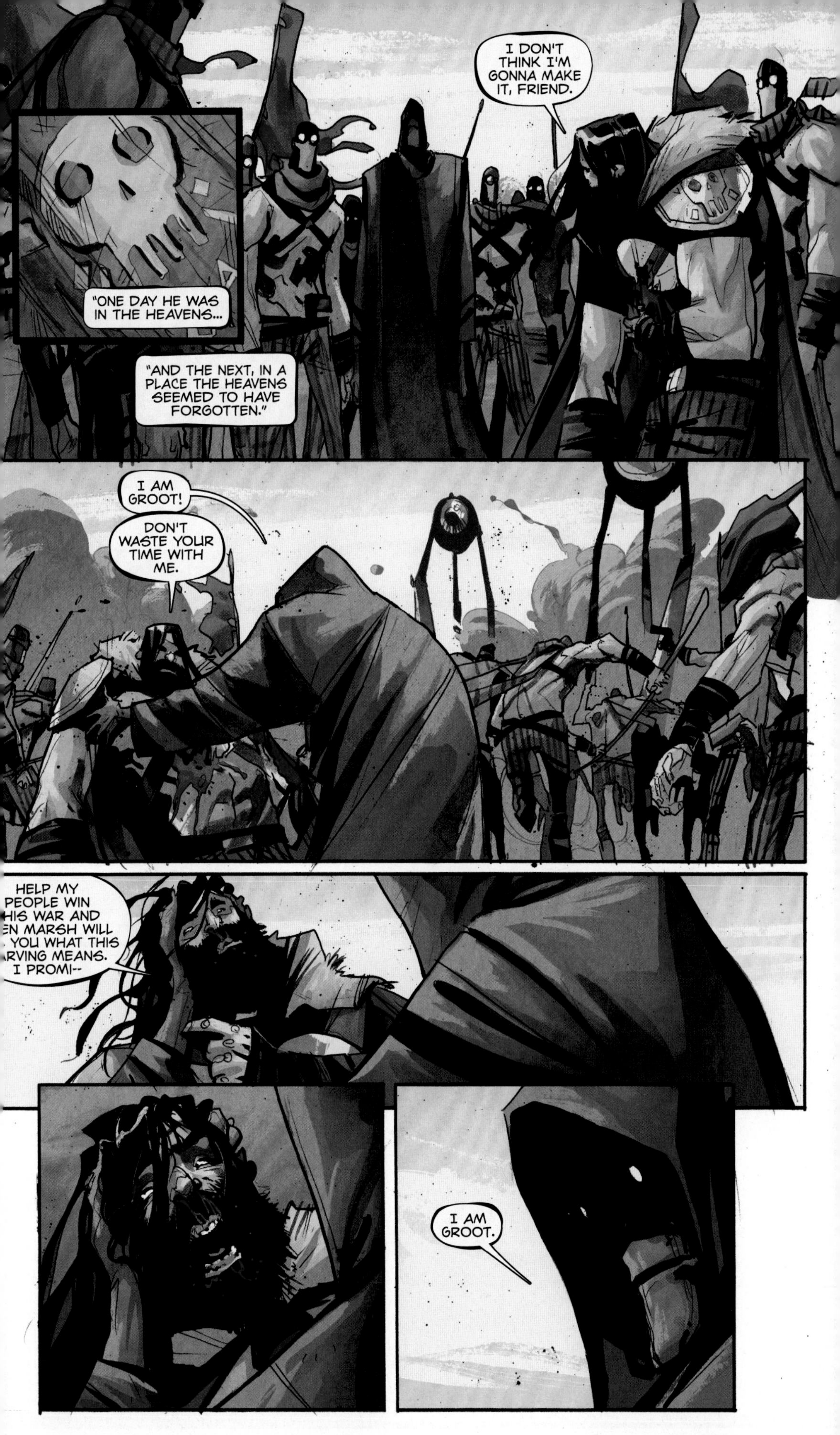
"ONE DAY HE WAS IN THE HEAVENS...
"AND THE NEXT, IN A PLACE THE HEAVENS SEEMED TO HAVE FORGOTTEN."
I DON'T THINK I'M GONNA MAKE IT, FRIEND.
I AM GROOT!
DON'T WASTE YOUR TIME WITH ME.
HELP MY PEOPLE WIN HIS WAR AND EN MARSH WILL YOU WHAT THIS RVING MEANS. I PROMI--
I AM GROOT.

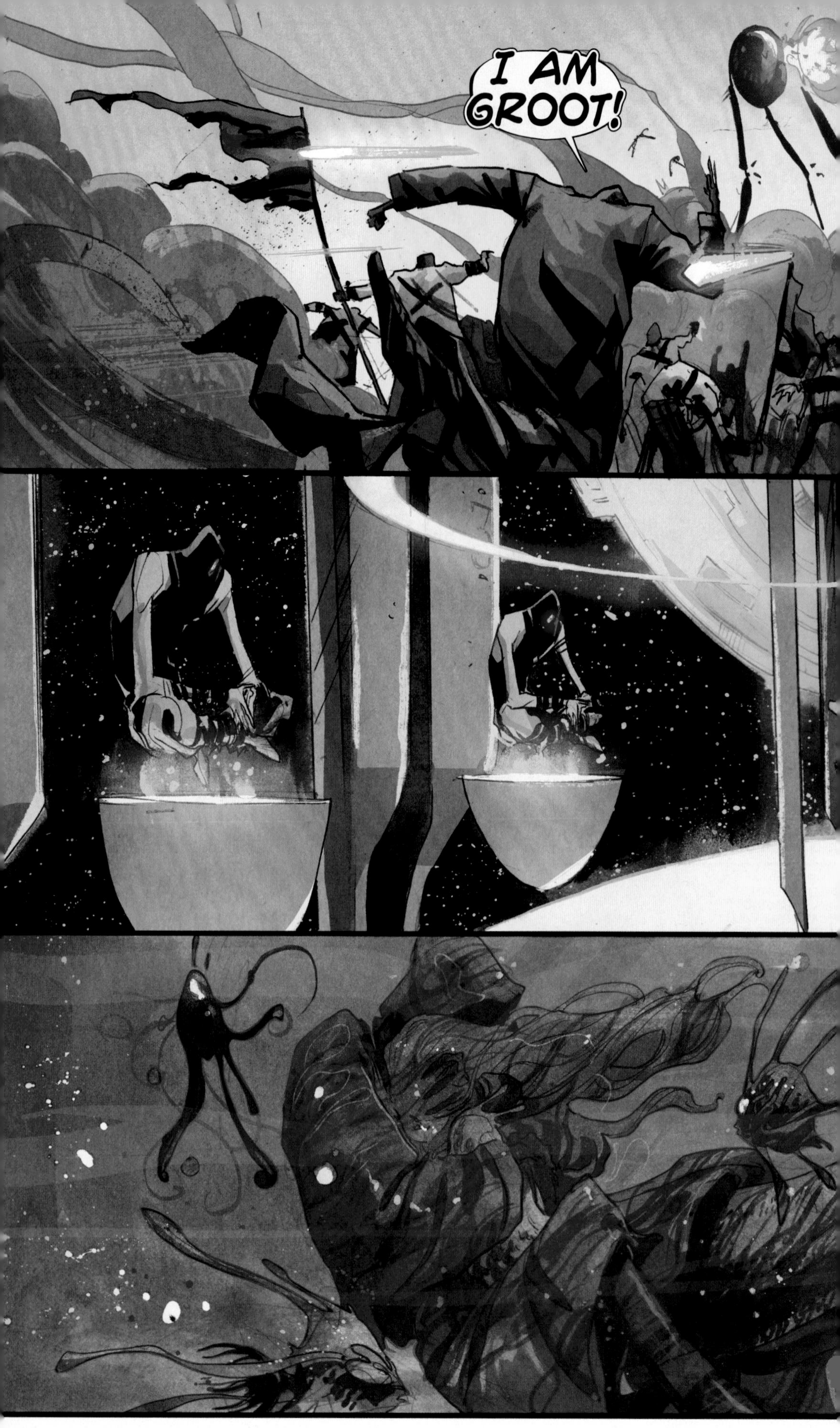
I AM GROOT!

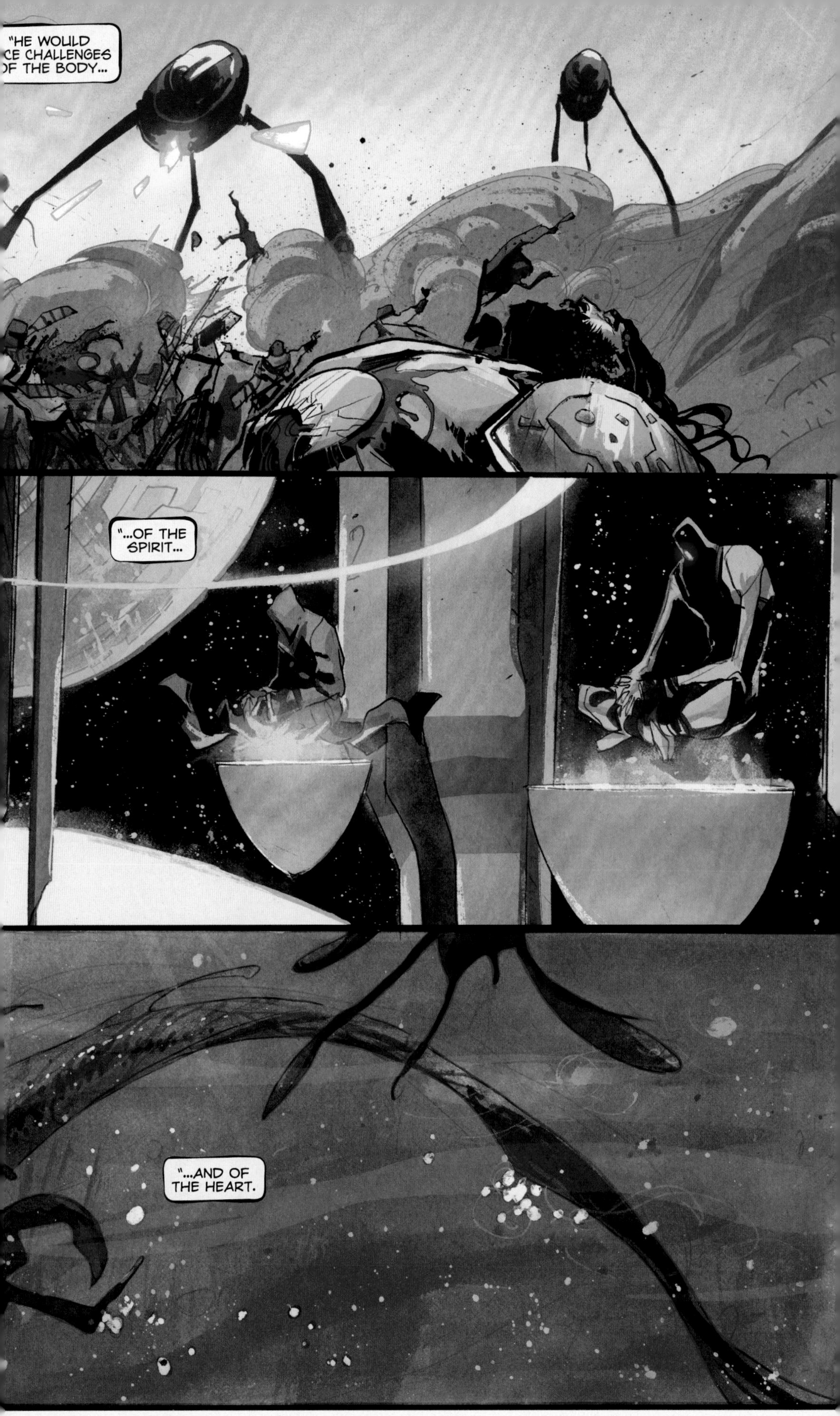
"HE WOULD CE CHALLENGES F THE BODY...
"...OF THE SPIRIT...
"...AND OF THE HEART.

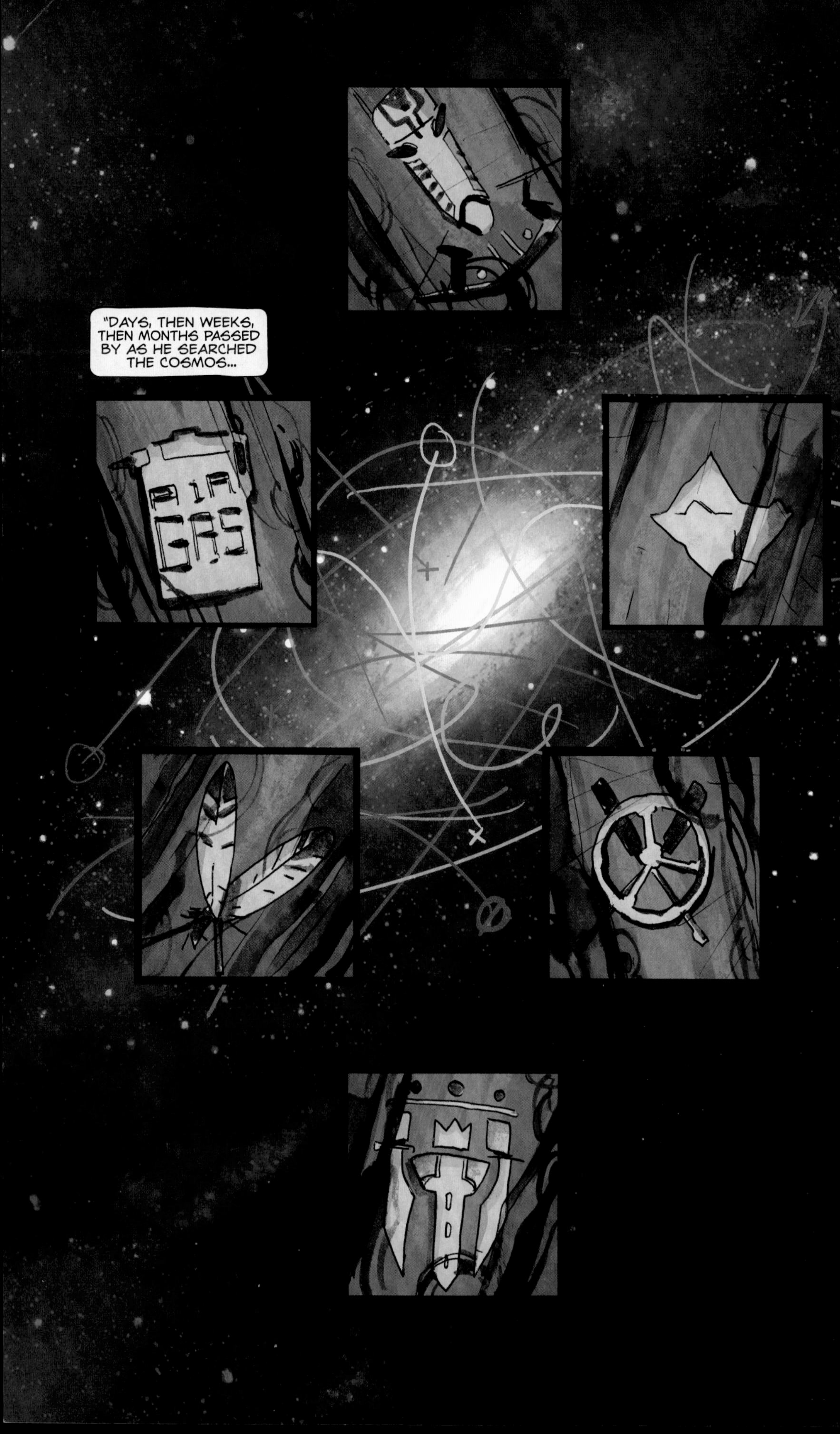
"DAYS, THEN WEEKS, THEN MONTHS PASSED BY AS HE SEARCHED THE COSMOS...
AIR
GAS

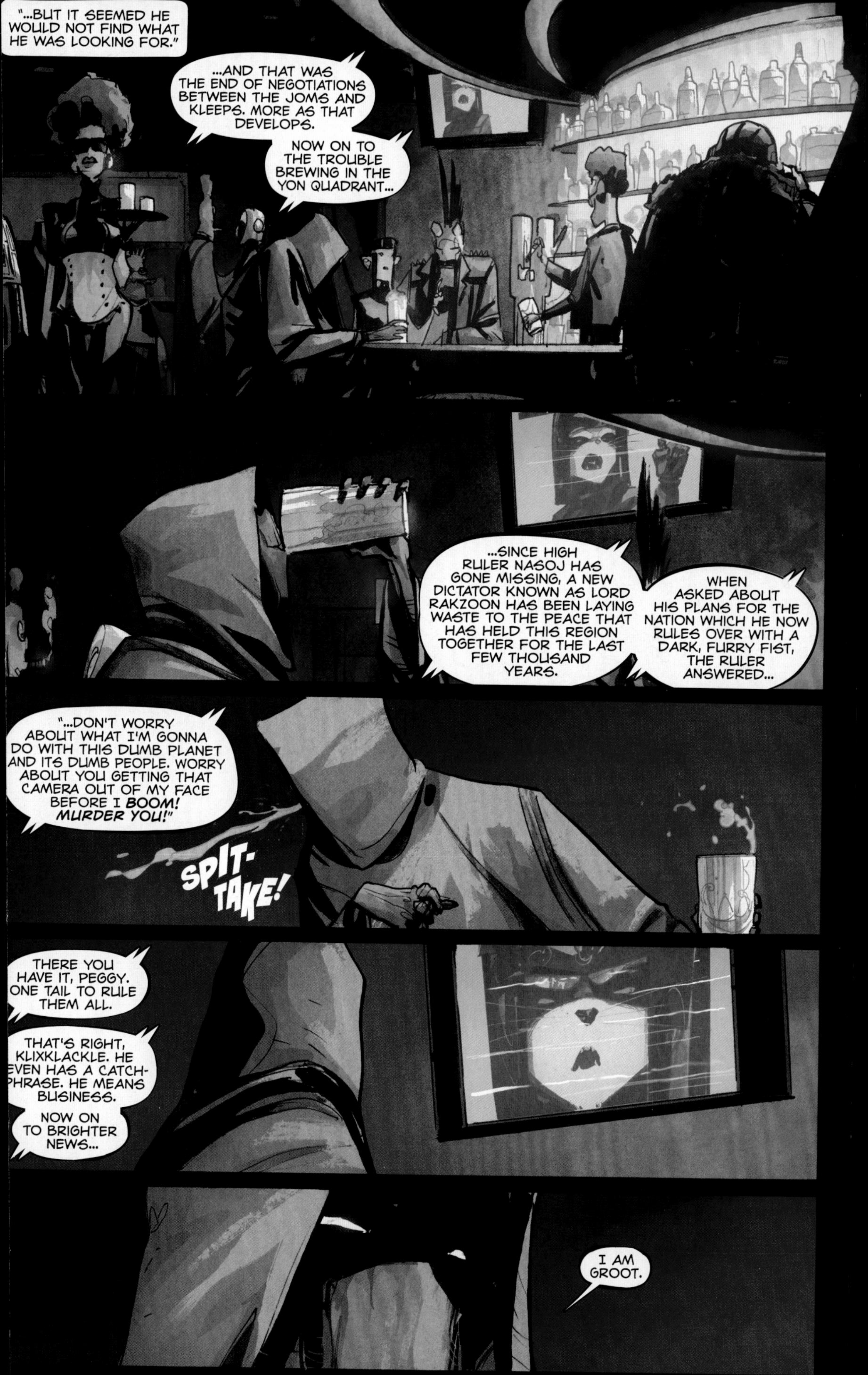
"...BUT IT SEEMED HE WOULD NOT FIND WHAT HE WAS LOOKING FOR."
...AND THAT WAS THE END OF NEGOTIATIONS BETWEEN THE JOMS AND KLEEPS. MORE AS THAT DEVELOPS.
NOW ON TO THE TROUBLE BREWING IN THE YON QUADRANT...
...SINCE HIGH RULER NASOJ HAS GONE MISSING, A NEW DICTATOR KNOWN AS LORD RAKZOON HAS BEEN LAYING WASTE TO THE PEACE THAT HAS HELD THIS REGION TOGETHER FOR THE LAST FEW THOUSAND YEARS.
WHEN ASKED ABOUT HIS PLANS FOR THE NATION WHICH HE NOW RULES OVER WITH A DARK, FURRY FIST, THE RULER ANSWERED...
"...DON'T WORRY ABOUT WHAT I'M GONNA DO WITH THIS DUMB PLANET AND ITS DUMB PEOPLE. WORRY ABOUT YOU GETTING THAT CAMERA OUT OF MY FACE BEFORE I BOOM! MURDER YOU!"
SPIT-TAKE!
THERE YOU HAVE IT, PEGGY. ONE TAIL TO RULE THEM ALL.
THAT'S RIGHT, KLIXKLACKLE. HE EVEN HAS A CATCH-PHRASE. HE MEANS BUSINESS.
NOW ON TO BRIGHTER NEWS...
I AM GROOT.

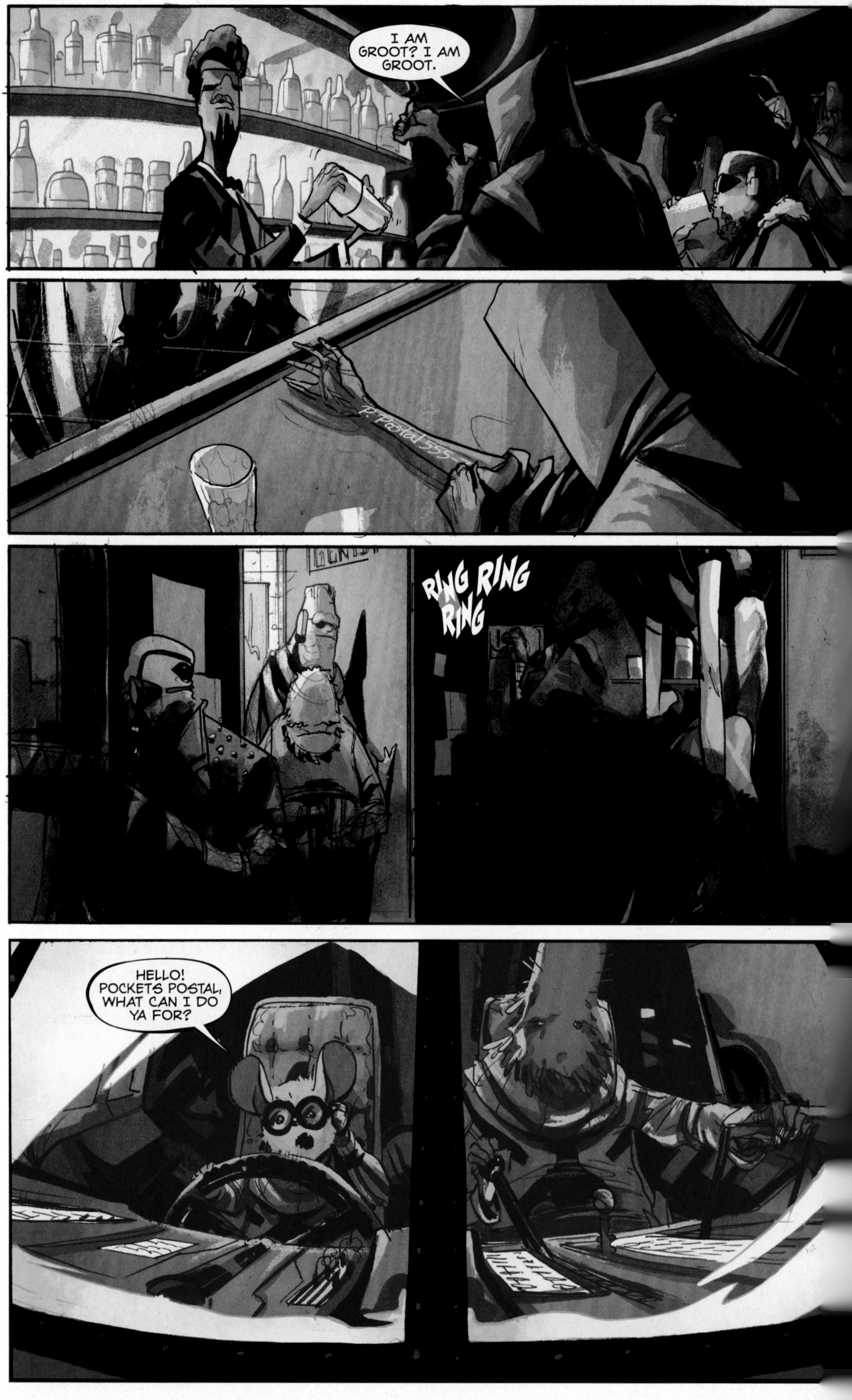
I AM GROOT? I AM GROOT.
RING RING RING
HELLO! POCKETS POSTAL, WHAT CAN I DO YA FOR?

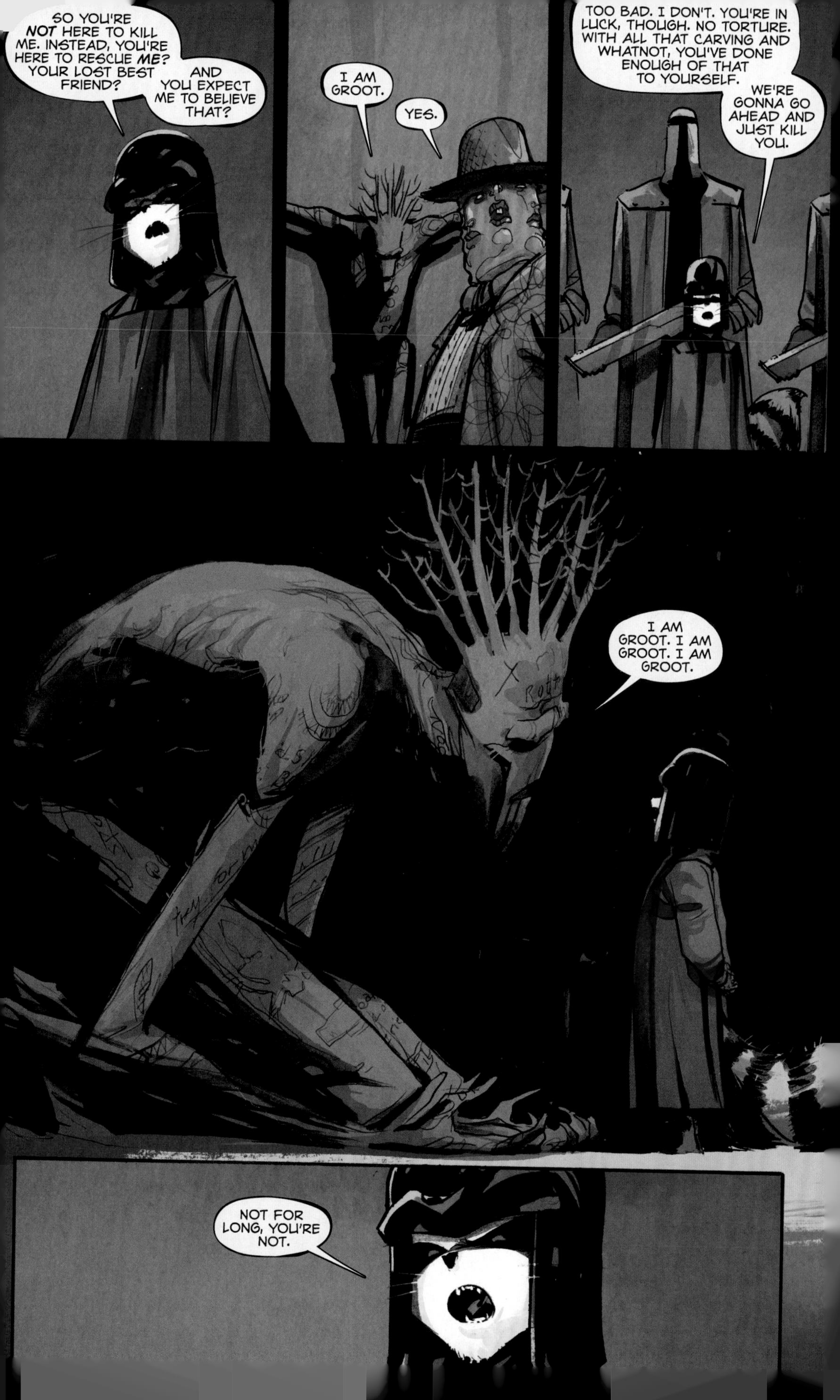
SO YOU'RE *NOT* HERE TO KILL ME. INSTEAD, YOU'RE HERE TO RESCUE *ME*? YOUR LOST BEST FRIEND?
AND YOU EXPECT ME TO BELIEVE THAT?
I AM GROOT.
YES.
TOO BAD. I DON'T. YOU'RE IN LUCK, THOUGH. NO TORTURE. WITH ALL THAT CARVING AND WHATNOT, YOU'VE DONE ENOUGH OF THAT TO YOURSELF.
WE'RE GONNA GO AHEAD AND JUST KILL YOU.
I AM GROOT. I AM GROOT. I AM GROOT.
NOT FOR LONG, YOU'RE NOT.

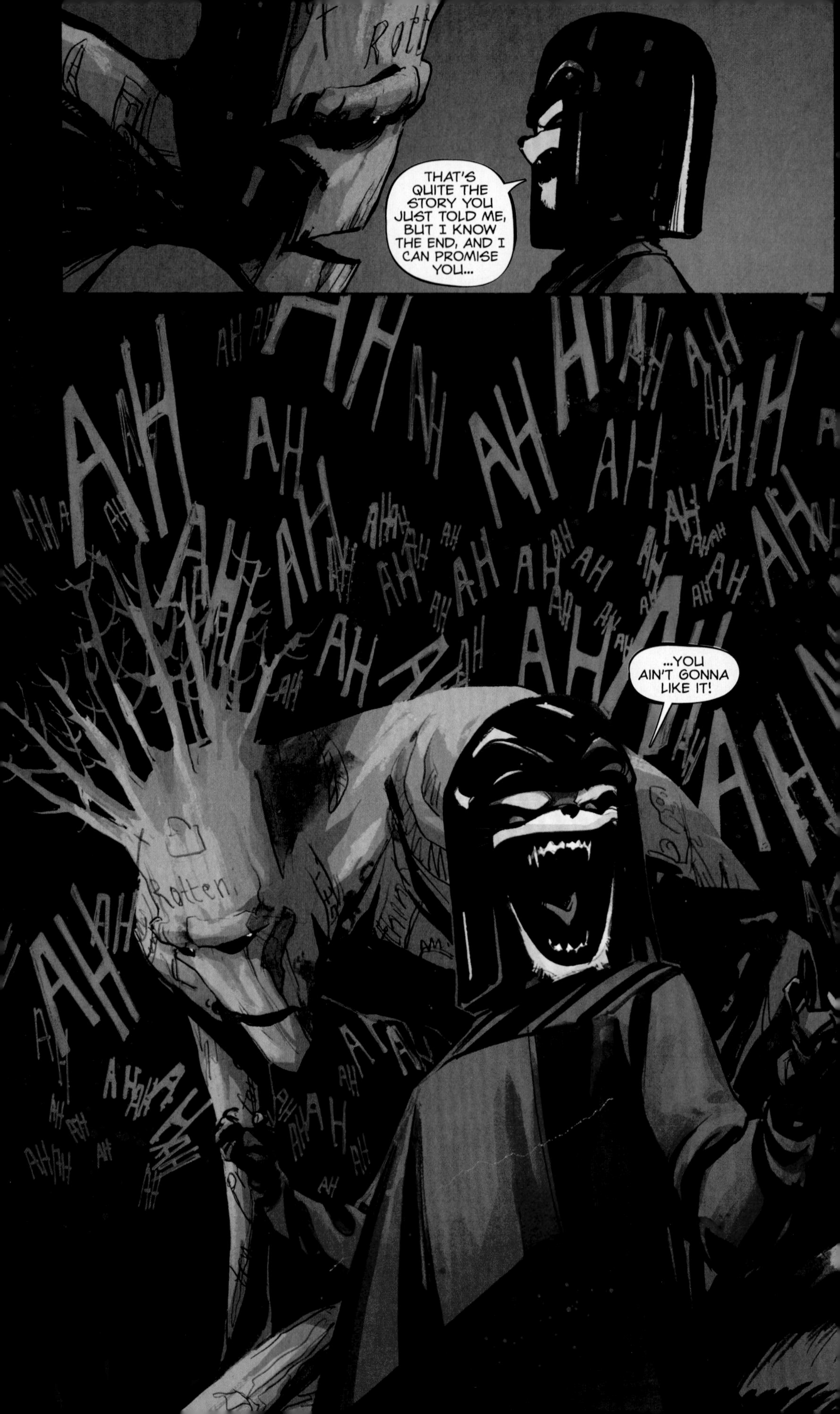
THAT'S QUITE THE STORY YOU JUST TOLD ME, BUT I KNOW THE END, AND I CAN PROMISE YOU...
AH AH AH AH AH AH AH AH
...YOU AIN'T GONNA LIKE IT!

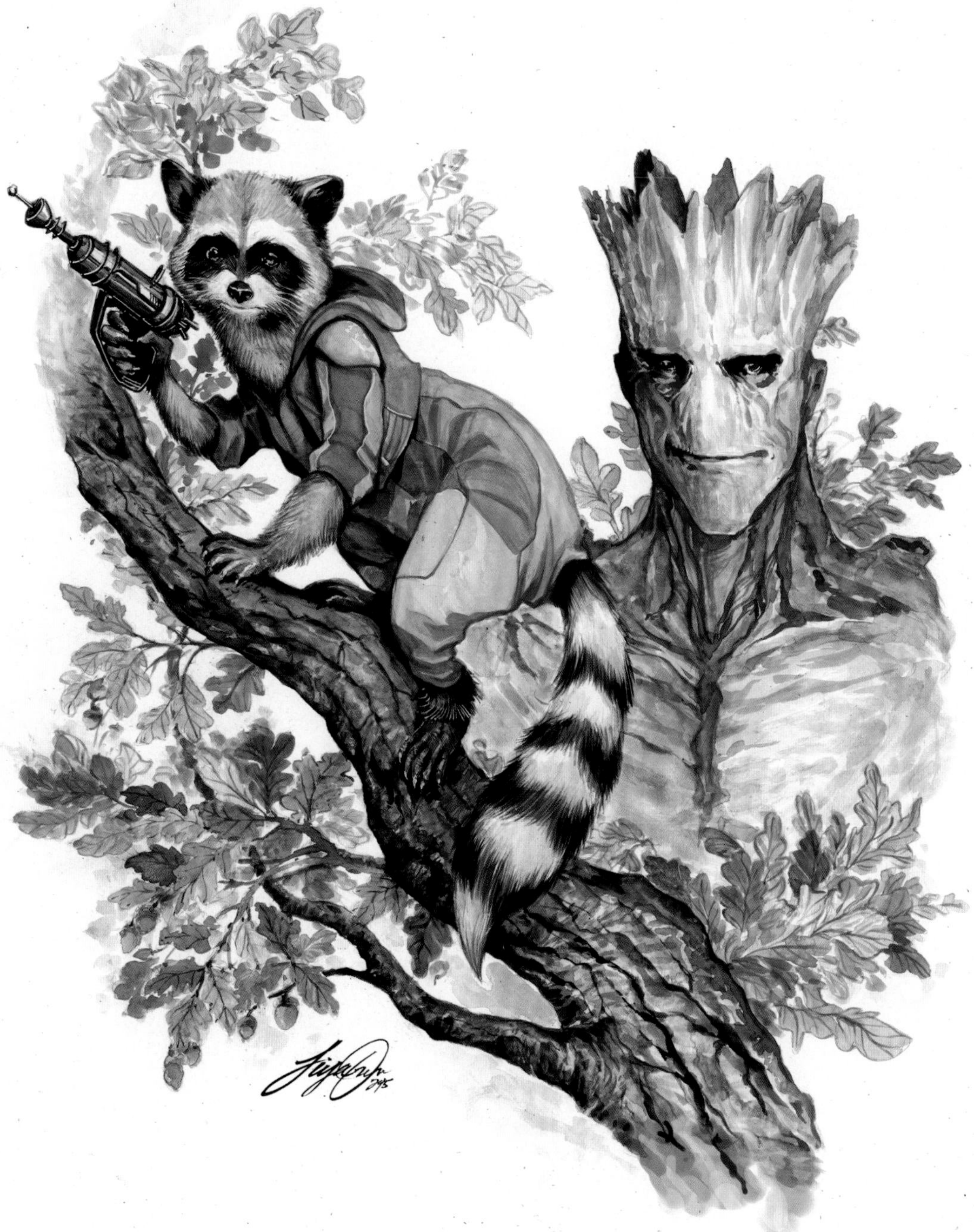

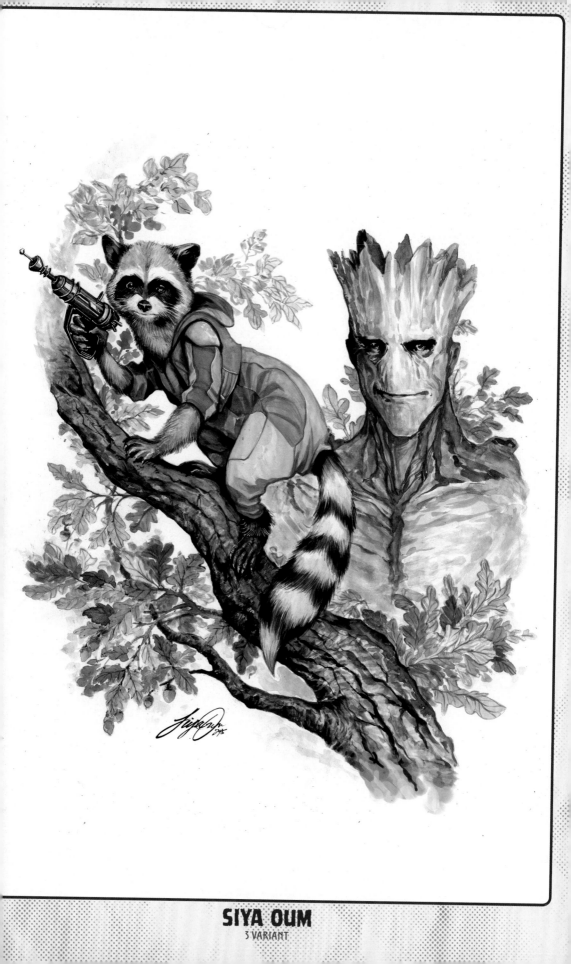

SIYA OUM
3 VARIANT

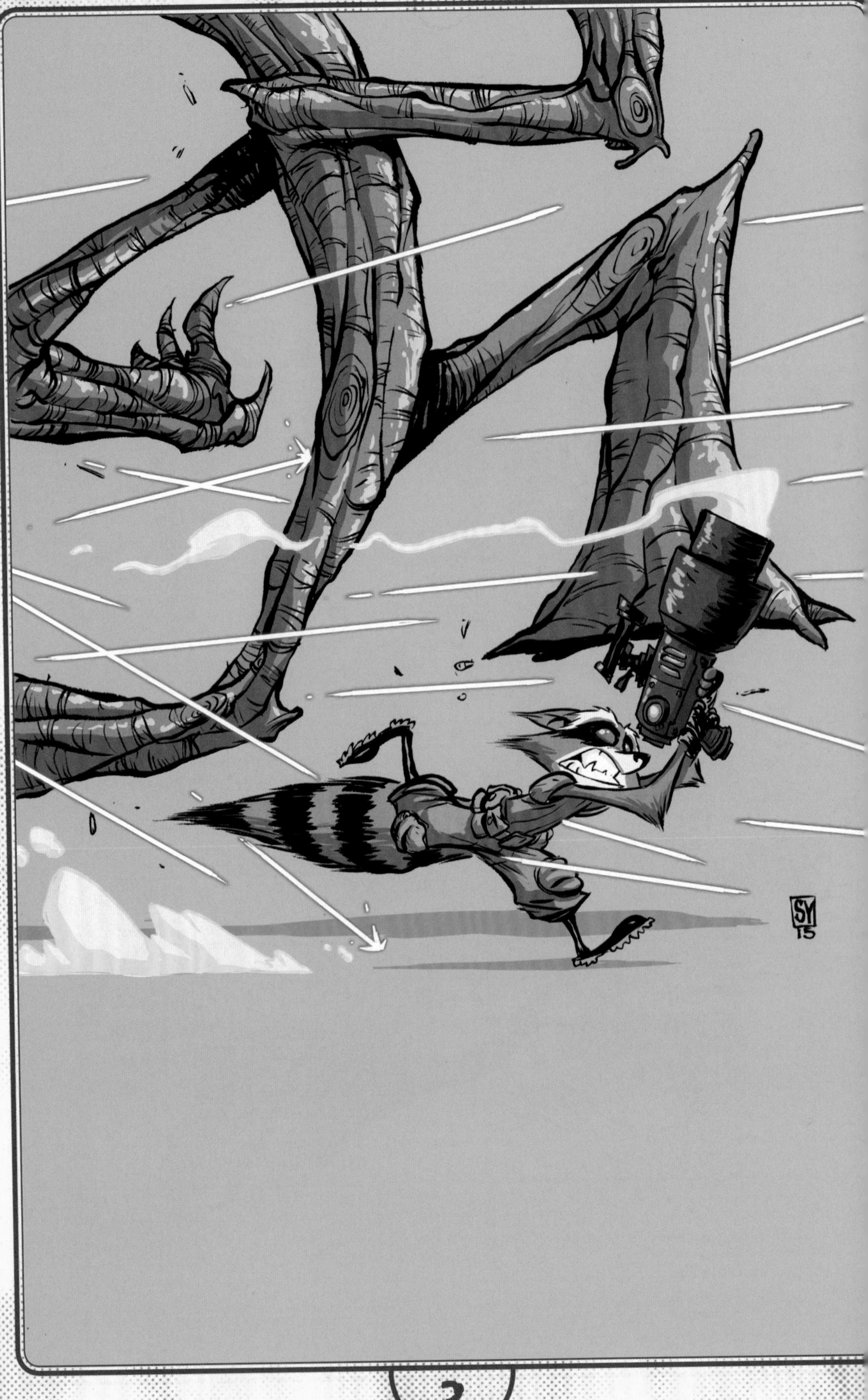

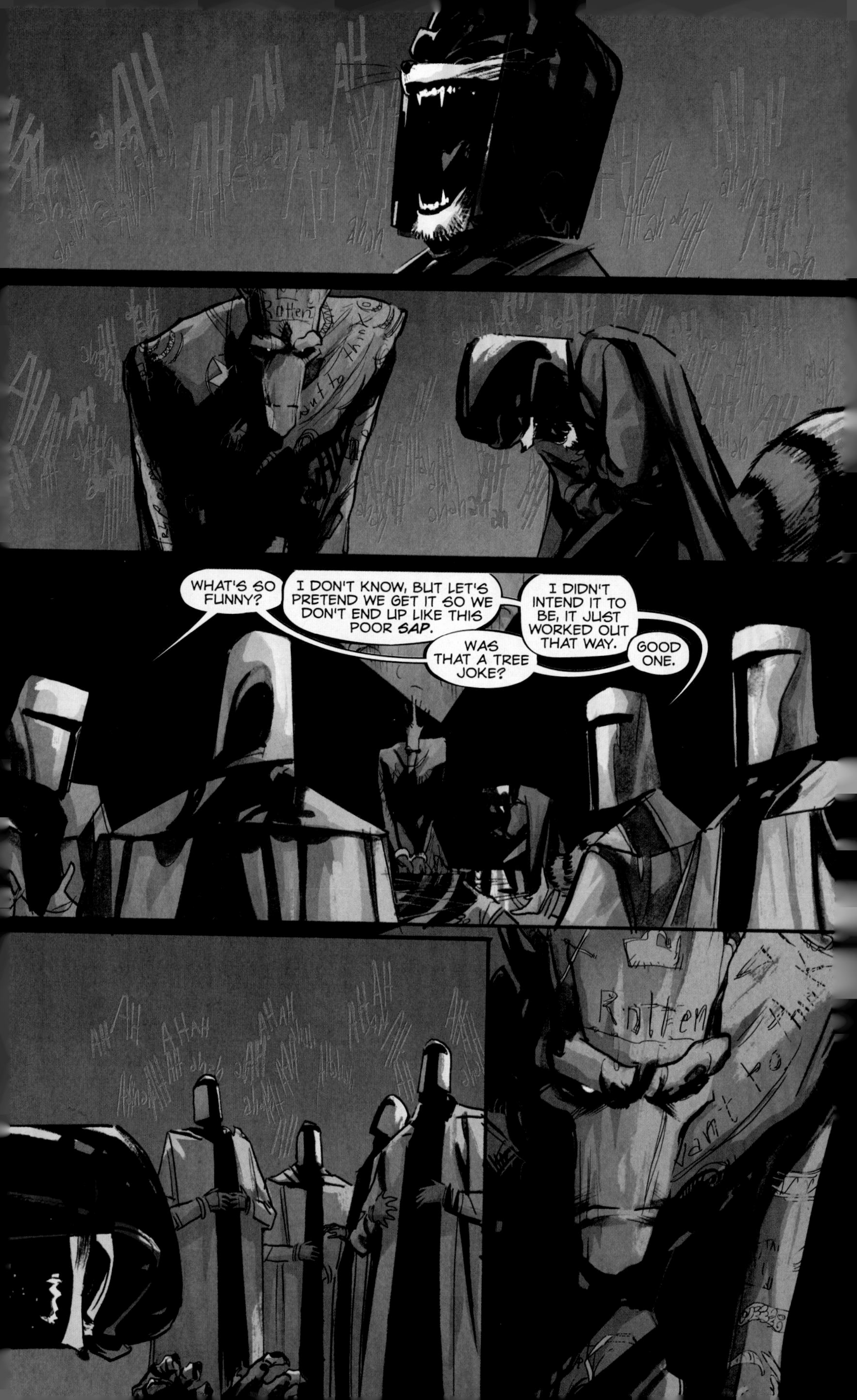

WHAT'S SO FUNNY?
I DON'T KNOW, BUT LET'S PRETEND WE GET IT SO WE DON'T END UP LIKE THIS POOR **SAP**.
WAS THAT A TREE JOKE?
I DIDN'T INTEND IT TO BE, IT JUST WORKED OUT THAT WAY.
GOOD ONE.
Rotten

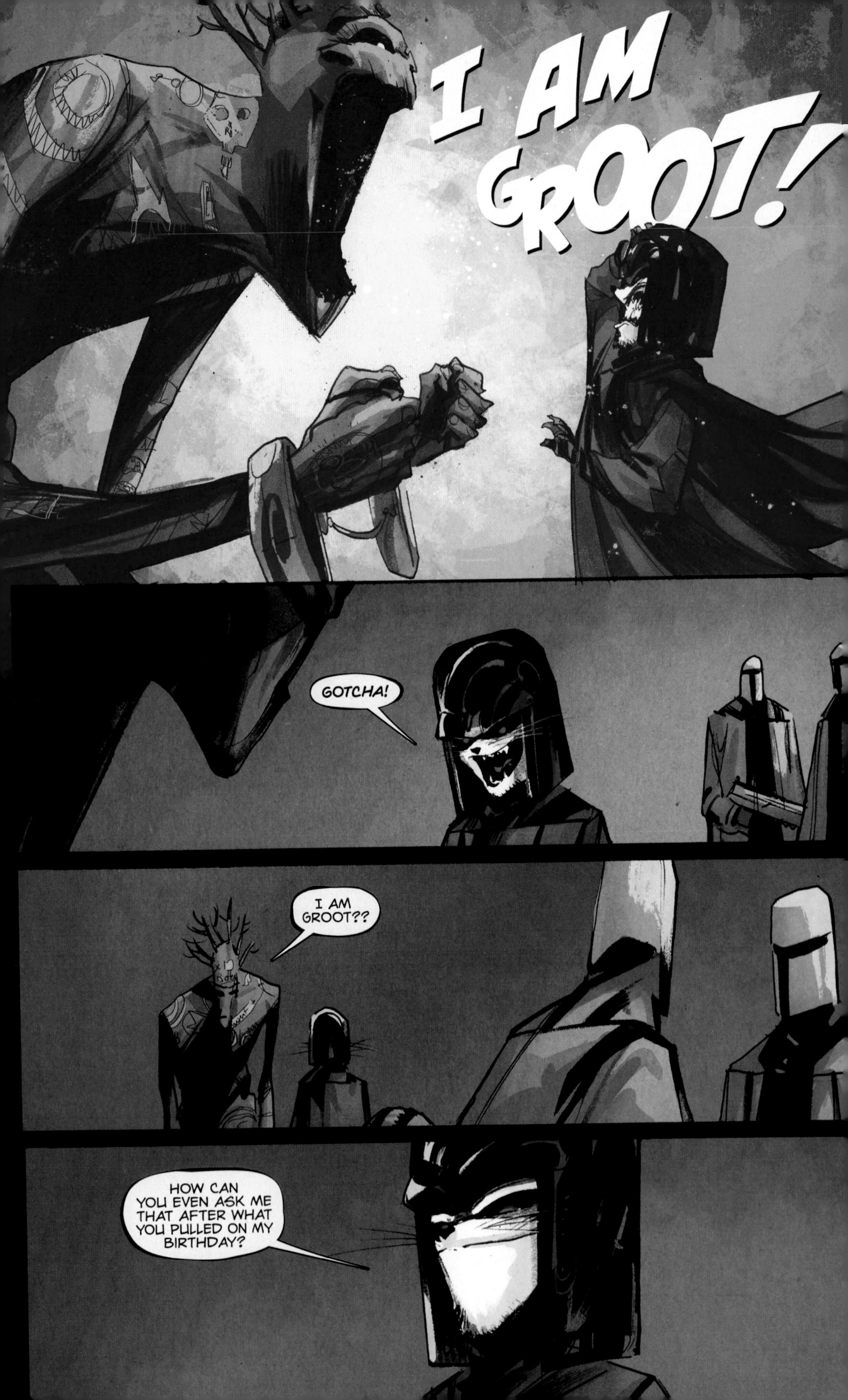
I AM GROOT!
GOTCHA!
I AM GROOT??
HOW CAN YOU EVEN ASK ME THAT AFTER WHAT YOU PULLED ON MY BIRTHDAY?

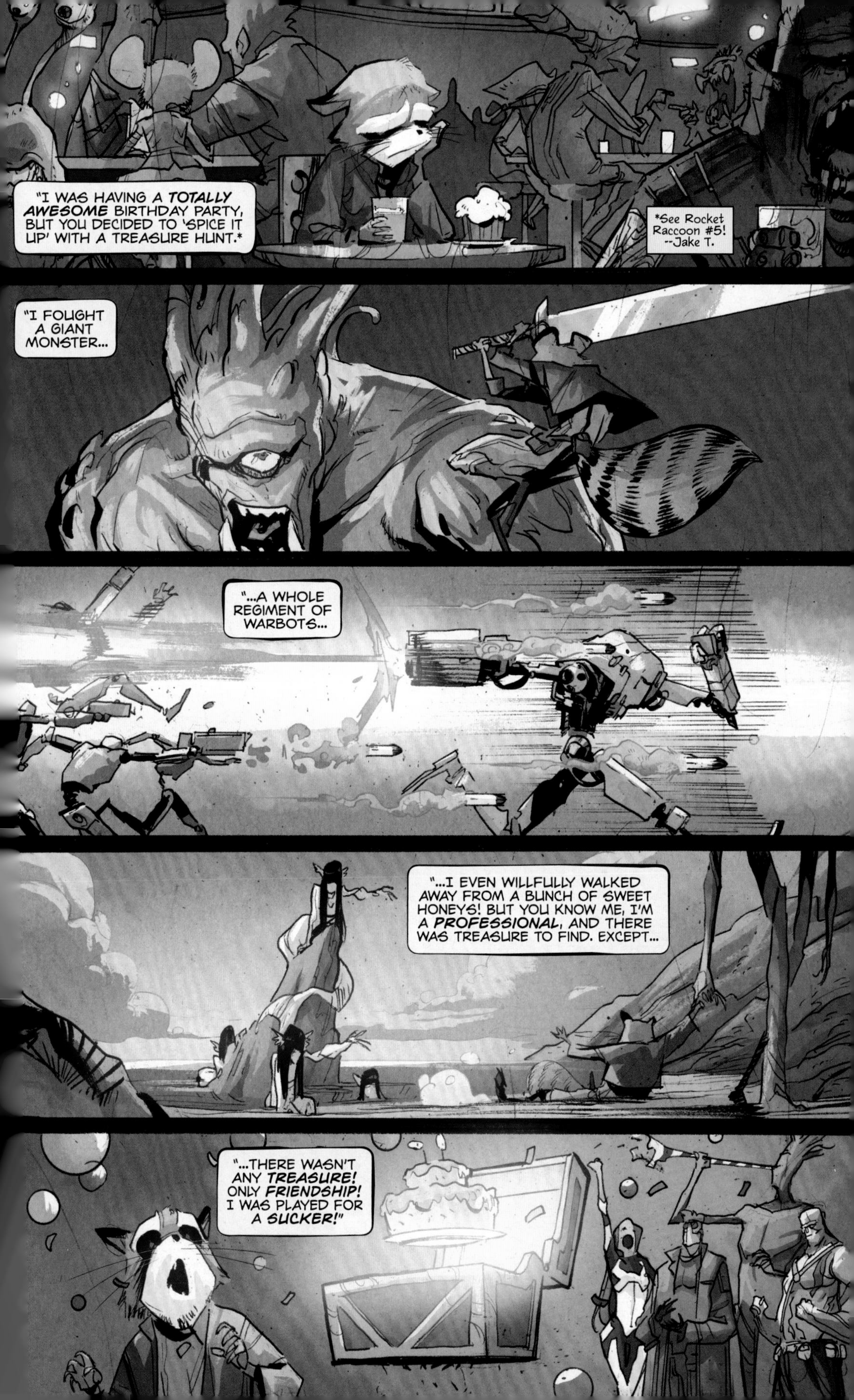
"I WAS HAVING A TOTALLY AWESOME BIRTHDAY PARTY, BUT YOU DECIDED TO 'SPICE IT UP' WITH A TREASURE HUNT.*
*See Rocket Raccoon #5! --Jake T.
"I FOUGHT A GIANT MONSTER...
"...A WHOLE REGIMENT OF WARBOTS...
"...I EVEN WILLFULLY WALKED AWAY FROM A BUNCH OF SWEET HONEYS! BUT YOU KNOW ME, I'M A PROFESSIONAL, AND THERE WAS TREASURE TO FIND. EXCEPT...
"...THERE WASN'T ANY TREASURE! ONLY FRIENDSHIP! I WAS PLAYED FOR A SUCKER!"

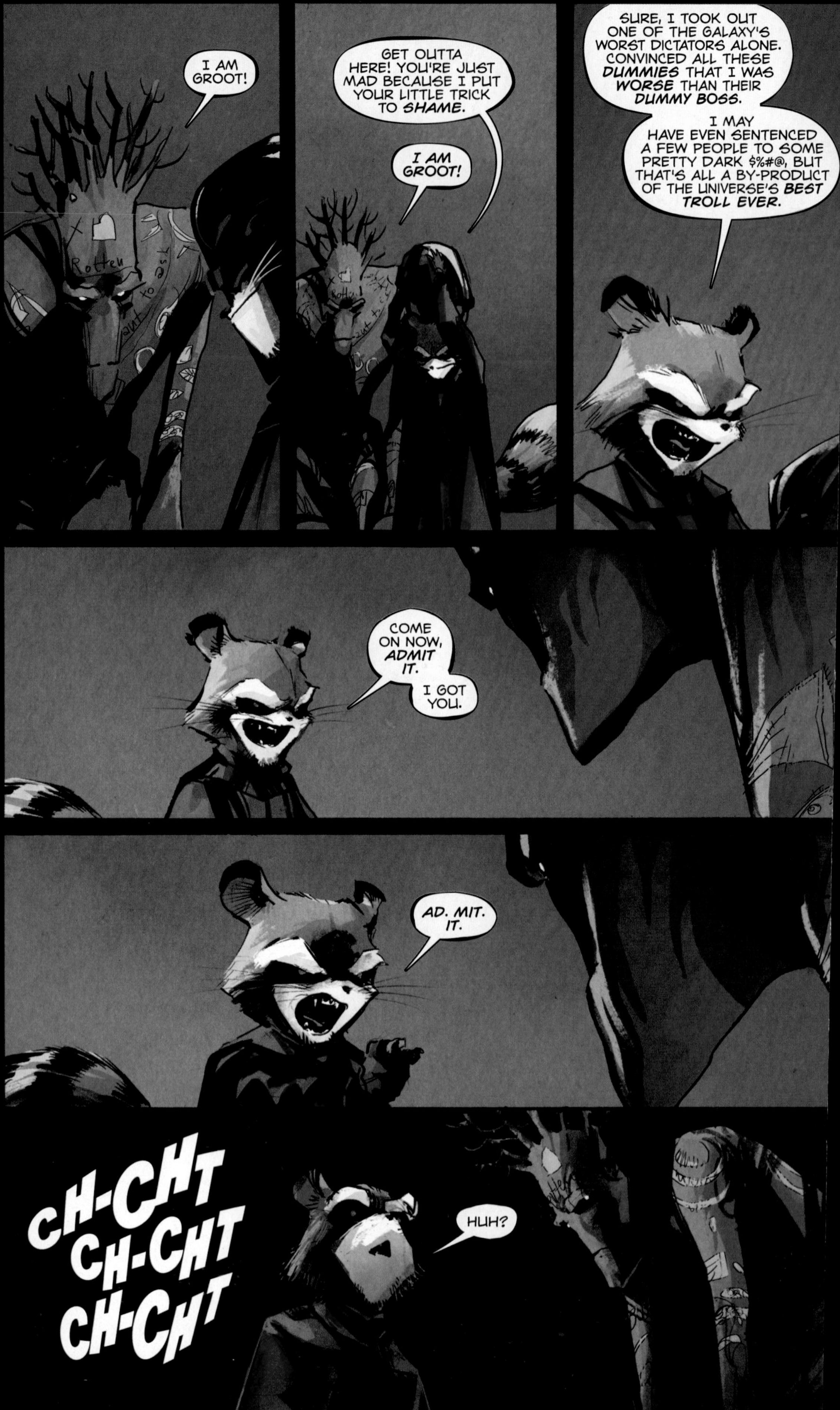
I AM GROOT!
GET OUTTA HERE! YOU'RE JUST MAD BECAUSE I PUT YOUR LITTLE TRICK TO SHAME.
I AM GROOT!
SURE, I TOOK OUT ONE OF THE GALAXY'S WORST DICTATORS ALONE. CONVINCED ALL THESE DUMMIES THAT I WAS WORSE THAN THEIR DUMMY BOSS.
I MAY HAVE EVEN SENTENCED A FEW PEOPLE TO SOME PRETTY DARK $%#@, BUT THAT'S ALL A BY-PRODUCT OF THE UNIVERSE'S BEST TROLL EVER.
COME ON NOW, ADMIT IT.
I GOT YOU.
AD. MIT. IT.
CH-CHT CH-CHT CH-CHT
HUH?

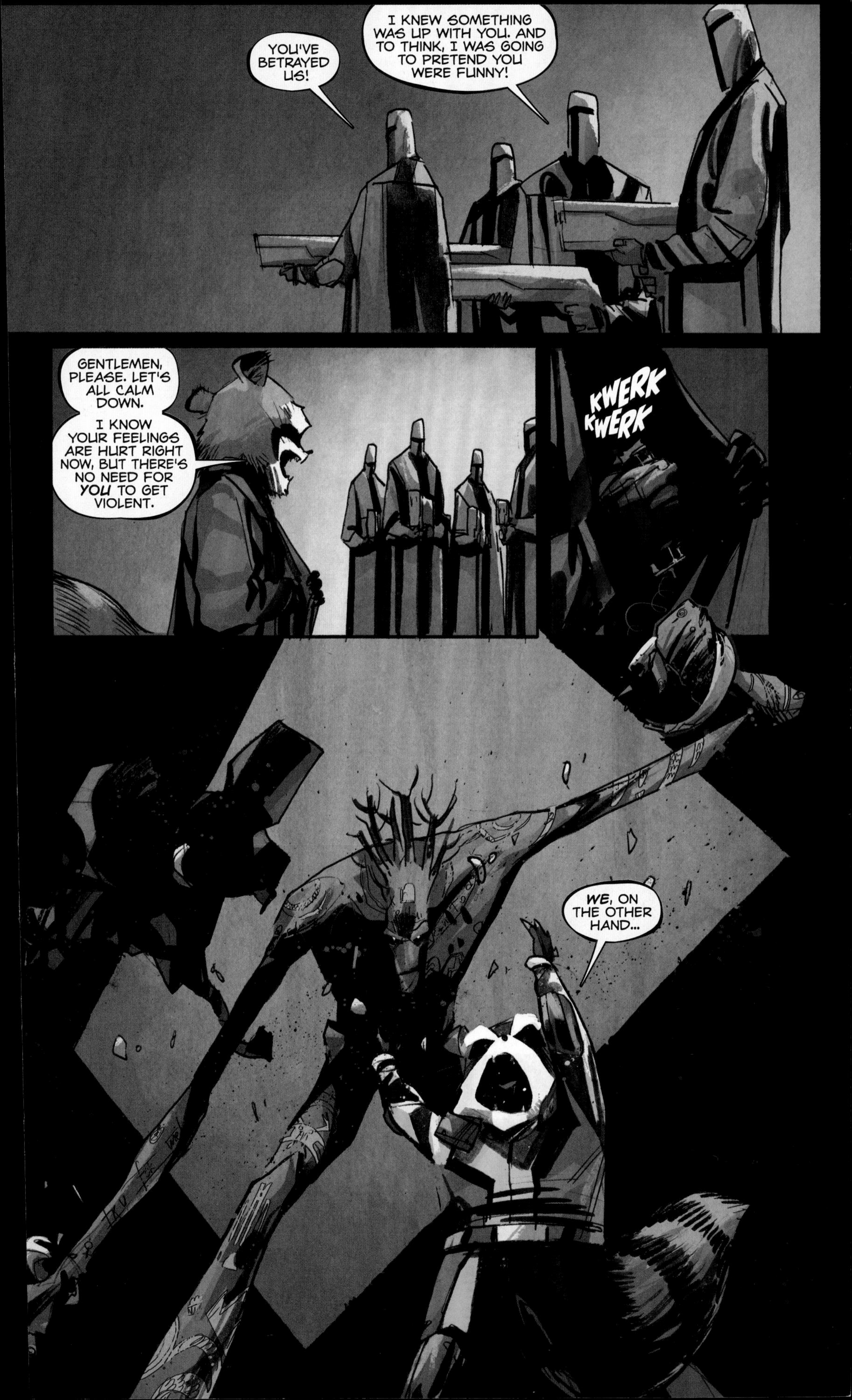
YOU'VE BETRAYED US!
I KNEW SOMETHING WAS UP WITH YOU. AND TO THINK, I WAS GOING TO PRETEND YOU WERE FUNNY!
GENTLEMEN, PLEASE. LET'S ALL CALM DOWN.
I KNOW YOUR FEELINGS ARE HURT RIGHT NOW, BUT THERE'S NO NEED FOR *YOU* TO GET VIOLENT.
KWERK KWERK
WE, ON THE OTHER HAND...

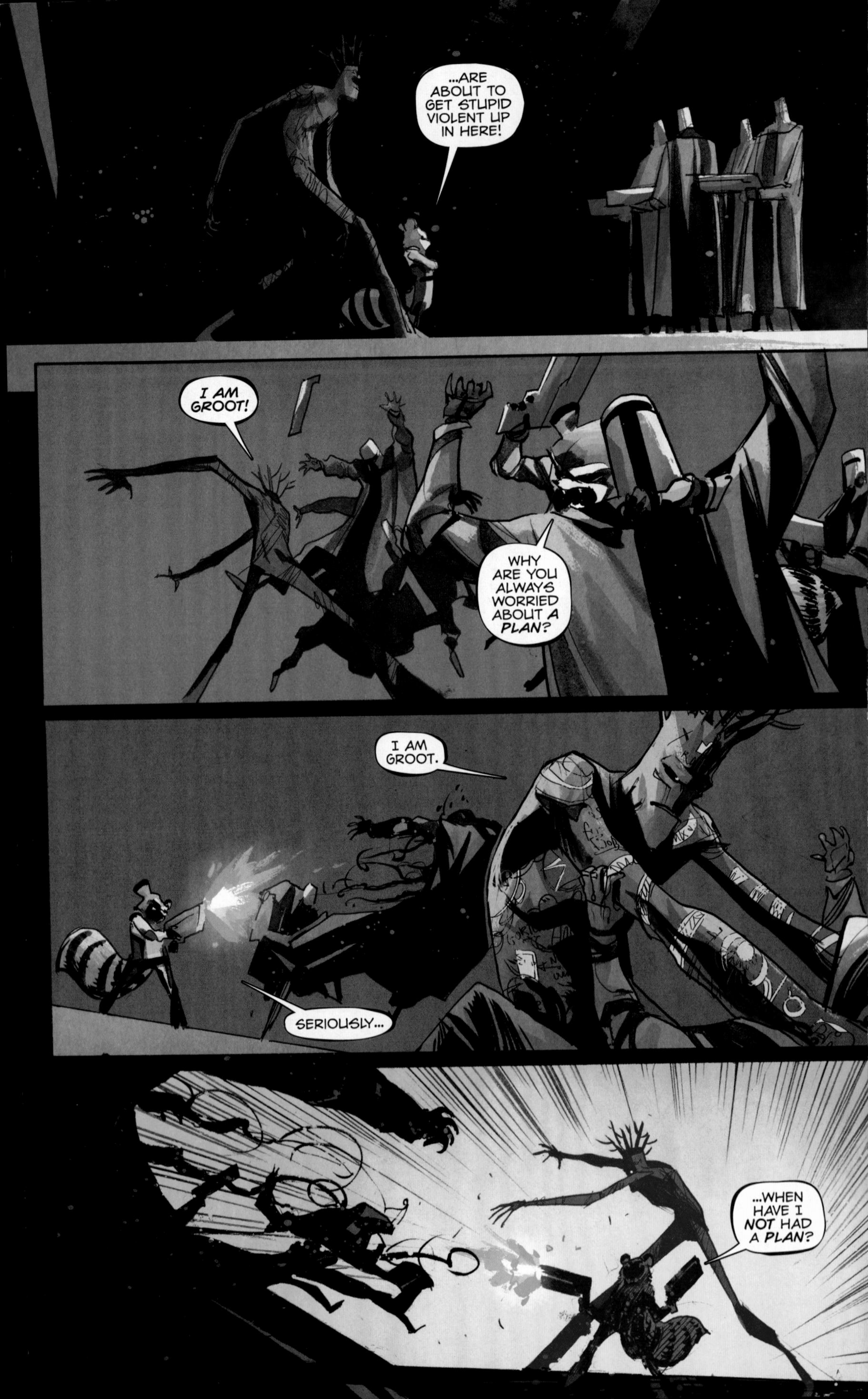
...ARE ABOUT TO GET STUPID VIOLENT UP IN HERE!
I AM GROOT!
WHY ARE YOU ALWAYS WORRIED ABOUT A PLAN?
I AM GROOT.
SERIOUSLY...
...WHEN HAVE I NOT HAD A PLAN?

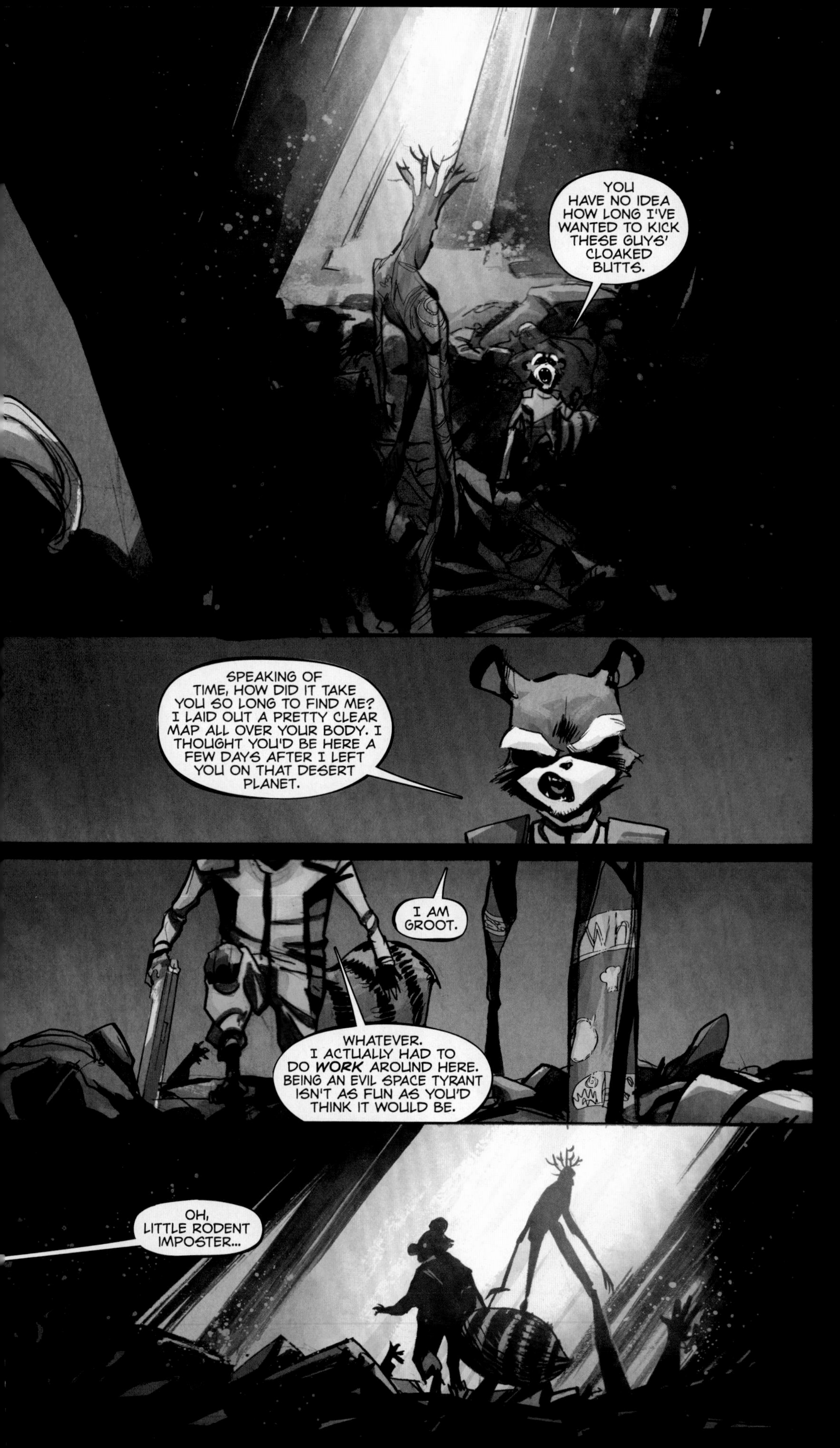
YOU HAVE NO IDEA HOW LONG I'VE WANTED TO KICK THESE GUYS' CLOAKED BUTTS.
SPEAKING OF TIME, HOW DID IT TAKE YOU SO LONG TO FIND ME? I LAID OUT A PRETTY CLEAR MAP ALL OVER YOUR BODY. I THOUGHT YOU'D BE HERE A FEW DAYS AFTER I LEFT YOU ON THAT DESERT PLANET.
I AM GROOT.
WHATEVER. I ACTUALLY HAD TO DO *WORK* AROUND HERE. BEING AN EVIL SPACE TYRANT ISN'T AS FUN AS YOU'D THINK IT WOULD BE.
OH, LITTLE RODENT IMPOSTER...

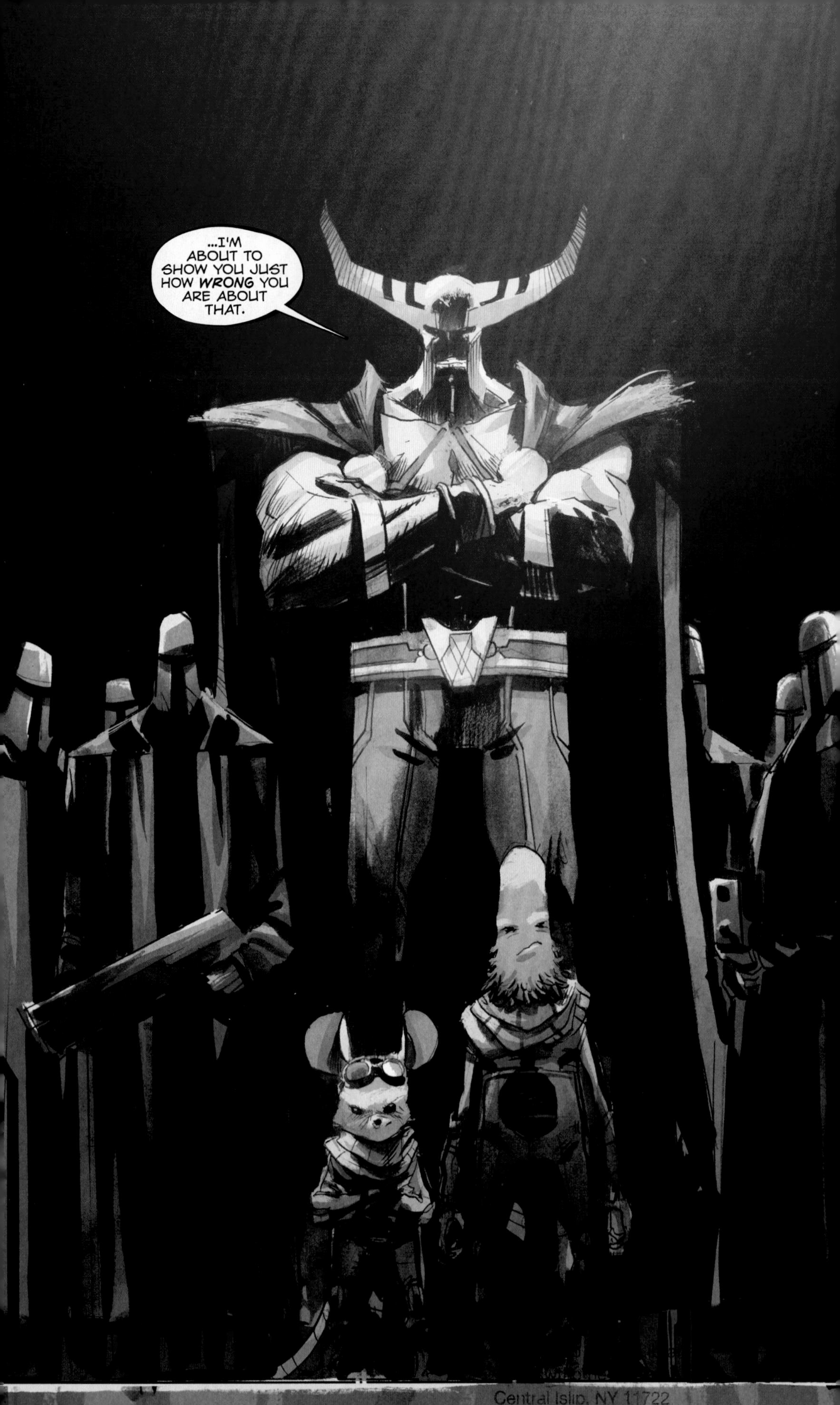
...I'M ABOUT TO SHOW YOU JUST HOW *WRONG* YOU ARE ABOUT THAT.

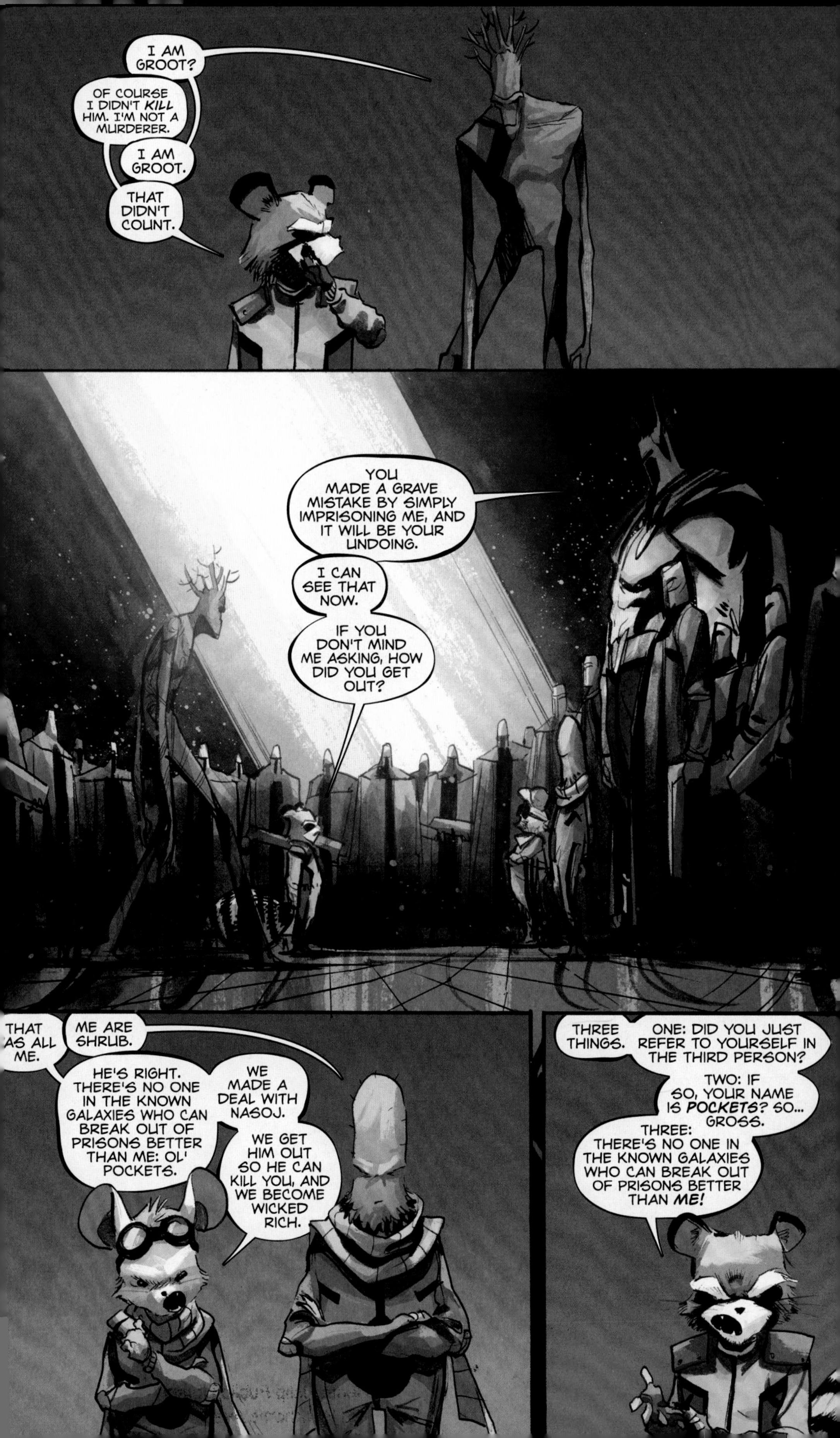
I AM GROOT?
OF COURSE I DIDN'T *KILL* HIM. I'M NOT A MURDERER.
I AM GROOT.
THAT DIDN'T COUNT.
YOU MADE A GRAVE MISTAKE BY SIMPLY IMPRISONING ME, AND IT WILL BE YOUR UNDOING.
I CAN SEE THAT NOW.
IF YOU DON'T MIND ME ASKING, HOW DID YOU GET OUT?
THAT AS ALL ME.
ME ARE SHRUB.
HE'S RIGHT. THERE'S NO ONE IN THE KNOWN GALAXIES WHO CAN BREAK OUT OF PRISONS BETTER THAN ME: OL' POCKETS.
WE MADE A DEAL WITH NASOJ.
WE GET HIM OUT SO HE CAN KILL YOU, AND WE BECOME WICKED RICH.
THREE THINGS.
ONE: DID YOU JUST REFER TO YOURSELF IN THE THIRD PERSON?
TWO: IF SO, YOUR NAME IS *POCKETS?* SO... GROSS.
THREE: THERE'S NO ONE IN THE KNOWN GALAXIES WHO CAN BREAK OUT OF PRISONS BETTER THAN *ME!*

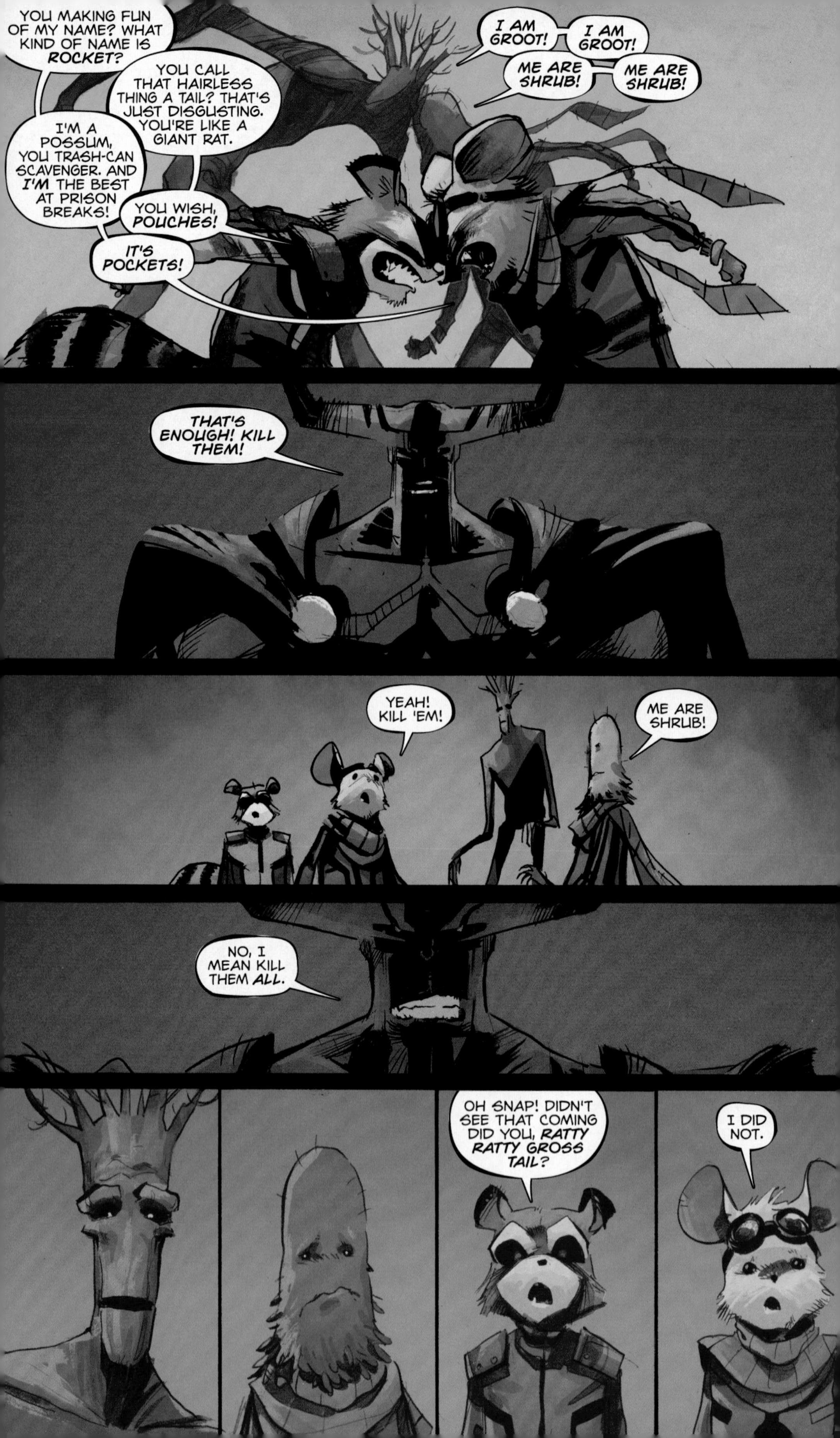
YOU MAKING FUN OF MY NAME? WHAT KIND OF NAME IS ROCKET?
I'M A POSSUM, YOU TRASH-CAN SCAVENGER. AND I'M THE BEST AT PRISON BREAKS!
YOU CALL THAT HAIRLESS THING A TAIL? THAT'S JUST DISGUSTING. YOU'RE LIKE A GIANT RAT.
YOU WISH, POUCHES!
IT'S POCKETS!
I AM GROOT!
I AM GROOT!
ME ARE SHRUB!
ME ARE SHRUB!
THAT'S ENOUGH! KILL THEM!
YEAH! KILL 'EM!
ME ARE SHRUB!
NO, I MEAN KILL THEM ALL.
OH SNAP! DIDN'T SEE THAT COMING DID YOU, RATTY RATTY GROSS TAIL?
I DID NOT.

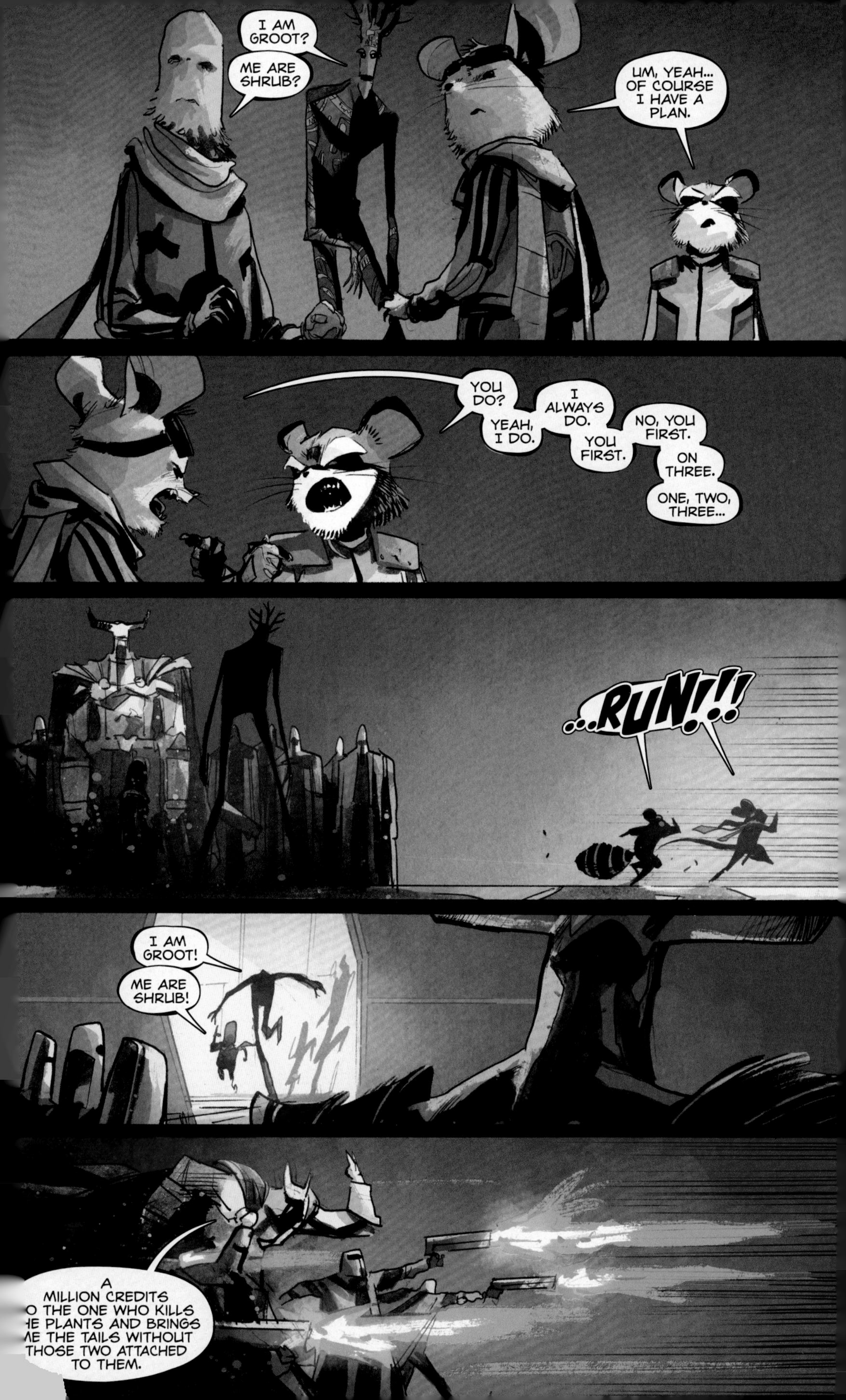
I AM GROOT?
ME ARE SHRUB?
UM, YEAH... OF COURSE I HAVE A PLAN.
YOU DO?
YEAH, I DO.
I ALWAYS DO.
YOU FIRST.
NO, YOU FIRST.
ON THREE.
ONE, TWO, THREE...
...RUN!!!
I AM GROOT!
ME ARE SHRUB!
A MILLION CREDITS TO THE ONE WHO KILLS THE PLANTS AND BRINGS ME THE TAILS WITHOUT THOSE TWO ATTACHED TO THEM.

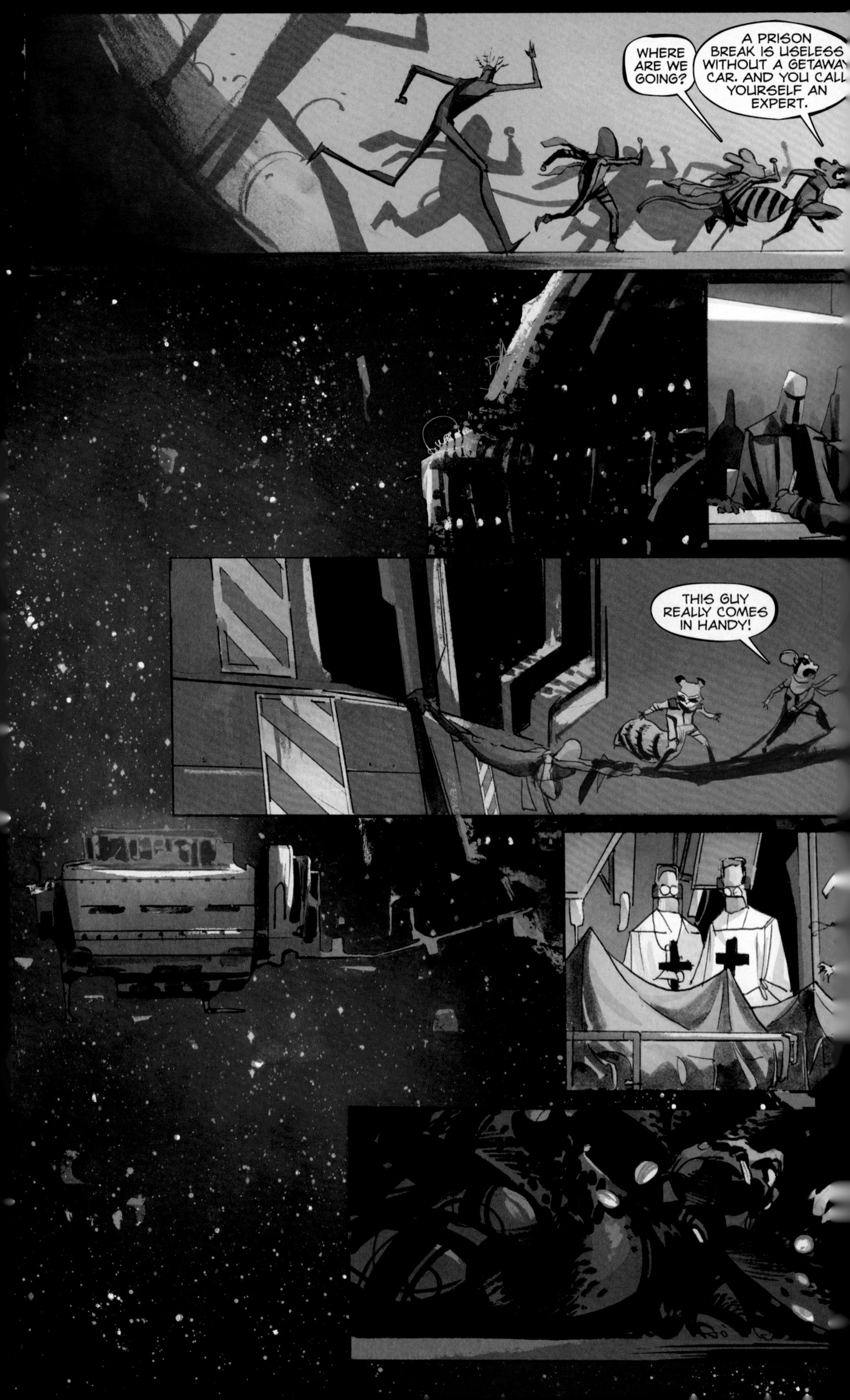
WHERE ARE WE GOING?
A PRISON BREAK IS USELESS WITHOUT A GETAWAY CAR. AND YOU CALL YOURSELF AN EXPERT.
THIS GUY REALLY COMES IN HANDY!

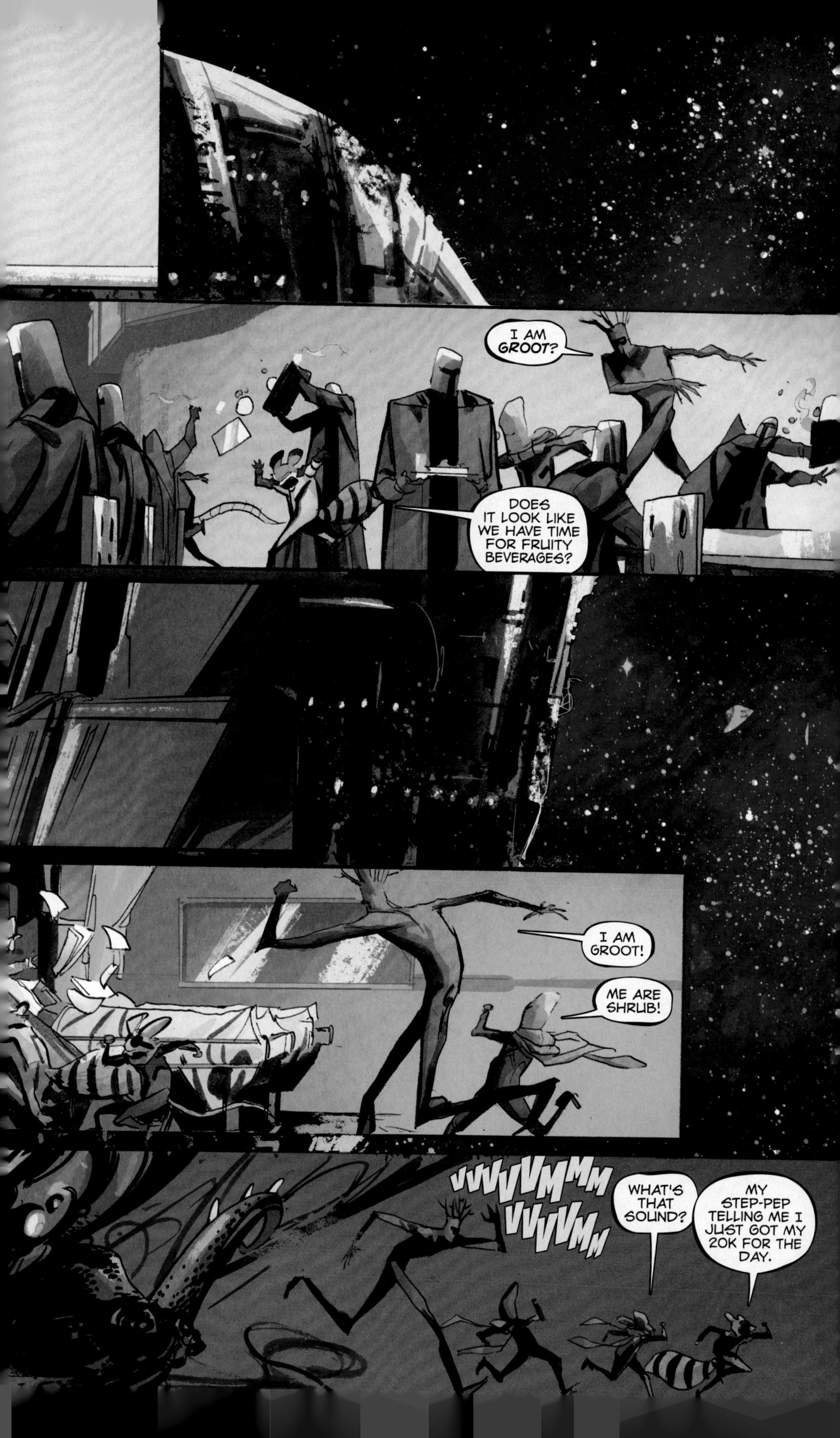
I AM GROOT?
DOES IT LOOK LIKE WE HAVE TIME FOR FRUITY BEVERAGES?
I AM GROOT!
ME ARE SHRUB!
VVVVVMMMM
VVVVMM
WHAT'S THAT SOUND?
MY STEP-PEP TELLING ME I JUST GOT MY 20K FOR THE DAY.

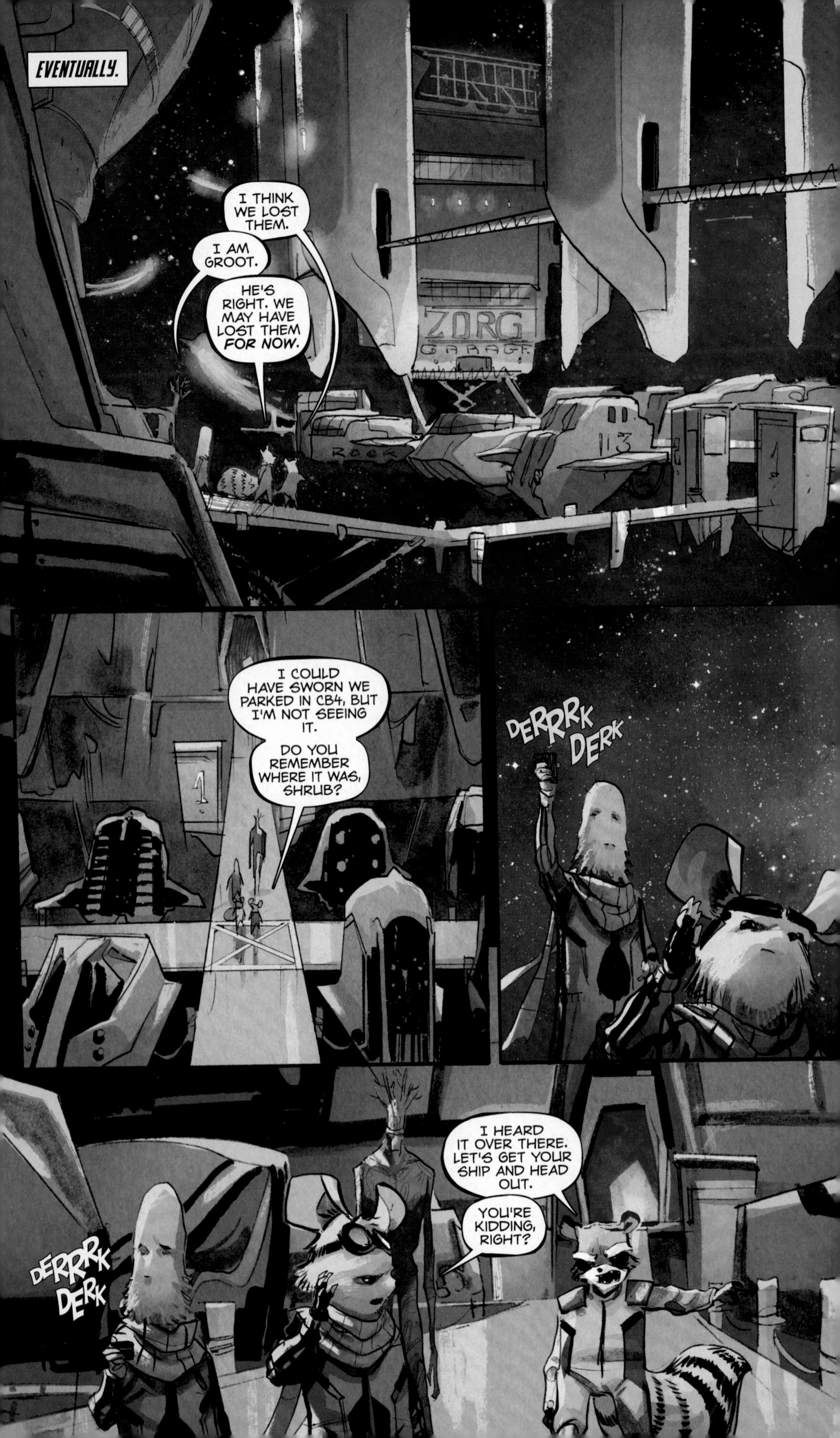

EVENTUALLY.
I THINK WE LOST THEM.
I AM GROOT.
HE'S RIGHT. WE MAY HAVE LOST THEM FOR NOW.
ZORG GARAGE
ROCK
113
I COULD HAVE SWORN WE PARKED IN CB4, BUT I'M NOT SEEING IT.
DO YOU REMEMBER WHERE IT WAS, SHRUB?
DERRRK DERK
I HEARD IT OVER THERE. LET'S GET YOUR SHIP AND HEAD OUT.
YOU'RE KIDDING, RIGHT?
DERRRK DERK

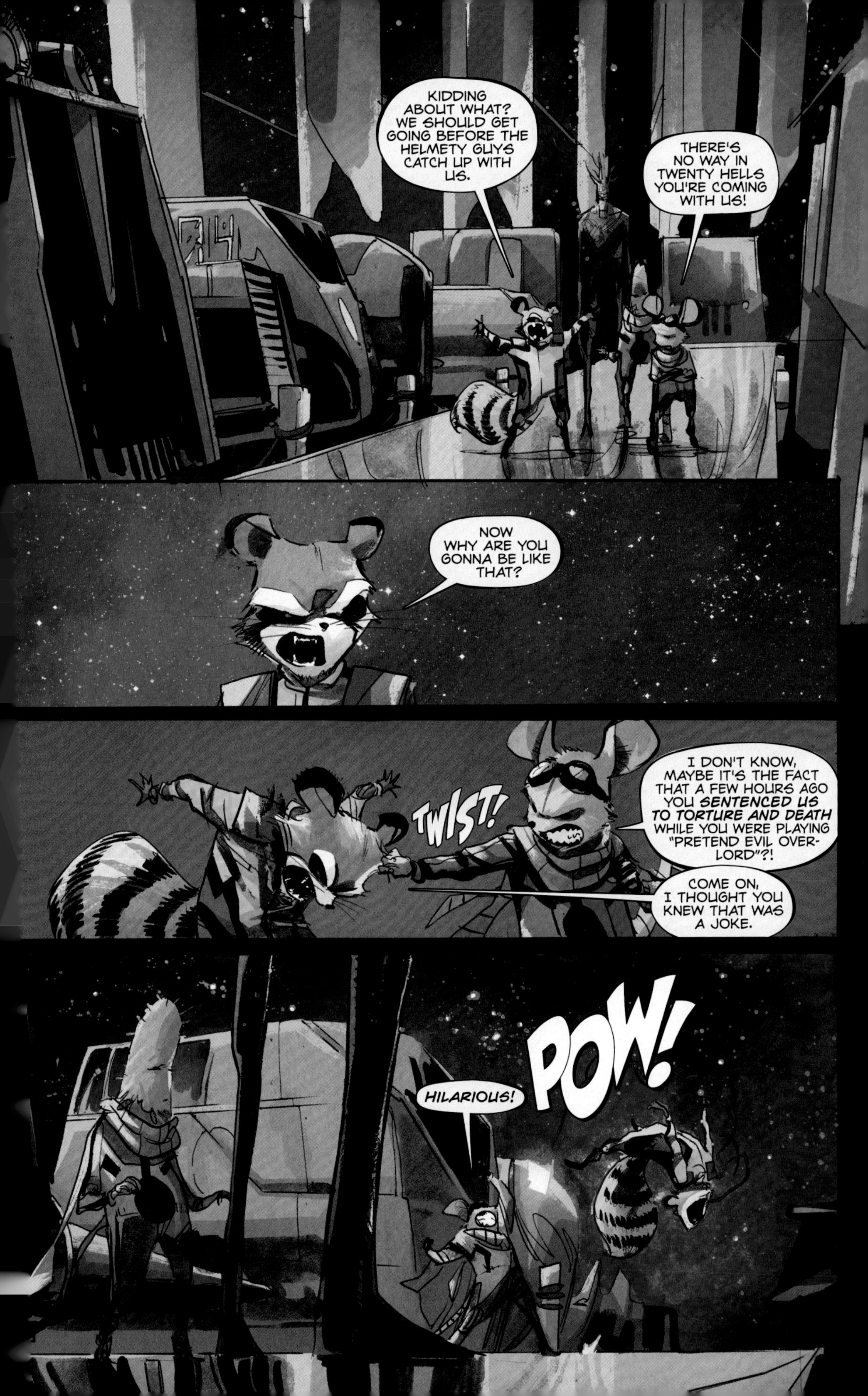
KIDDING ABOUT WHAT? WE SHOULD GET GOING BEFORE THE HELMETY GUYS CATCH UP WITH US.
THERE'S NO WAY IN TWENTY HELLS YOU'RE COMING WITH US!
NOW WHY ARE YOU GONNA BE LIKE THAT?
I DON'T KNOW, MAYBE IT'S THE FACT THAT A FEW HOURS AGO YOU *SENTENCED US TO TORTURE AND DEATH* WHILE YOU WERE PLAYING "PRETEND EVIL OVER-LORD"?!
TWIST!
COME ON, I THOUGHT YOU KNEW THAT WAS A JOKE.
HILARIOUS!
POW!

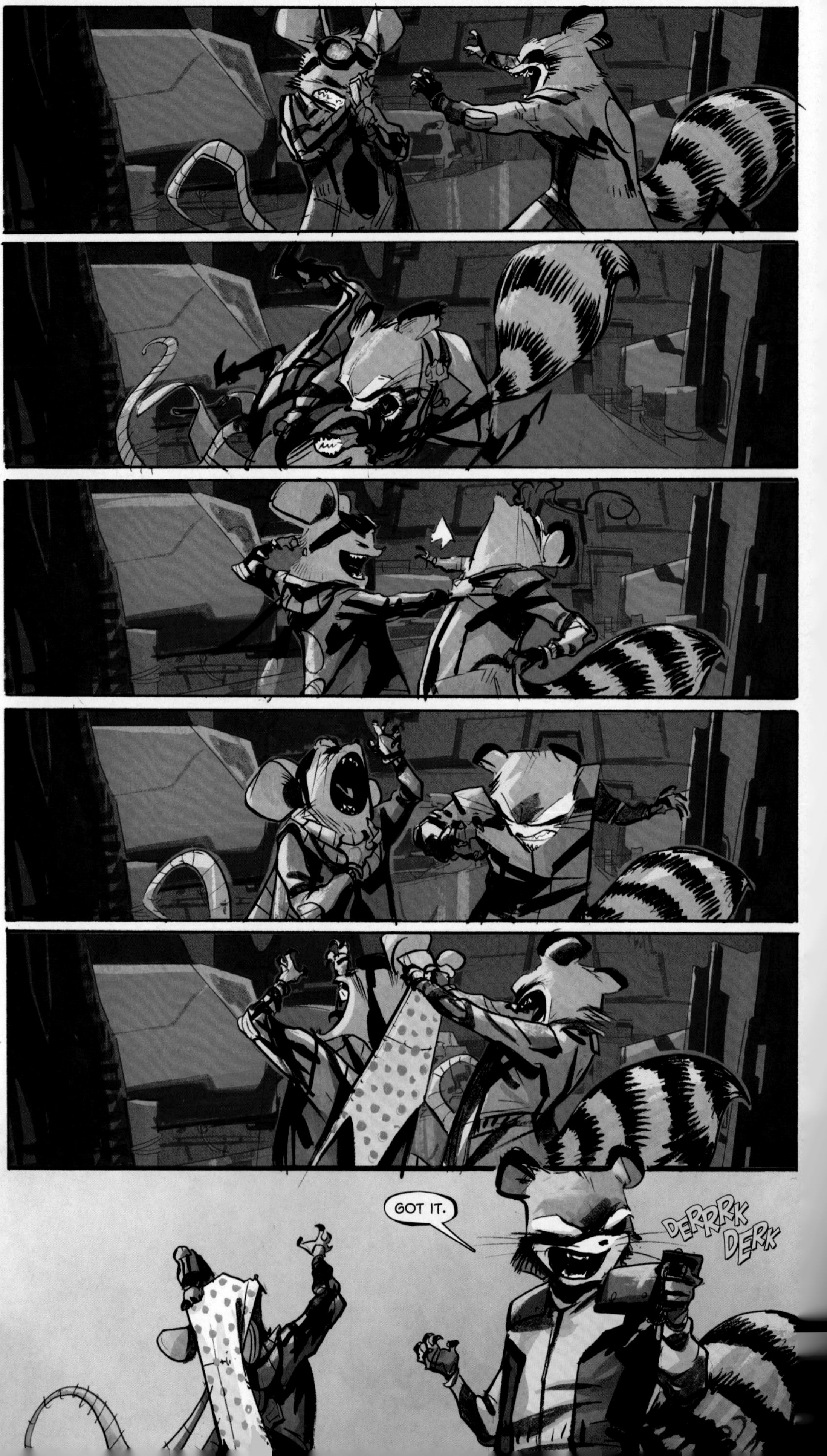
GOT IT.
DERRRK DERK

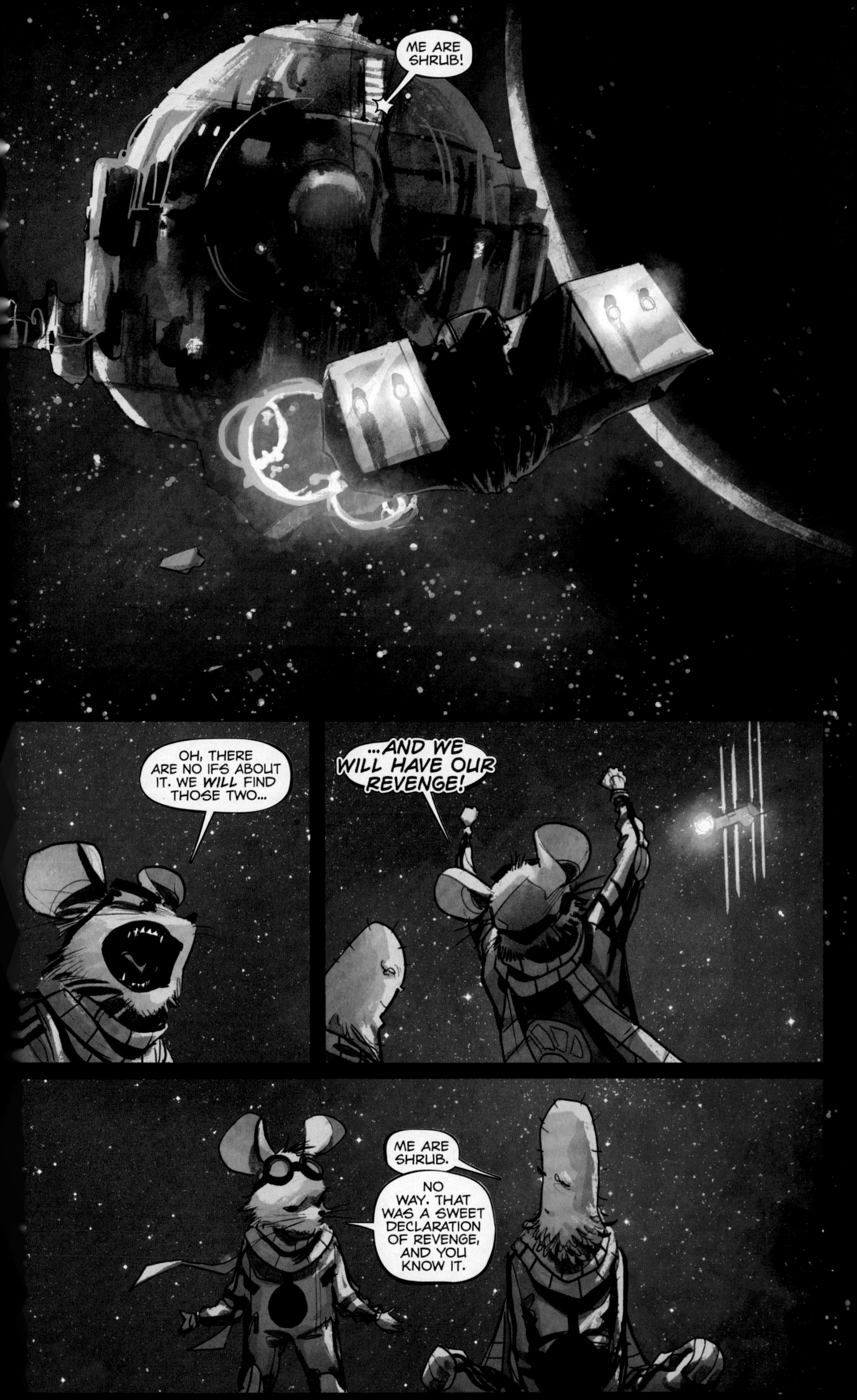
ME ARE SHRUB!
OH, THERE ARE NO IFS ABOUT IT. WE *WILL* FIND THOSE TWO...
...AND WE WILL HAVE OUR REVENGE!
ME ARE SHRUB.
NO WAY. THAT WAS A SWEET DECLARATION OF REVENGE, AND YOU KNOW IT.

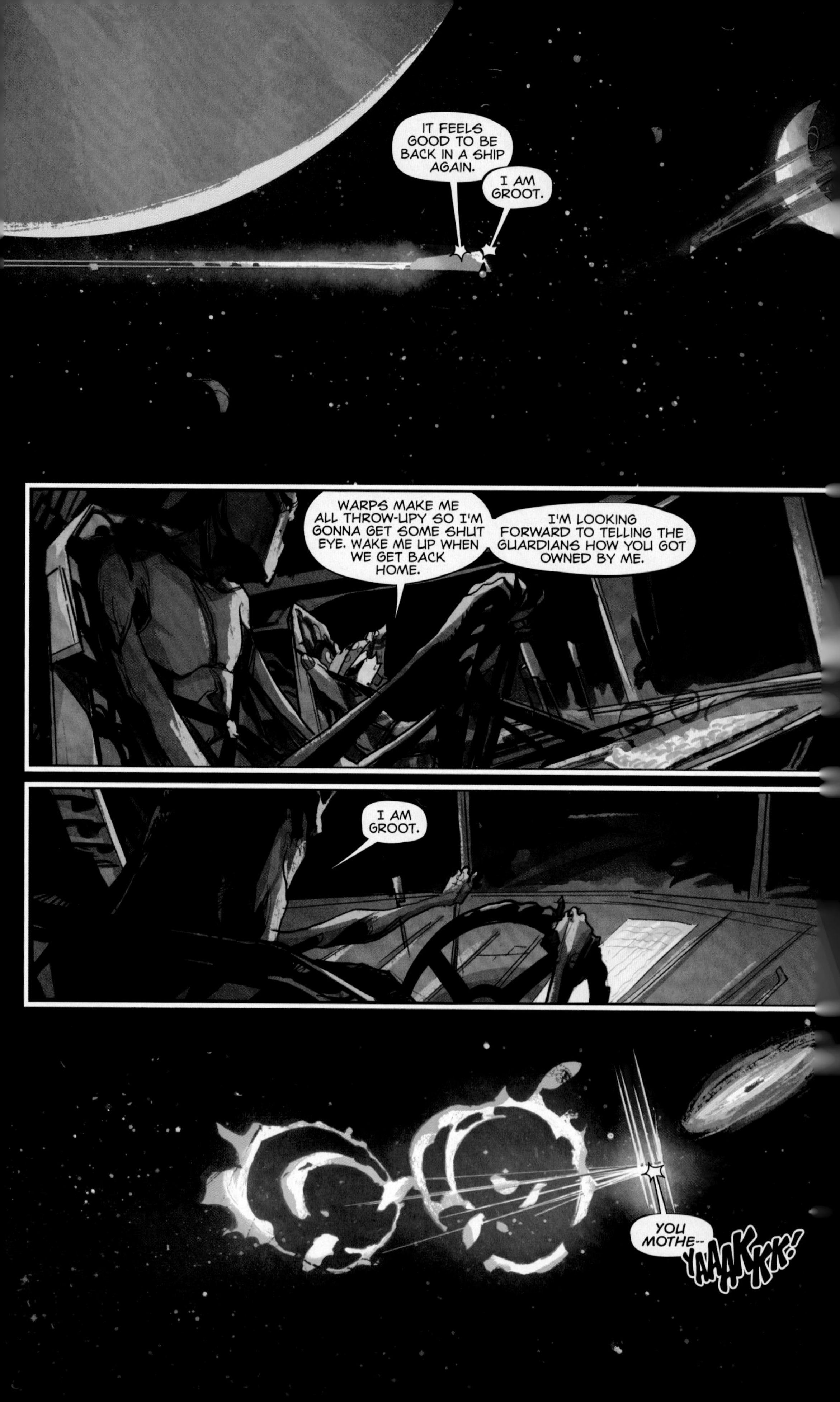
IT FEELS GOOD TO BE BACK IN A SHIP AGAIN.
I AM GROOT.
WARPS MAKE ME ALL THROW-UPY SO I'M GONNA GET SOME SHUT EYE. WAKE ME UP WHEN WE GET BACK HOME.
I'M LOOKING FORWARD TO TELLING THE GUARDIANS HOW YOU GOT OWNED BY ME.
I AM GROOT.
YOU MOTHE--
YAAAKKKK!

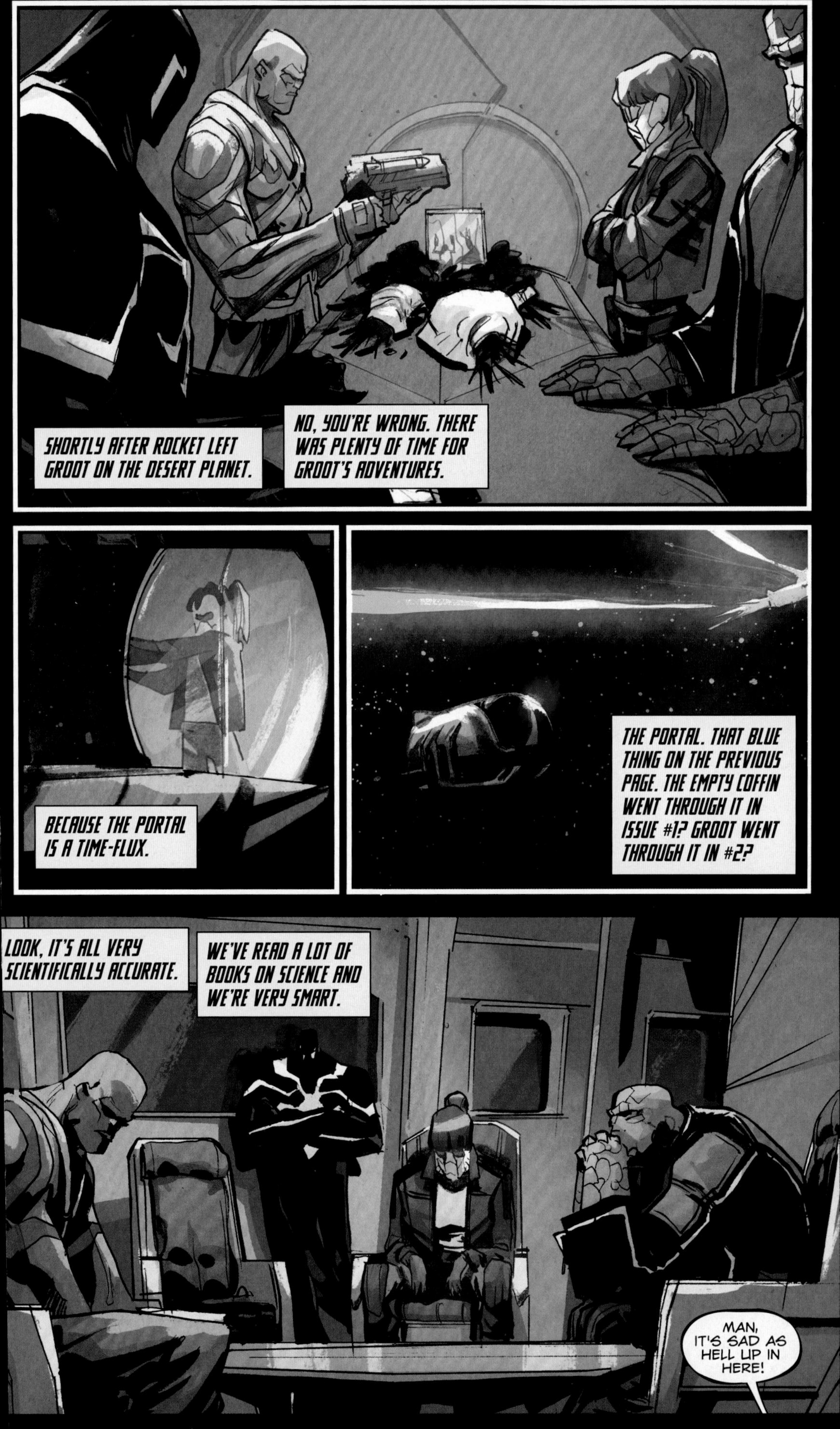
SHORTLY AFTER ROCKET LEFT GROOT ON THE DESERT PLANET.
NO, YOU'RE WRONG. THERE WAS PLENTY OF TIME FOR GROOT'S ADVENTURES.
BECAUSE THE PORTAL IS A TIME-FLUX.
THE PORTAL. THAT BLUE THING ON THE PREVIOUS PAGE. THE EMPTY COFFIN WENT THROUGH IT IN ISSUE #1? GROOT WENT THROUGH IT IN #2?
LOOK, IT'S ALL VERY SCIENTIFICALLY ACCURATE.
WE'VE READ A LOT OF BOOKS ON SCIENCE AND WE'RE VERY SMART.
MAN, IT'S SAD AS HELL UP IN HERE!

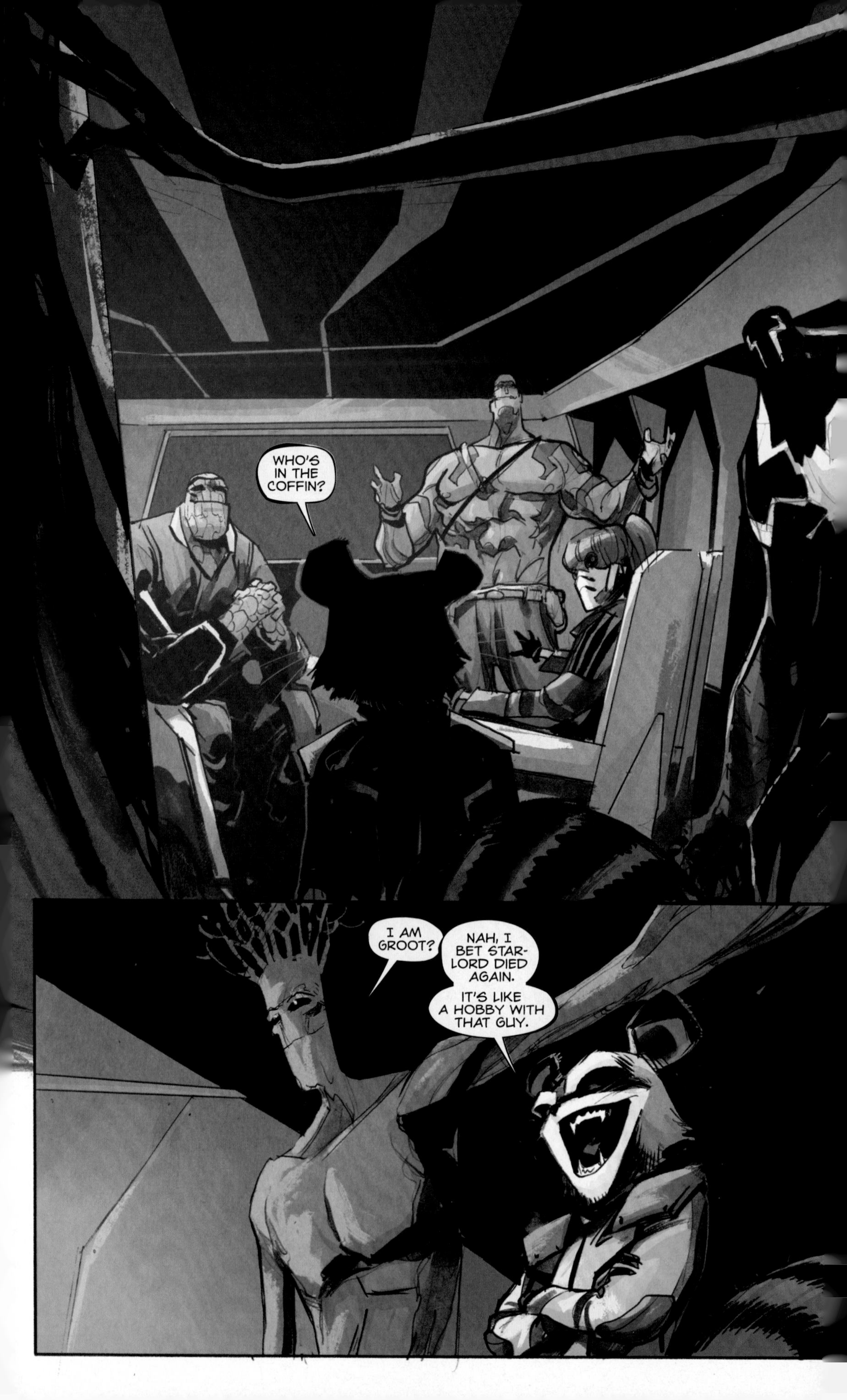

WHO'S IN THE COFFIN?
I AM GROOT?
NAH, I BET STAR-LORD DIED AGAIN.
IT'S LIKE A HOBBY WITH THAT GUY.

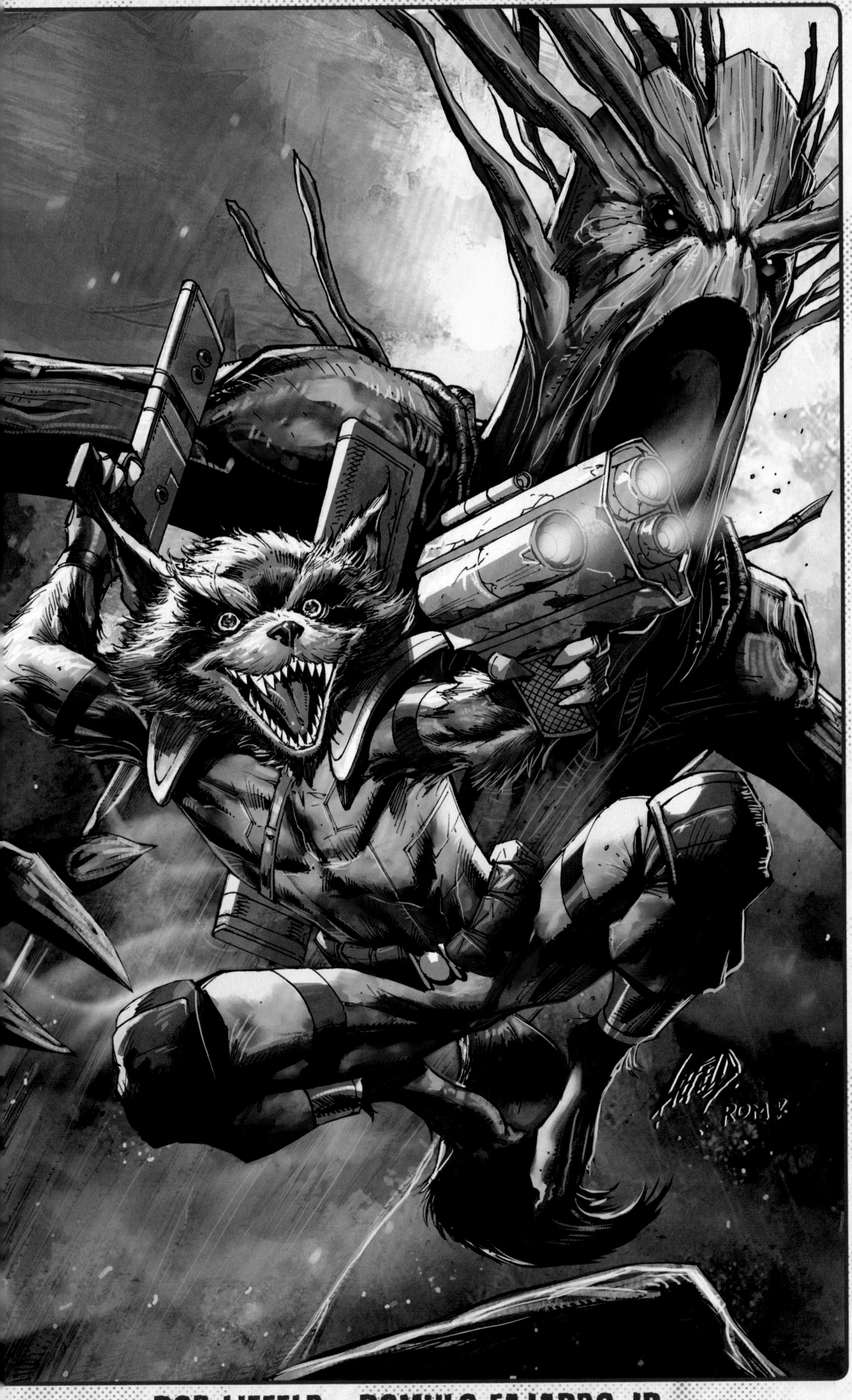

ROM B.

ROB LIEFELD & ROMULO FAJARDO JR.
4 VARIANT

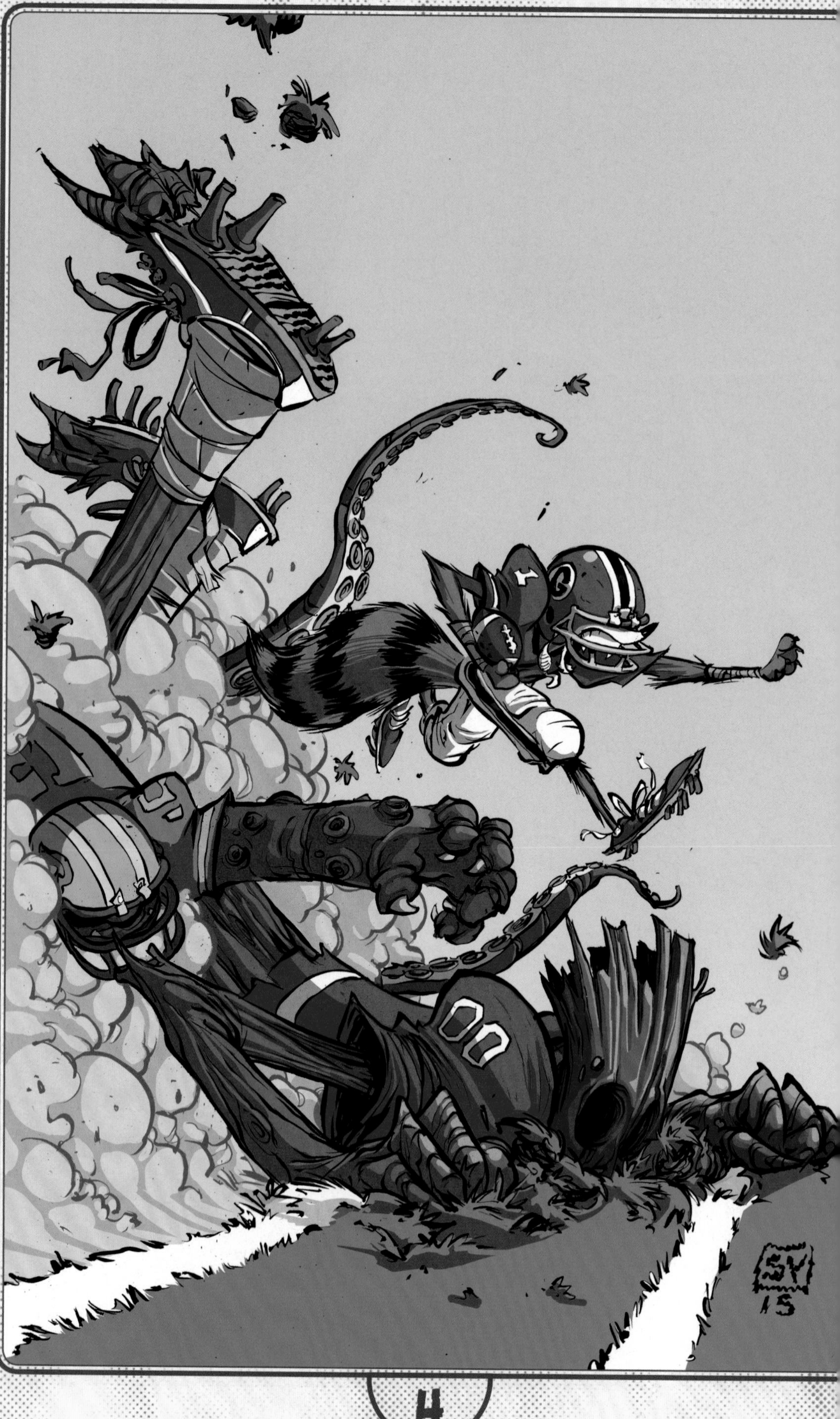

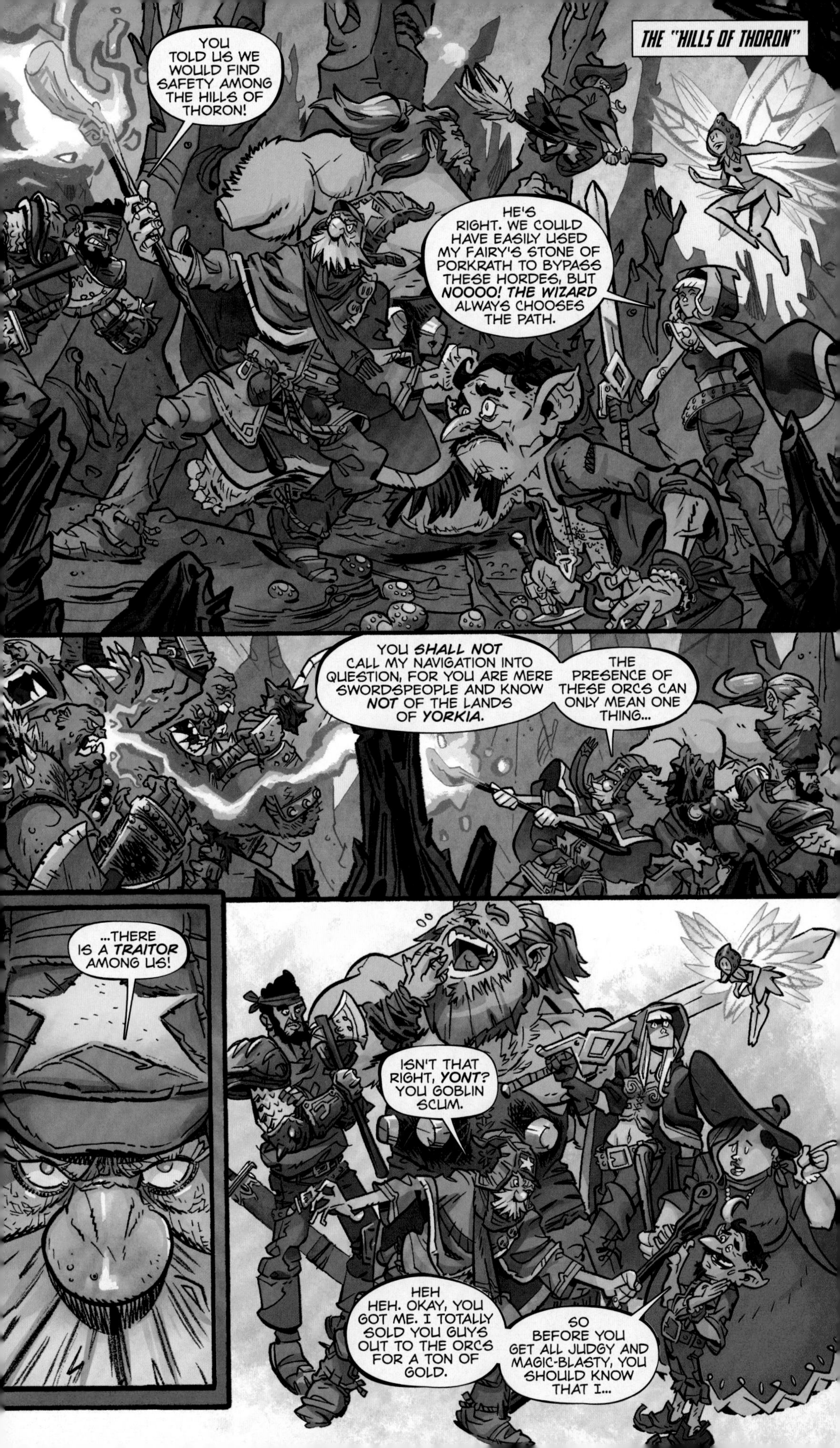
THE "HILLS OF THORON"
YOU TOLD US WE WOULD FIND SAFETY AMONG THE HILLS OF THORON!
HE'S RIGHT. WE COULD HAVE EASILY USED MY FAIRY'S STONE OF PORKRATH TO BYPASS THESE HORDES, BUT NOOOO! THE WIZARD ALWAYS CHOOSES THE PATH.
YOU SHALL NOT CALL MY NAVIGATION INTO QUESTION, FOR YOU ARE MERE SWORDSPEOPLE AND KNOW NOT OF THE LANDS OF YORKIA.
THE PRESENCE OF THESE ORCS CAN ONLY MEAN ONE THING...
...THERE IS A TRAITOR AMONG US!
ISN'T THAT RIGHT, YONT? YOU GOBLIN SCUM.
HEH HEH. OKAY, YOU GOT ME. I TOTALLY SOLD YOU GUYS OUT TO THE ORCS FOR A TON OF GOLD.
SO BEFORE YOU GET ALL JUDGY AND MAGIC-BLASTY, YOU SHOULD KNOW THAT I...

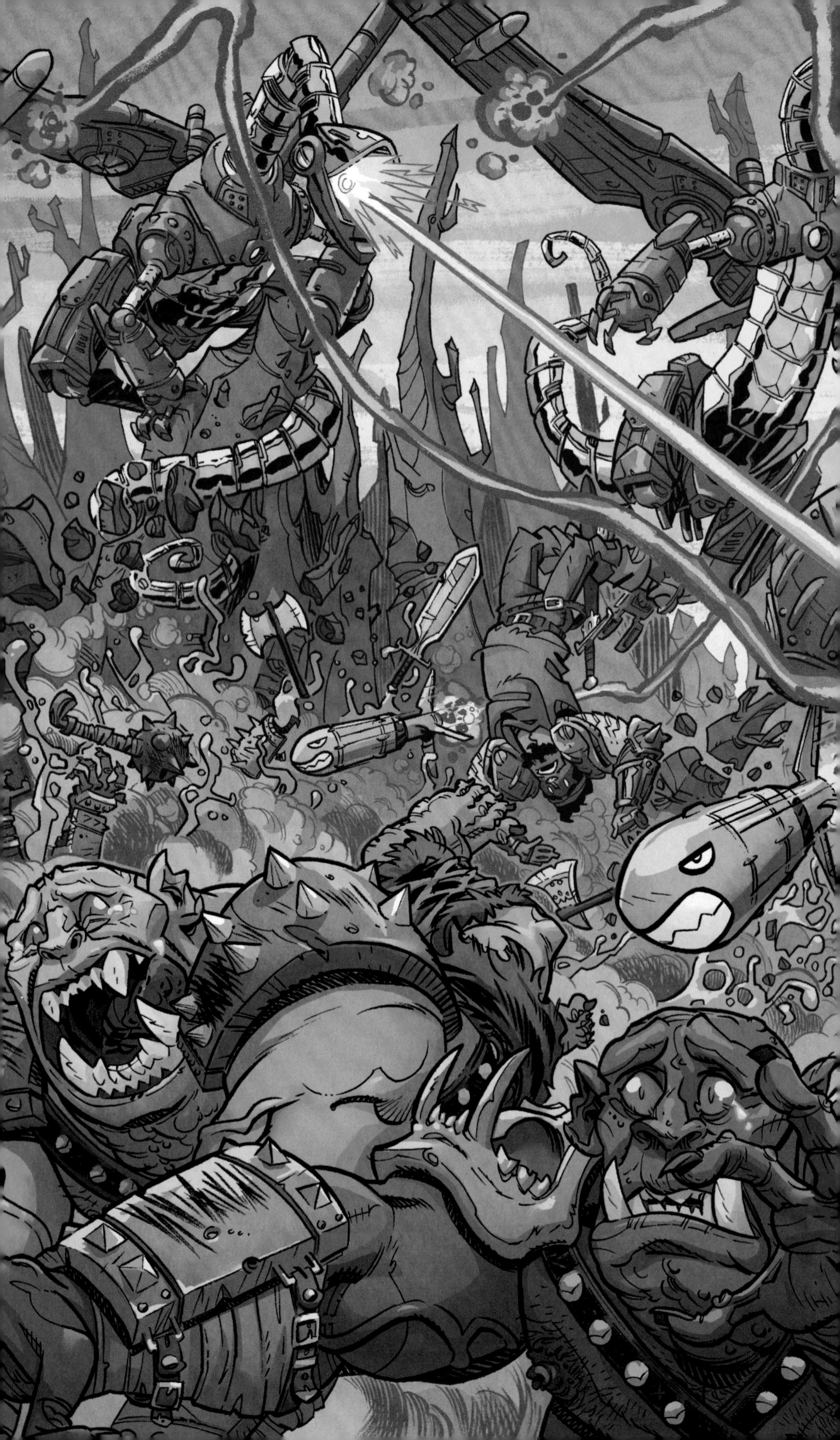

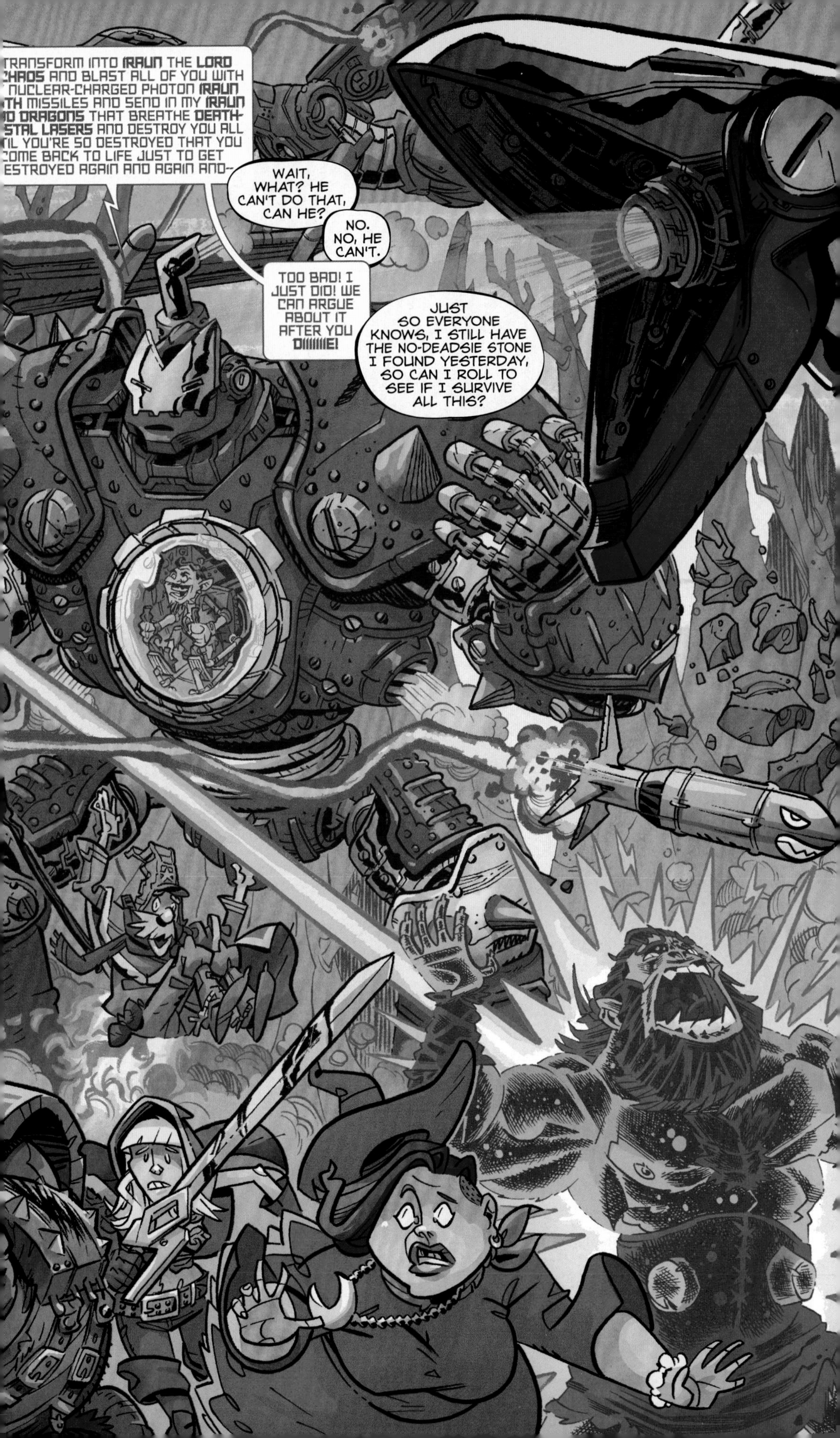
TRANSFORM INTO IRAUN THE LORD CHAOS AND BLAST ALL OF YOU WITH NUCLEAR-CHARGED PHOTON IRAUN TH MISSILES AND SEND IN MY IRAUN D DRAGONS THAT BREATHE DEATH-STAL LASERS AND DESTROY YOU ALL TIL YOU'RE SO DESTROYED THAT YOU COME BACK TO LIFE JUST TO GET ESTROYED AGAIN AND AGAIN AND--
WAIT, WHAT? HE CAN'T DO THAT, CAN HE?
NO. NO, HE CAN'T.
TOO BAD! I JUST DID! WE CAN ARGUE ABOUT IT AFTER YOU DIIIIIIE!
JUST SO EVERYONE KNOWS, I STILL HAVE THE NO-DEADSIE STONE I FOUND YESTERDAY, SO CAN I ROLL TO SEE IF I SURVIVE ALL THIS?

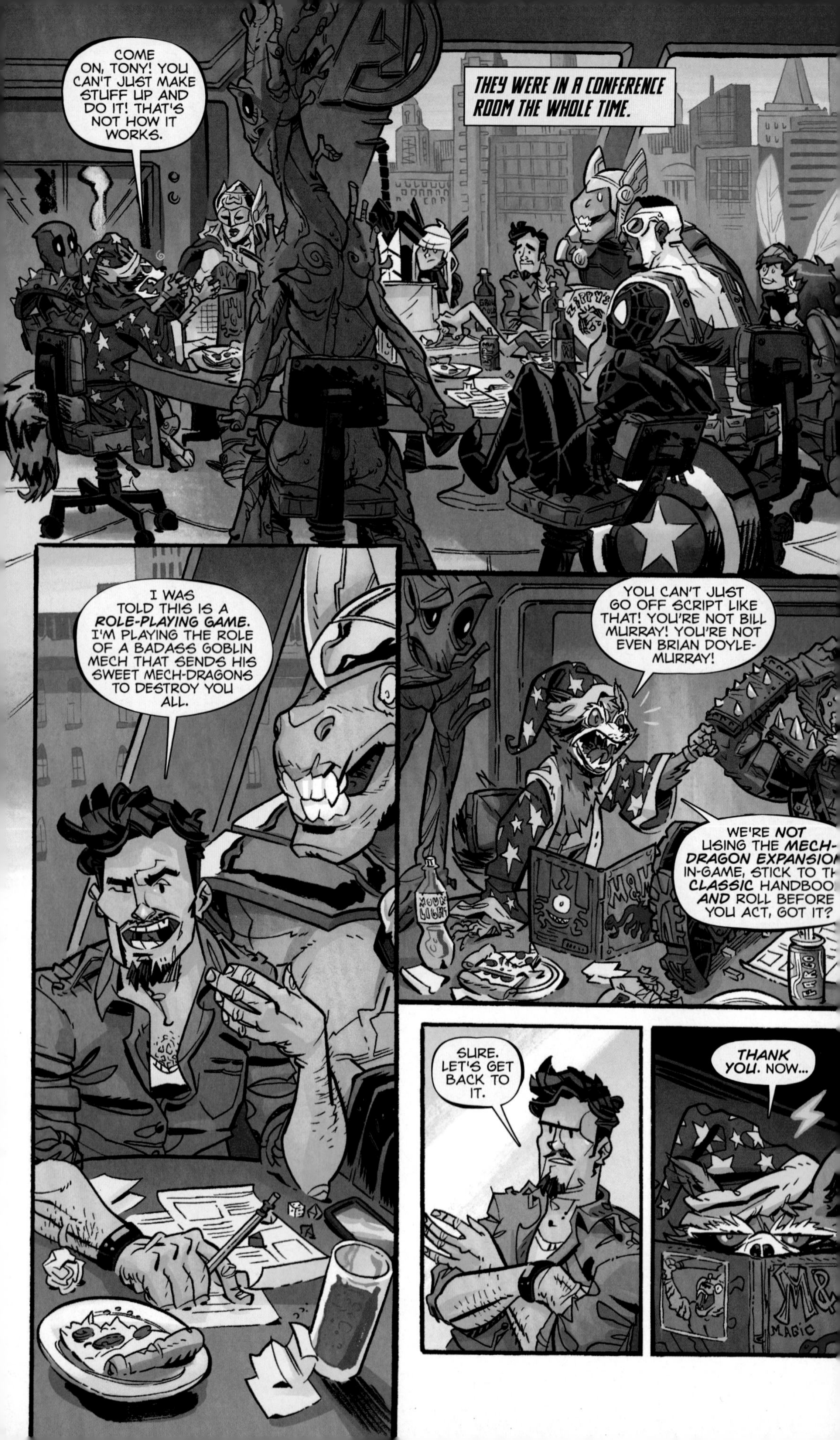
COME ON, TONY! YOU CAN'T JUST MAKE STUFF UP AND DO IT! THAT'S NOT HOW IT WORKS.
THEY WERE IN A CONFERENCE ROOM THE WHOLE TIME.
I WAS TOLD THIS IS A ROLE-PLAYING GAME. I'M PLAYING THE ROLE OF A BADASS GOBLIN MECH THAT SENDS HIS SWEET MECH-DRAGONS TO DESTROY YOU ALL.
YOU CAN'T JUST GO OFF SCRIPT LIKE THAT! YOU'RE NOT BILL MURRAY! YOU'RE NOT EVEN BRIAN DOYLE-MURRAY!
WE'RE NOT USING THE MECH-DRAGON EXPANSIO IN-GAME, STICK TO TH CLASSIC HANDBOO AND ROLL BEFORE YOU ACT, GOT IT?
SURE. LET'S GET BACK TO IT.
THANK YOU. NOW...
MAGIC

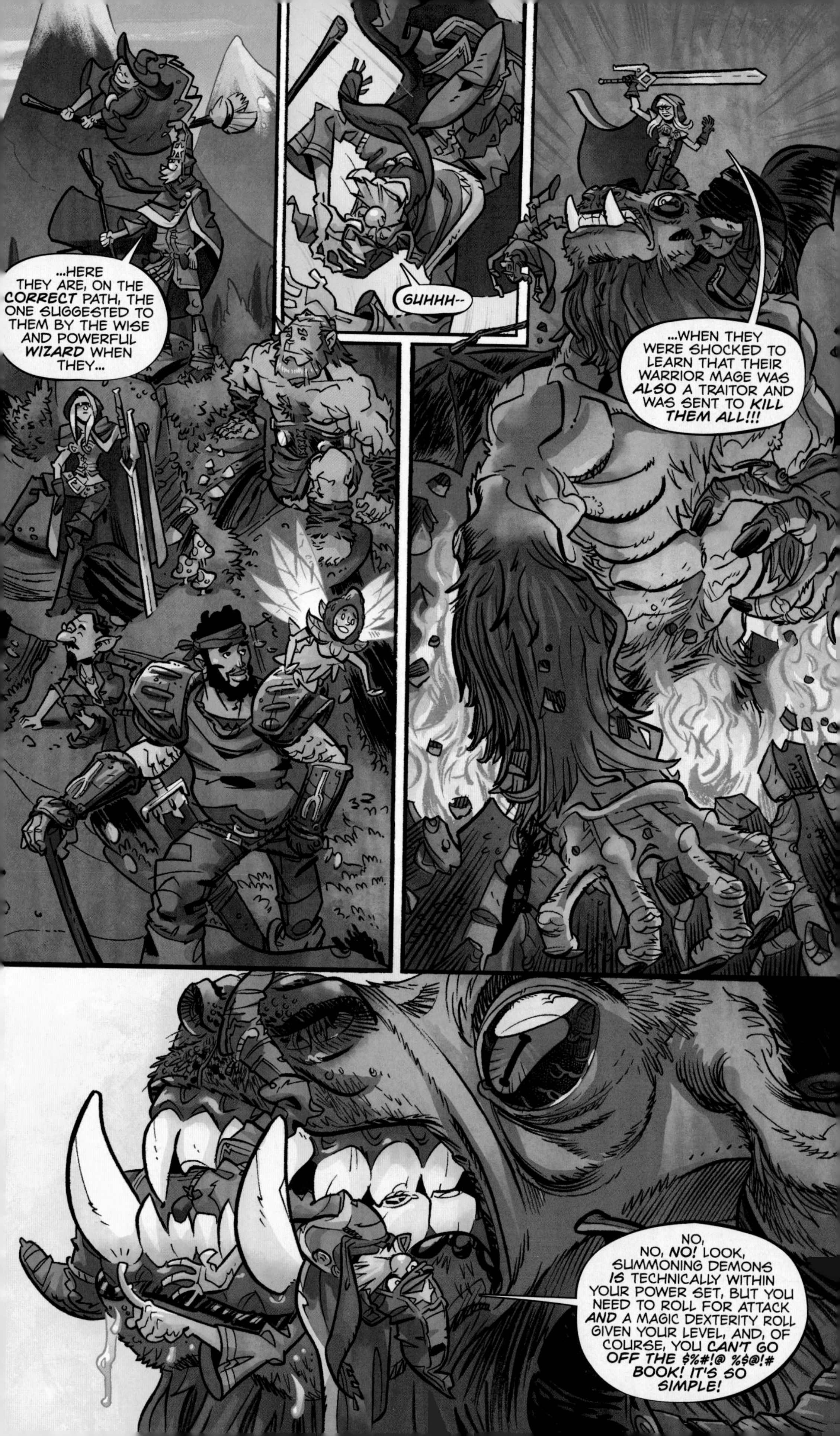
...HERE THEY ARE, ON THE **CORRECT** PATH, THE ONE SUGGESTED TO THEM BY THE WISE AND POWERFUL **WIZARD** WHEN THEY...
GUHHH--
...WHEN THEY WERE SHOCKED TO LEARN THAT THEIR WARRIOR MAGE WAS **ALSO** A TRAITOR AND WAS SENT TO **KILL THEM ALL!!!**
NO, NO, **NO!** LOOK, SUMMONING DEMONS **IS** TECHNICALLY WITHIN YOUR POWER SET, BUT YOU NEED TO ROLL FOR ATTACK **AND** A MAGIC DEXTERITY ROLL GIVEN YOUR LEVEL, AND, OF COURSE, YOU **CAN'T GO OFF THE $%#!@ %$@!# BOOK! IT'S SO SIMPLE!**

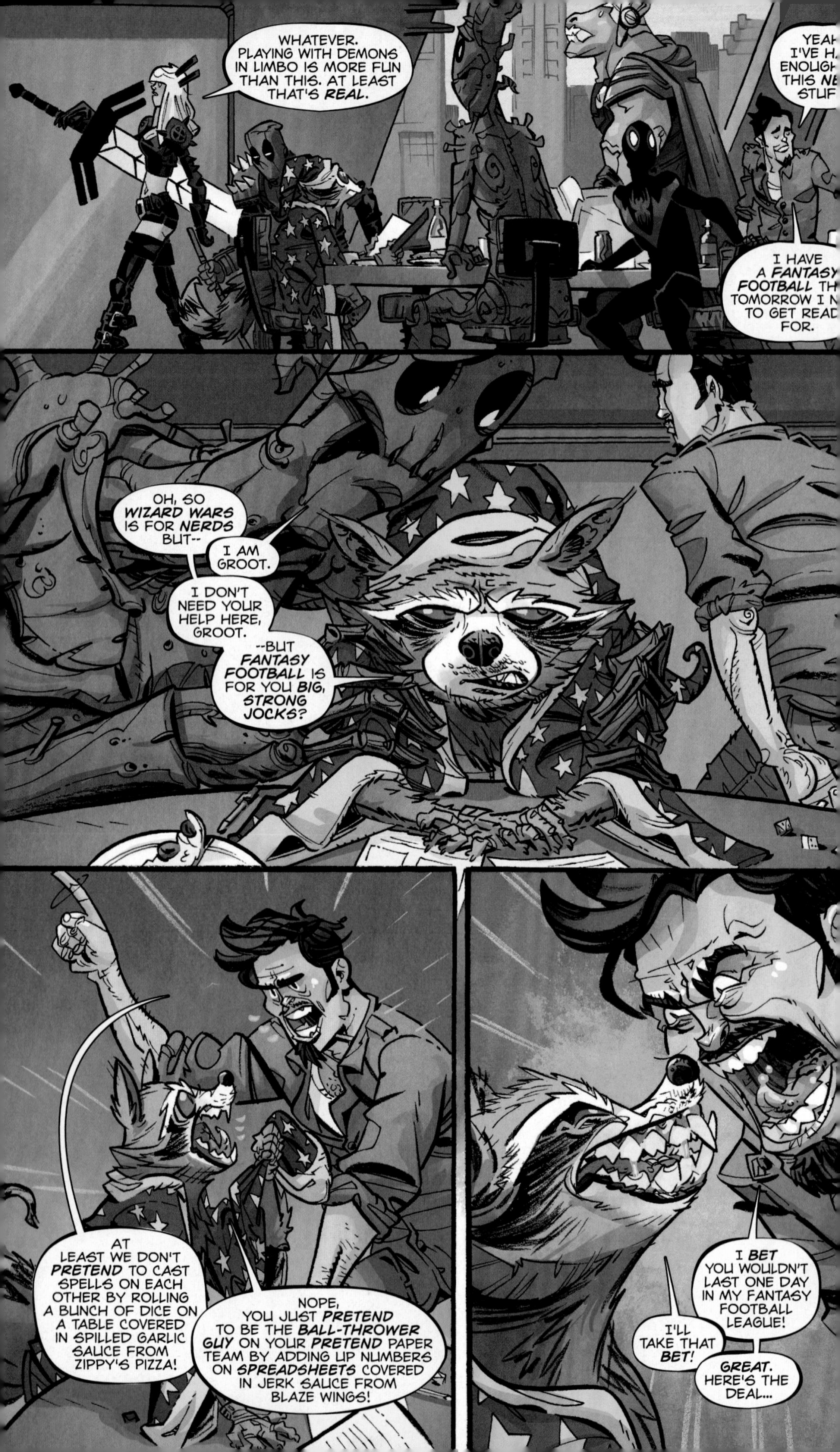
WHATEVER. PLAYING WITH DEMONS IN LIMBO IS MORE FUN THAN THIS. AT LEAST THAT'S *REAL*.
YEAH I'VE HA ENOUGH THIS NE STUF
I HAVE A *FANTASY FOOTBALL* TH TOMORROW I N TO GET READ FOR.
OH, SO *WIZARD WARS* IS FOR *NERDS* BUT--
I AM GROOT.
I DON'T NEED YOUR HELP HERE, GROOT.
--BUT *FANTASY FOOTBALL* IS FOR YOU *BIG, STRONG JOCKS?*
AT LEAST WE DON'T *PRETEND* TO CAST SPELLS ON EACH OTHER BY ROLLING A BUNCH OF DICE ON A TABLE COVERED IN SPILLED GARLIC SAUCE FROM ZIPPY'S PIZZA!
NOPE, YOU JUST *PRETEND* TO BE THE *BALL-THROWER GUY* ON YOUR *PRETEND* PAPER TEAM BY ADDING UP NUMBERS ON *SPREADSHEETS* COVERED IN JERK SAUCE FROM BLAZE WINGS!
I *BET* YOU WOULDN'T LAST ONE DAY IN MY FANTASY FOOTBALL LEAGUE!
I'LL TAKE THAT *BET!*
GREAT. HERE'S THE DEAL...

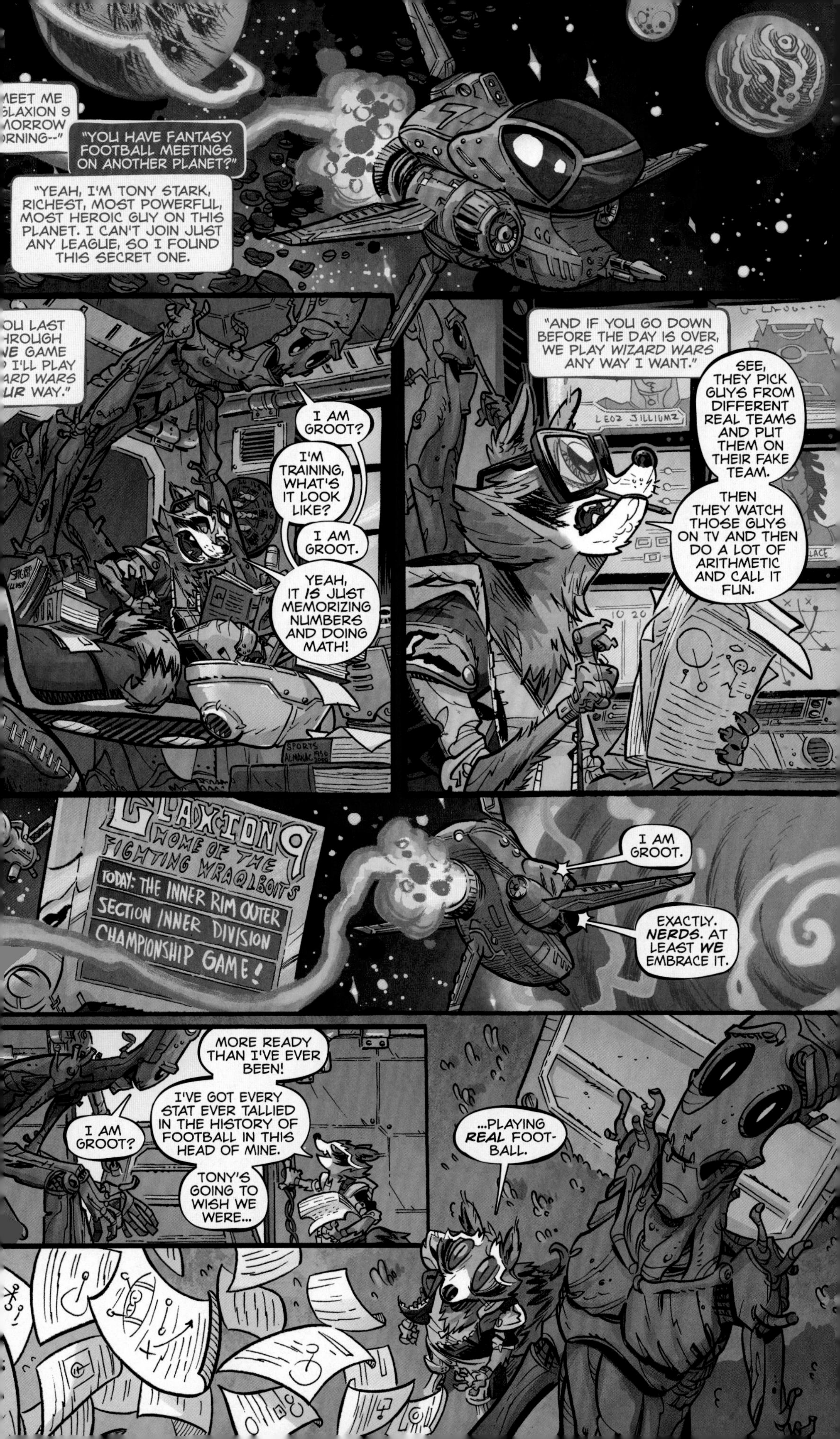
MEET ME
GLAXION 9
MORROW
RNING--"
"YOU HAVE FANTASY FOOTBALL MEETINGS ON ANOTHER PLANET?"
"YEAH, I'M TONY STARK, RICHEST, MOST POWERFUL, MOST HEROIC GUY ON THIS PLANET. I CAN'T JOIN JUST ANY LEAGUE, SO I FOUND THIS SECRET ONE.
OU LAST
HROUGH
NE GAME
I'LL PLAY
ARD WARS
UR WAY."
I AM GROOT?
I'M TRAINING, WHAT'S IT LOOK LIKE?
I AM GROOT.
YEAH, IT *IS* JUST MEMORIZING NUMBERS AND DOING MATH!
SPORTS ALMANAC
"AND IF YOU GO DOWN BEFORE THE DAY IS OVER, WE PLAY *WIZARD WARS* ANY WAY I WANT."
LEOZ JILLIUMZ
SEE, THEY PICK GUYS FROM DIFFERENT REAL TEAMS AND PUT THEM ON THEIR FAKE TEAM.
THEN THEY WATCH THOSE GUYS ON TV AND THEN DO A LOT OF ARITHMETIC AND CALL IT FUN.
GLAXION 9
HOME OF THE FIGHTING WRAQLBOITS
TODAY: THE INNER RIM OUTER SECTION INNER DIVISION CHAMPIONSHIP GAME!
I AM GROOT.
EXACTLY. **NERDS.** AT LEAST ***WE*** EMBRACE IT.
I AM GROOT?
MORE READY THAN I'VE EVER BEEN!
I'VE GOT EVERY STAT EVER TALLIED IN THE HISTORY OF FOOTBALL IN THIS HEAD OF MINE.
TONY'S GOING TO WISH WE WERE...
...PLAYING ***REAL*** FOOT-BALL.

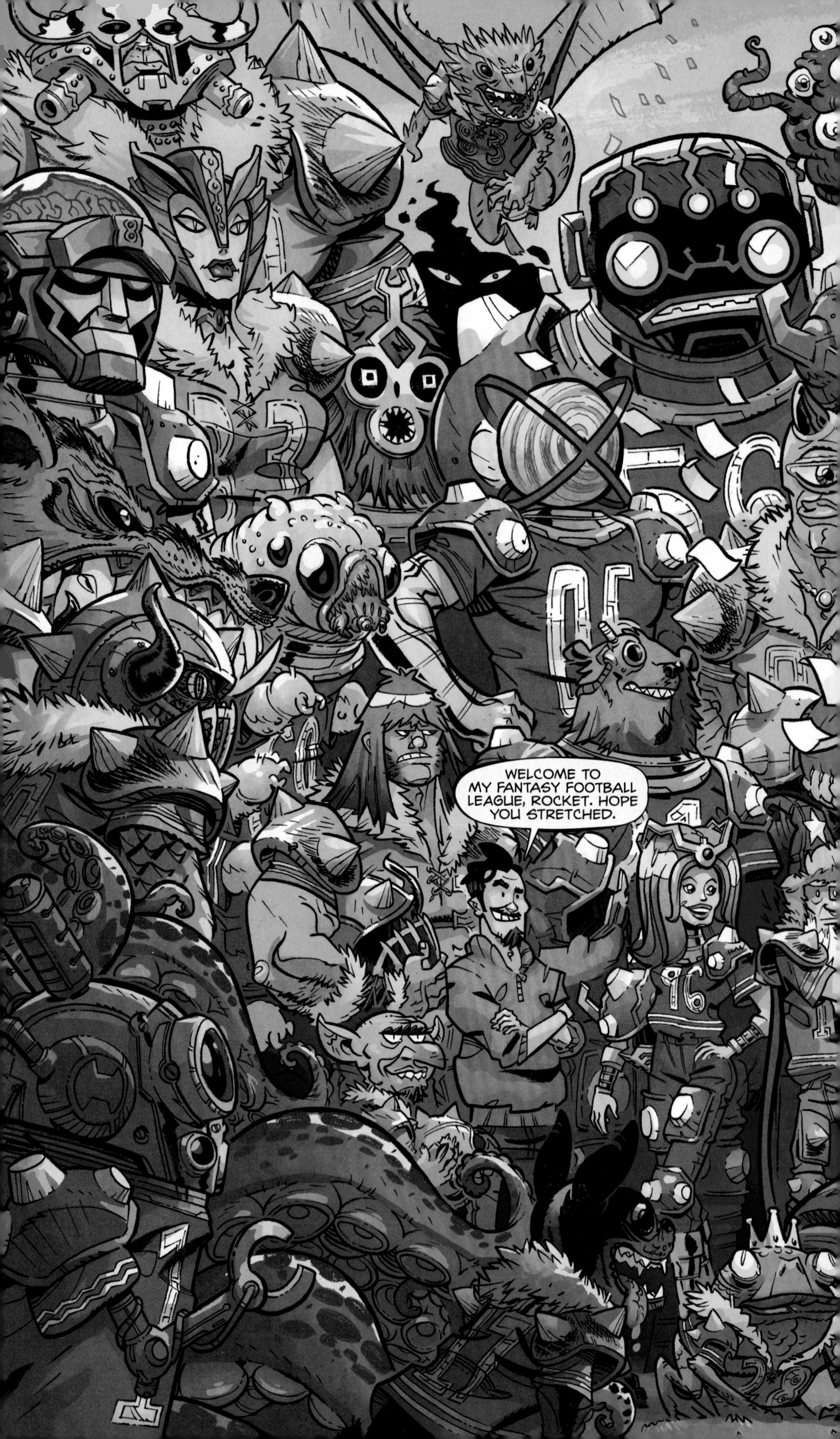
WELCOME TO MY FANTASY FOOTBALL LEAGUE, ROCKET. HOPE YOU STRETCHED.

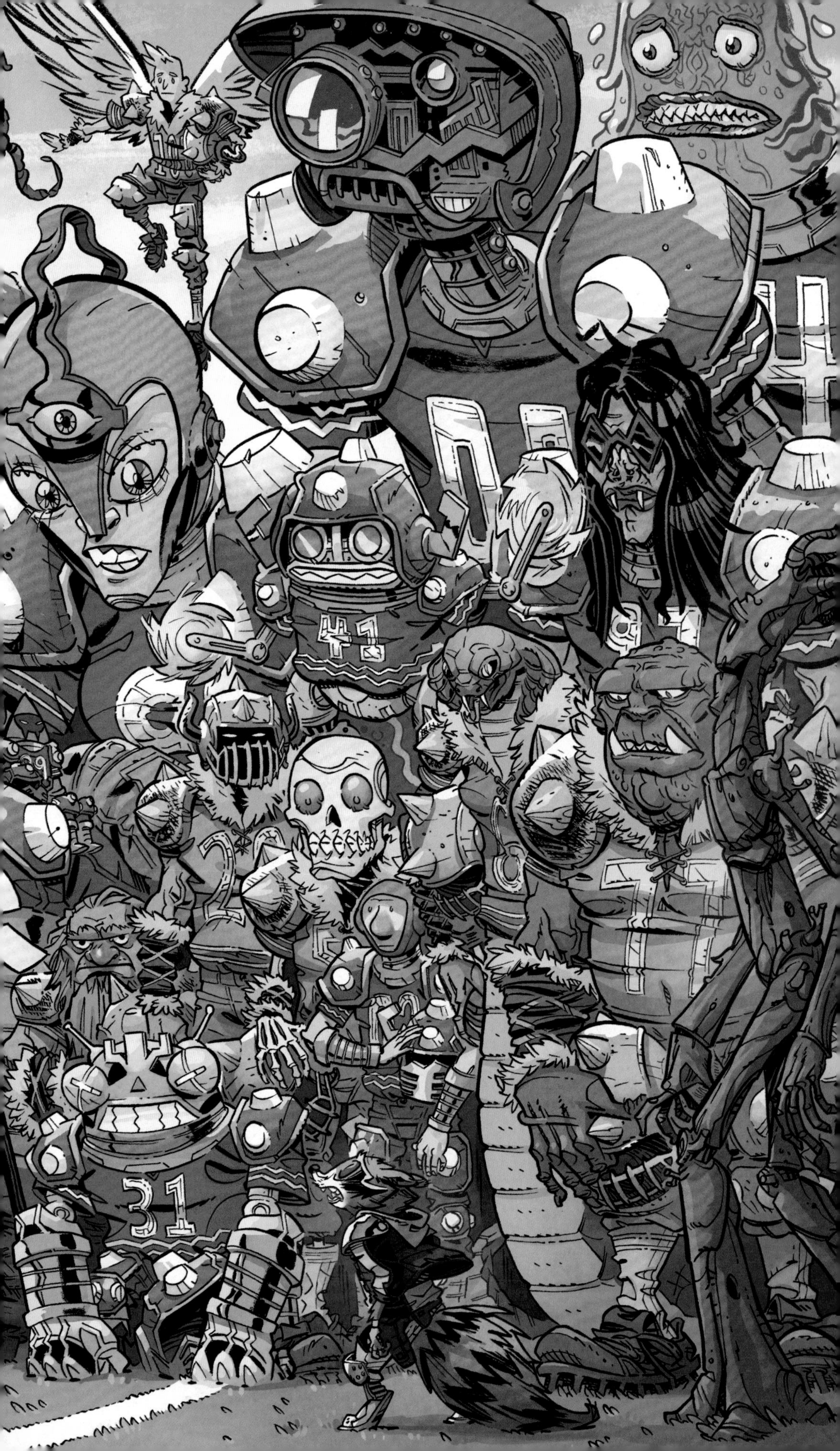

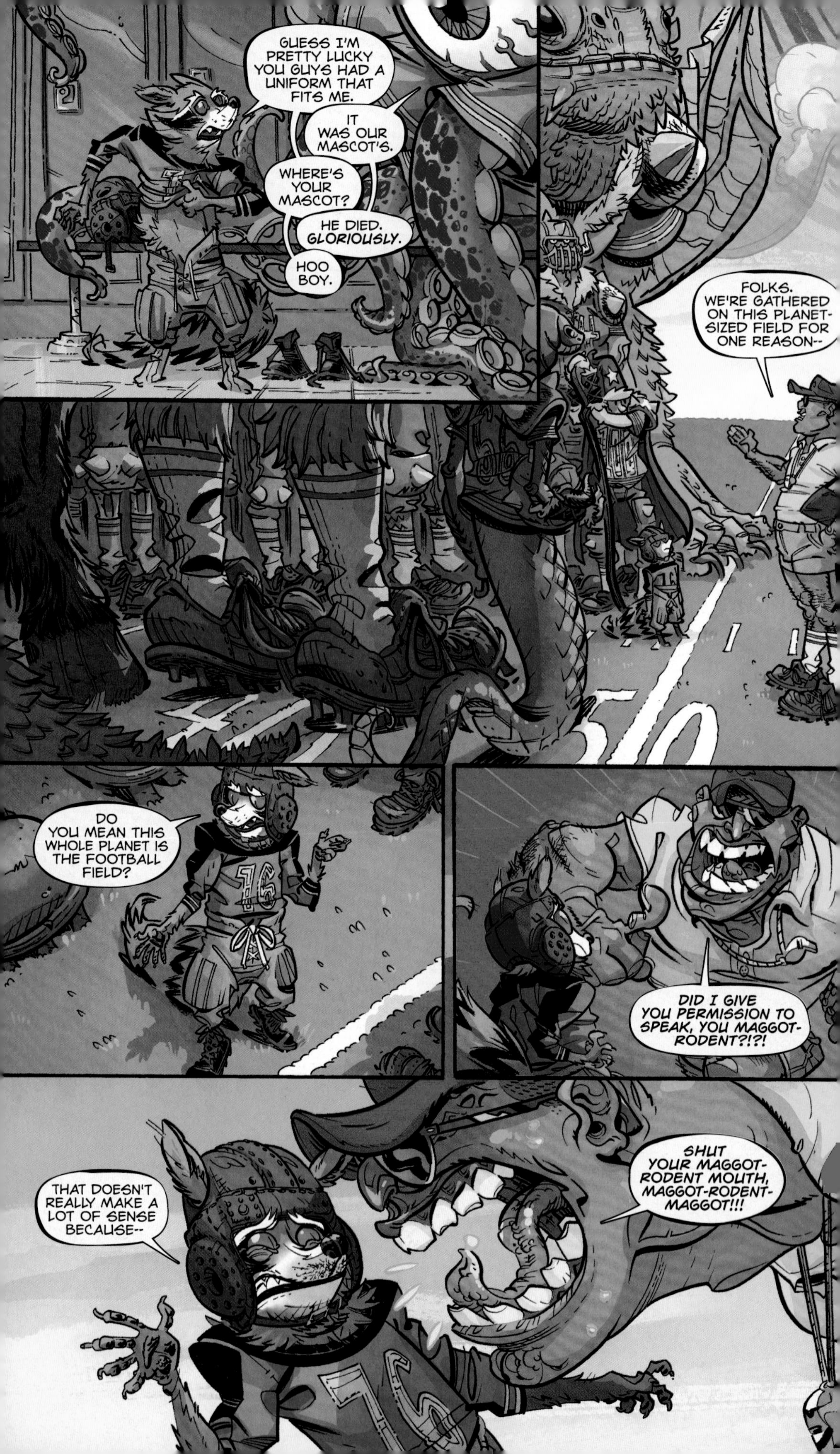
GUESS I'M PRETTY LUCKY YOU GUYS HAD A UNIFORM THAT FITS ME.
IT WAS OUR MASCOT'S.
WHERE'S YOUR MASCOT?
HE DIED. GLORIOUSLY.
HOO BOY.
FOLKS. WE'RE GATHERED ON THIS PLANET-SIZED FIELD FOR ONE REASON--
DO YOU MEAN THIS WHOLE PLANET IS THE FOOTBALL FIELD?
DID I GIVE YOU PERMISSION TO SPEAK, YOU MAGGOT-RODENT?!?!
THAT DOESN'T REALLY MAKE A LOT OF SENSE BECAUSE--
SHUT YOUR MAGGOT-RODENT MOUTH, MAGGOT-RODENT-MAGGOT!!!

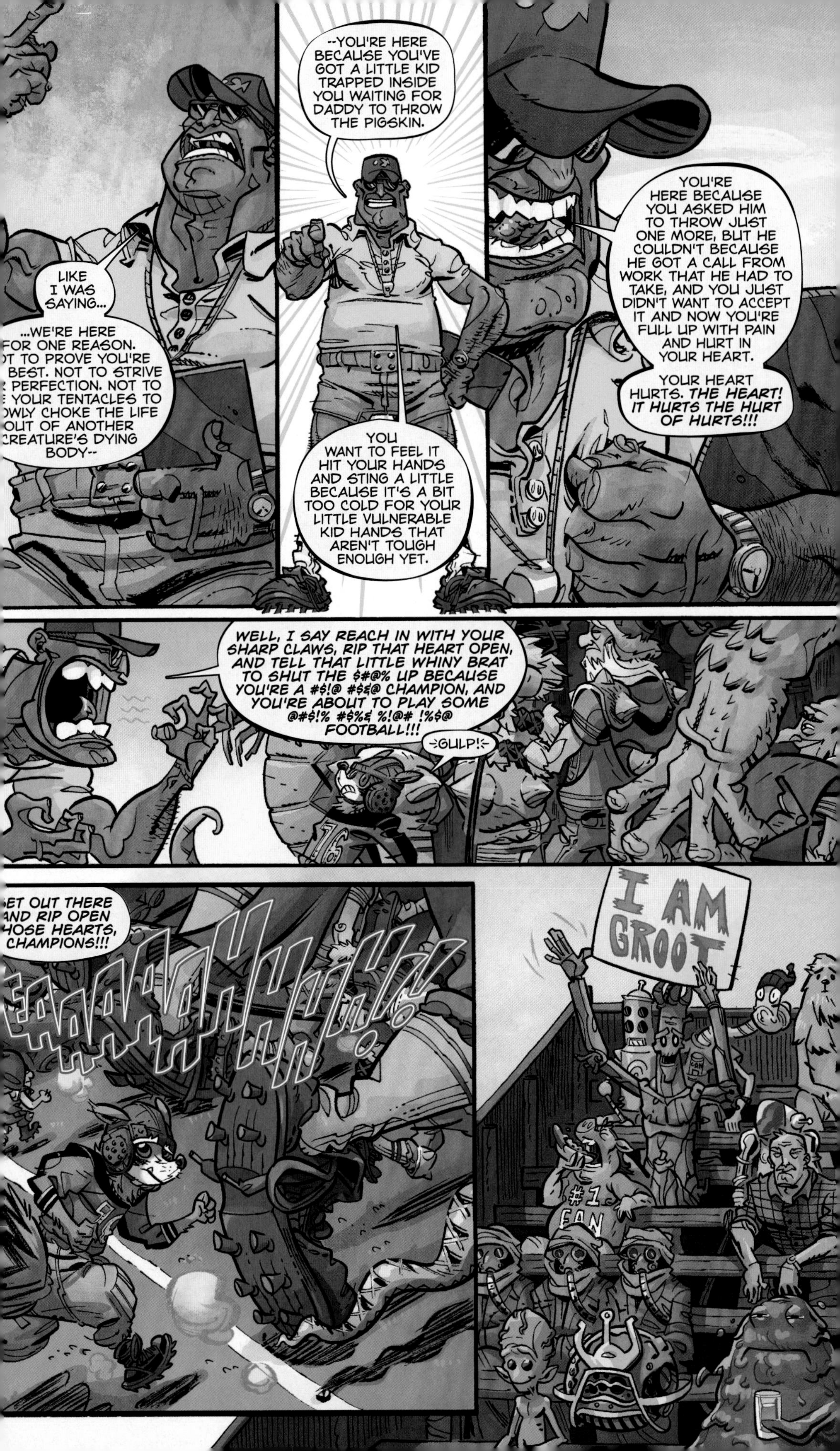
LIKE I WAS SAYING...
...WE'RE HERE FOR ONE REASON. OT TO PROVE YOU'RE BEST. NOT TO STRIVE PERFECTION. NOT TO E YOUR TENTACLES TO OWLY CHOKE THE LIFE OUT OF ANOTHER CREATURE'S DYING BODY--
--YOU'RE HERE BECAUSE YOU'VE GOT A LITTLE KID TRAPPED INSIDE YOU WAITING FOR DADDY TO THROW THE PIGSKIN.
YOU WANT TO FEEL IT HIT YOUR HANDS AND STING A LITTLE BECAUSE IT'S A BIT TOO COLD FOR YOUR LITTLE VULNERABLE KID HANDS THAT AREN'T TOUGH ENOUGH YET.
YOU'RE HERE BECAUSE YOU ASKED HIM TO THROW JUST ONE MORE, BUT HE COULDN'T BECAUSE HE GOT A CALL FROM WORK THAT HE HAD TO TAKE, AND YOU JUST DIDN'T WANT TO ACCEPT IT AND NOW YOU'RE FULL UP WITH PAIN AND HURT IN YOUR HEART.
YOUR HEART HURTS. THE HEART! IT HURTS THE HURT OF HURTS!!!
WELL, I SAY REACH IN WITH YOUR SHARP CLAWS, RIP THAT HEART OPEN, AND TELL THAT LITTLE WHINY BRAT TO SHUT THE $#@% UP BECAUSE YOU'RE A #$!@ #$&@ CHAMPION, AND YOU'RE ABOUT TO PLAY SOME @#$!% #$%& %!@# !%$@ FOOTBALL!!!
-GULP!-
ET OUT THERE AND RIP OPEN HOSE HEARTS, CHAMPIONS!!!
EAAAAAAHHHHH!
I AM GROOT
#1 FAN

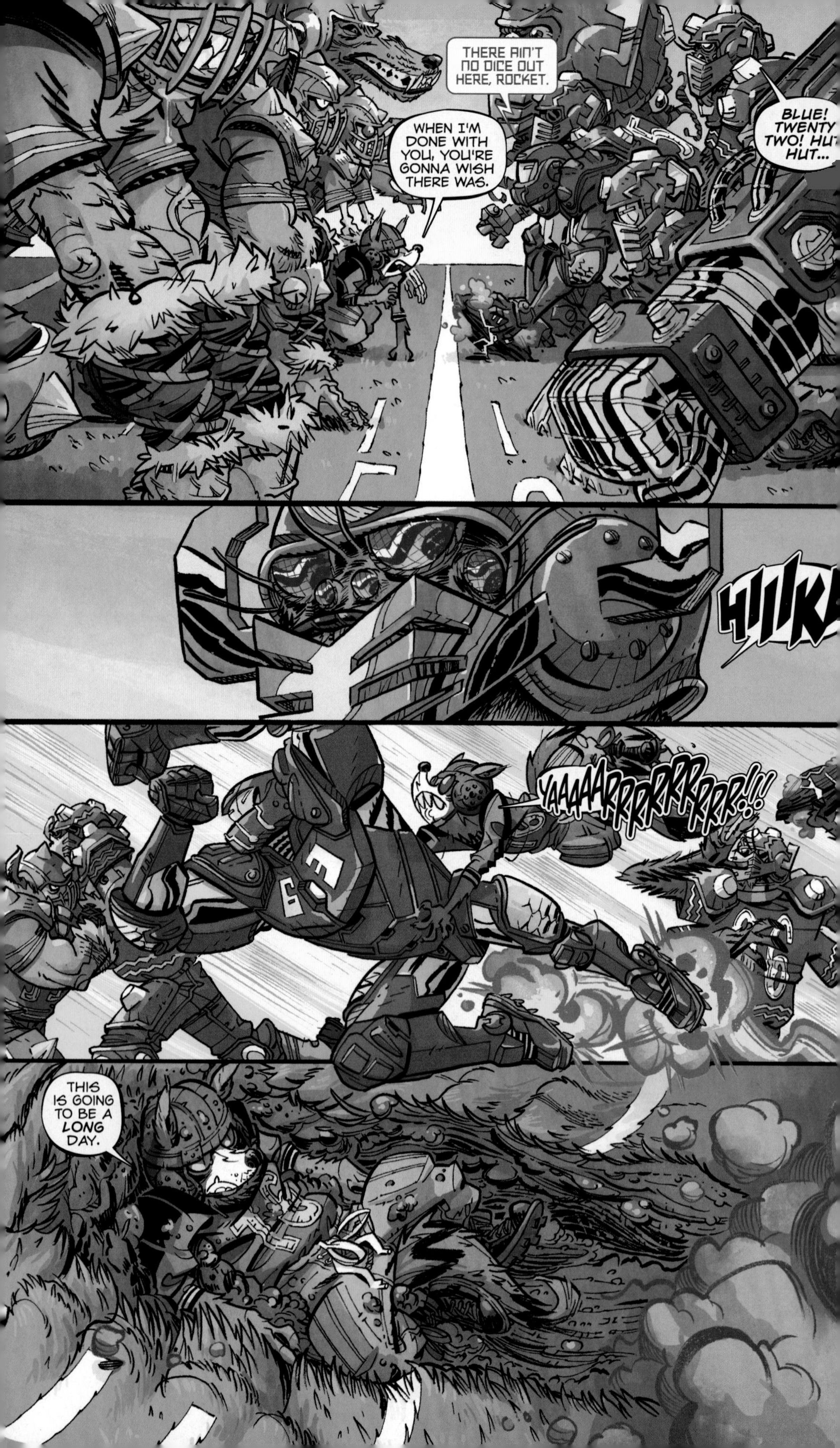
THERE AIN'T NO DICE OUT HERE, ROCKET.
WHEN I'M DONE WITH YOU, YOU'RE GONNA WISH THERE WAS.
BLUE! TWENTY TWO! HUT! HUT...
HUUK
YAAAAARRRRRRRRR!!!
THIS IS GOING TO BE A LONG DAY.

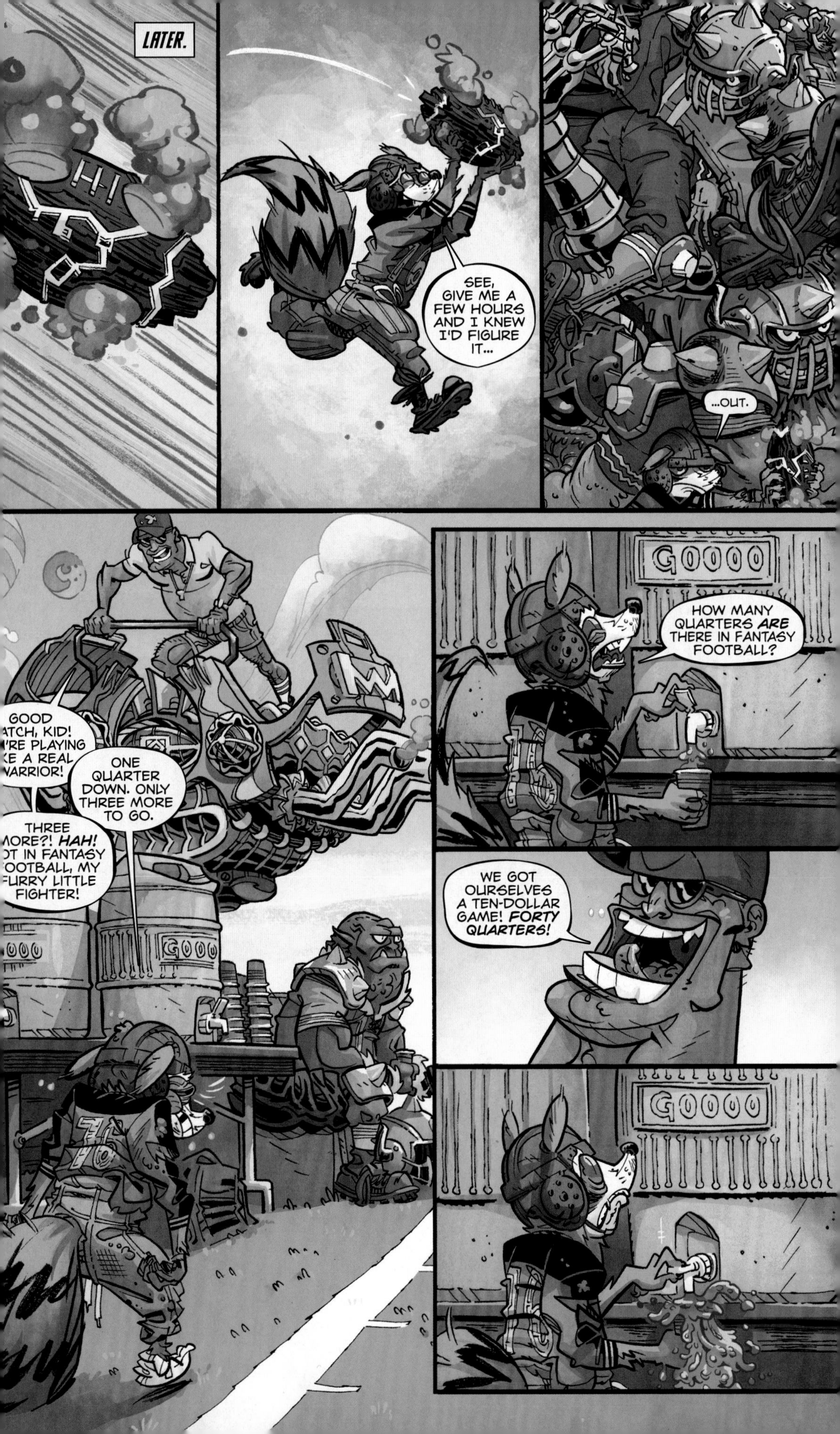
LATER.
HI
SEE, GIVE ME A FEW HOURS AND I KNEW I'D FIGURE IT...
...OUT.
GOOD
ATCH, KID!
'RE PLAYING
E A REAL
ARRIOR!
ONE QUARTER DOWN. ONLY THREE MORE TO GO.
THREE
ORE?! HAH!
OT IN FANTASY
OOTBALL, MY
FURRY LITTLE
FIGHTER!
GOOOO
HOW MANY QUARTERS ARE THERE IN FANTASY FOOTBALL?
WE GOT OURSELVES A TEN-DOLLAR GAME! FORTY QUARTERS!
GOOOO

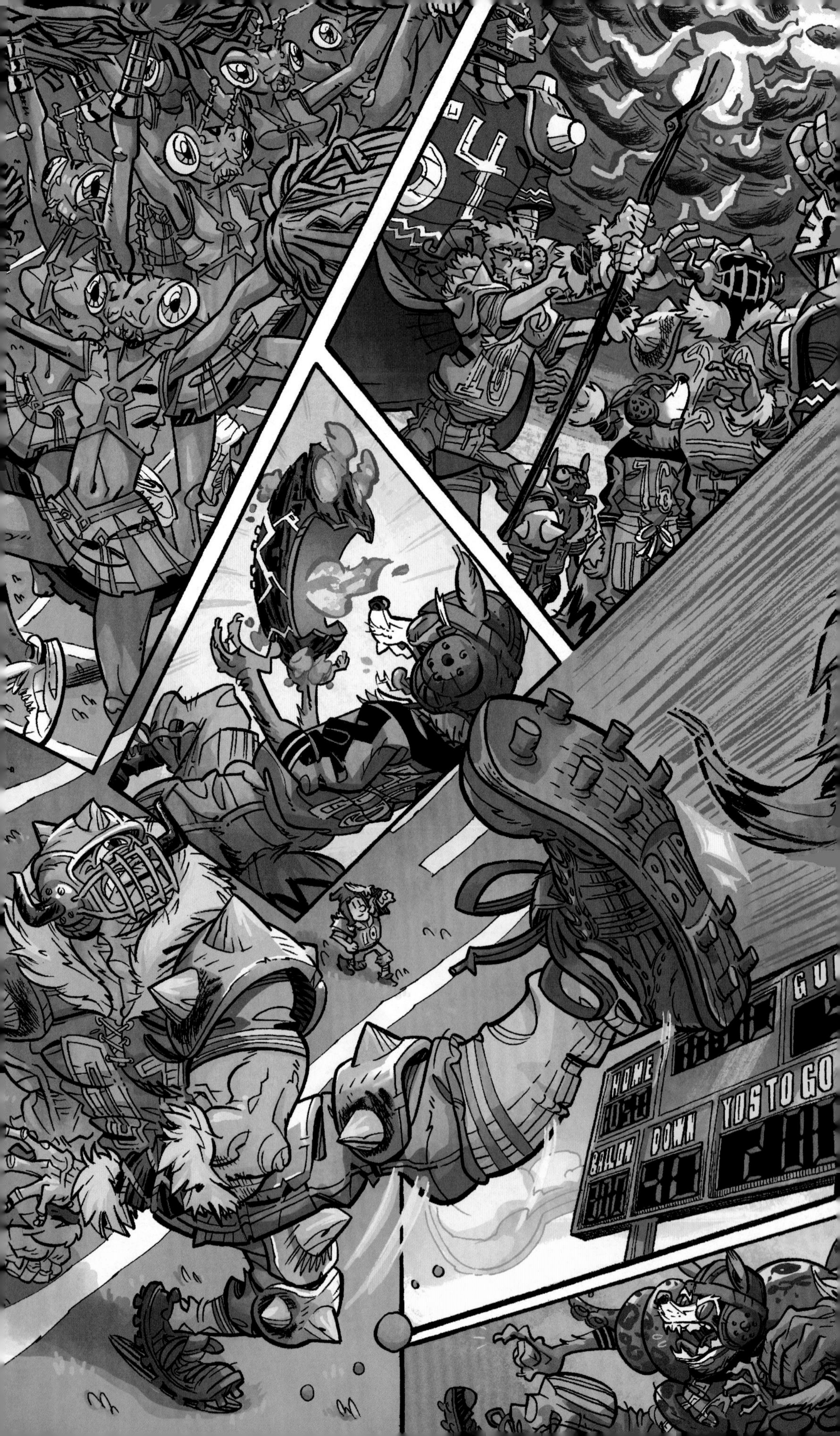
HOME
BALL ON
DOWN
YDS TO GO

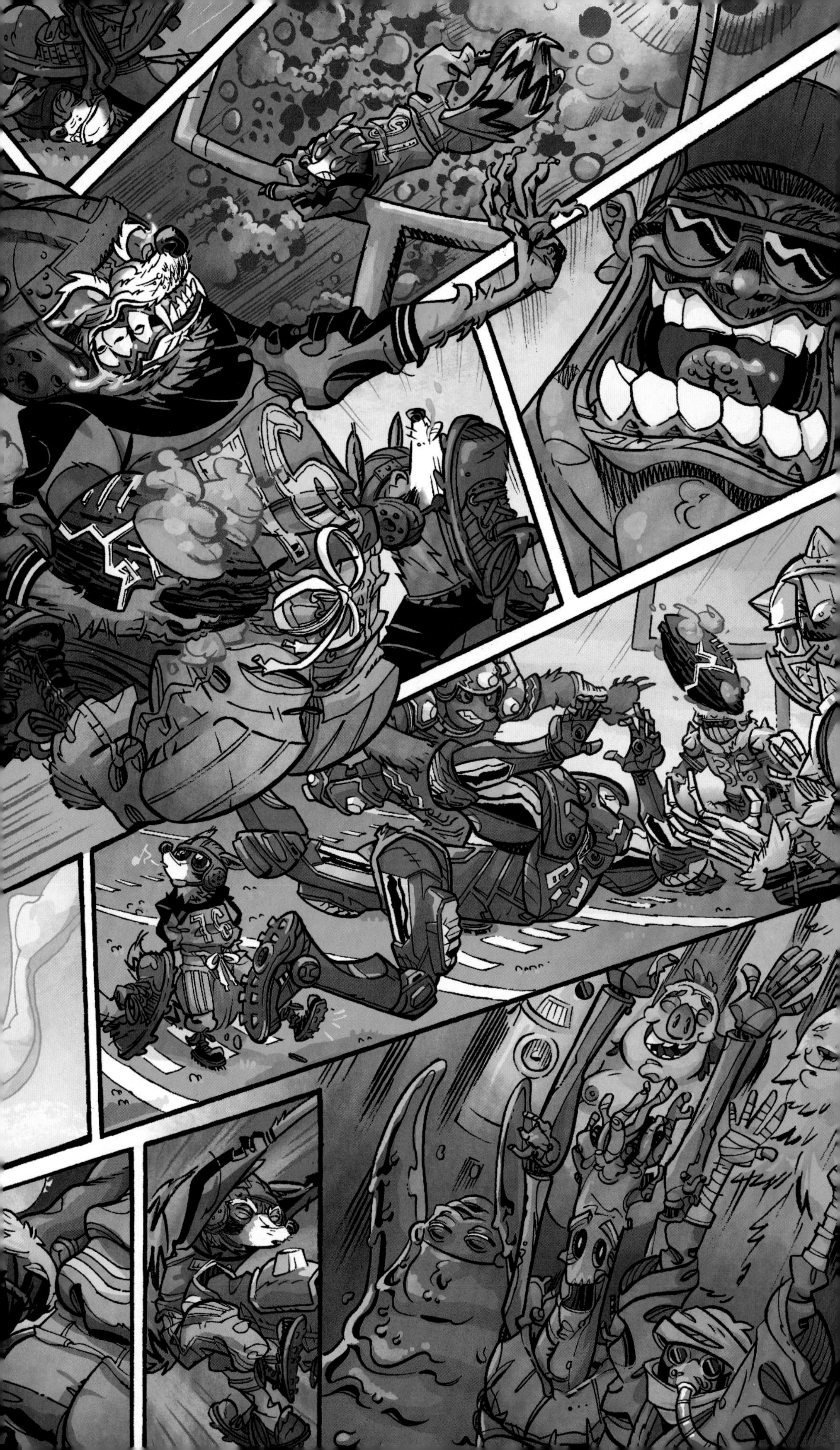

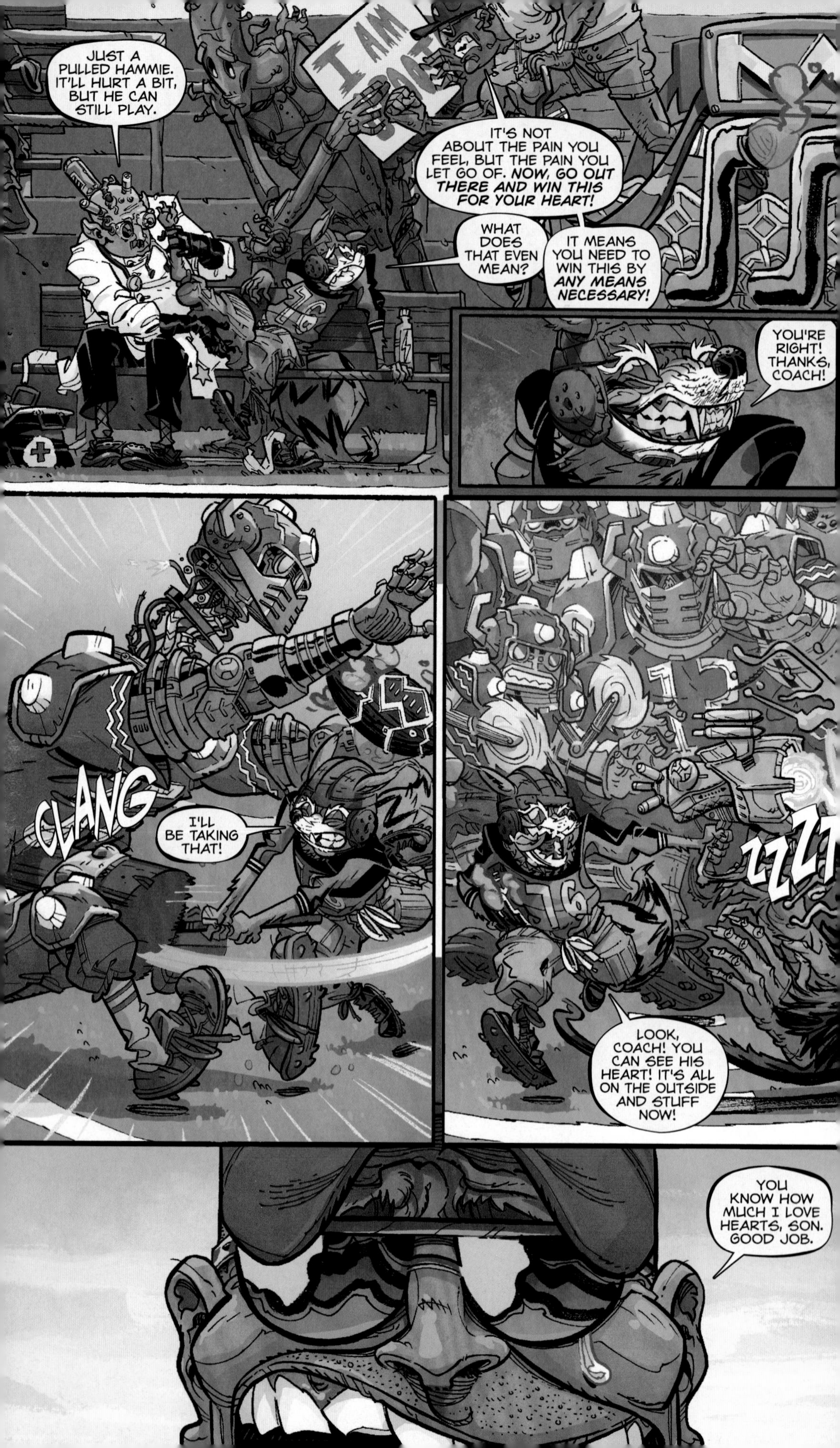

JUST A PULLED HAMMIE. IT'LL HURT A BIT, BUT HE CAN STILL PLAY.
I AM
IT'S NOT ABOUT THE PAIN YOU FEEL, BUT THE PAIN YOU LET GO OF. NOW, GO OUT THERE AND WIN THIS FOR YOUR HEART!
WHAT DOES THAT EVEN MEAN?
IT MEANS YOU NEED TO WIN THIS BY ANY MEANS NECESSARY!
YOU'RE RIGHT! THANKS, COACH!
CLANG
I'LL BE TAKING THAT!
ZZZZT
LOOK, COACH! YOU CAN SEE HIS HEART! IT'S ALL ON THE OUTSIDE AND STUFF NOW!
YOU KNOW HOW MUCH I LOVE HEARTS, SON. GOOD JOB.

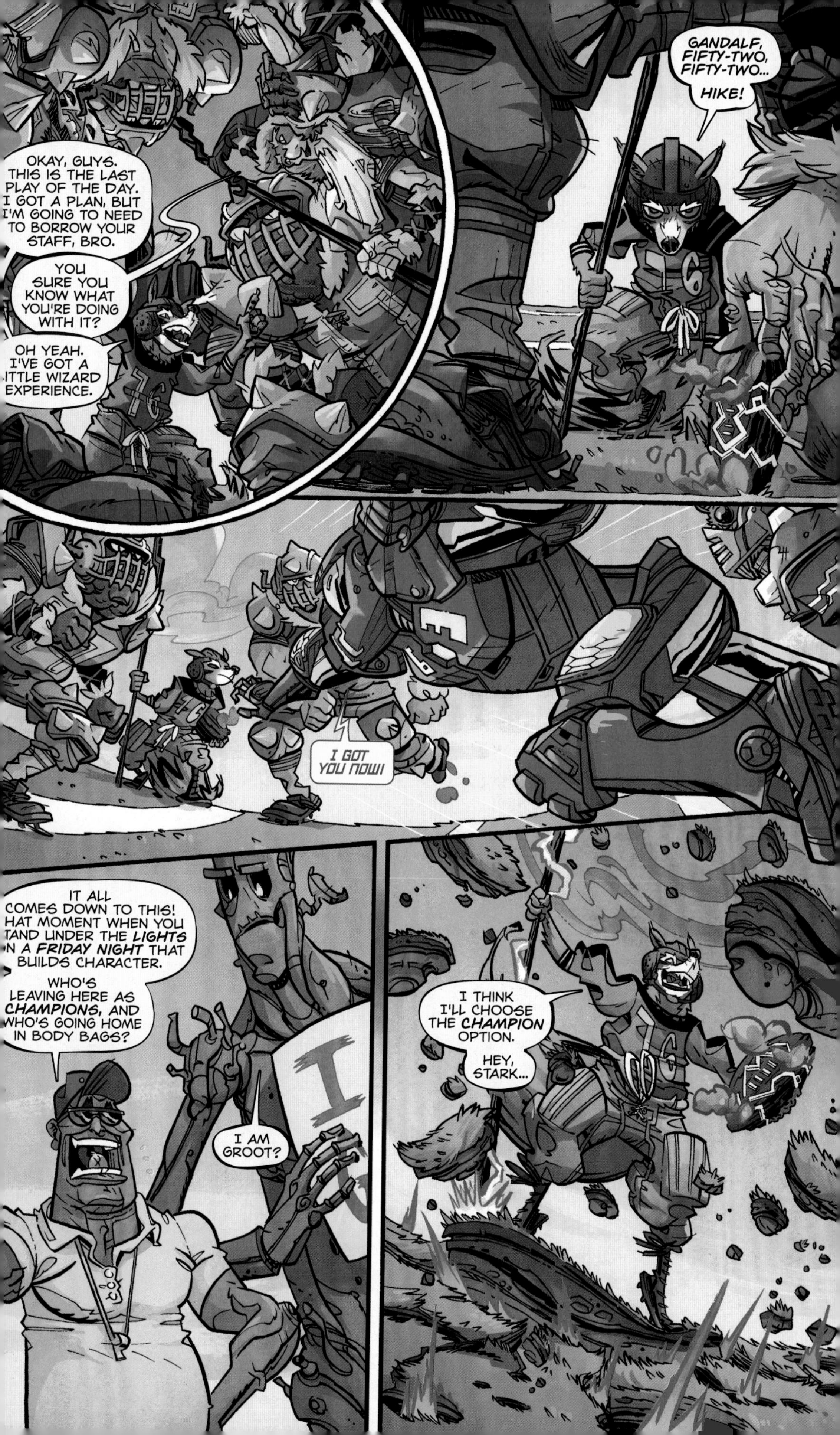
OKAY, GUYS. THIS IS THE LAST PLAY OF THE DAY. I GOT A PLAN, BUT I'M GOING TO NEED TO BORROW YOUR STAFF, BRO.
YOU SURE YOU KNOW WHAT YOU'RE DOING WITH IT?
OH YEAH. I'VE GOT A LITTLE WIZARD EXPERIENCE.
GANDALF, FIFTY-TWO, FIFTY-TWO...
HIKE!
I GOT YOU NOW!
IT ALL COMES DOWN TO THIS! THAT MOMENT WHEN YOU STAND UNDER THE LIGHTS ON A FRIDAY NIGHT THAT BUILDS CHARACTER.
WHO'S LEAVING HERE AS CHAMPIONS, AND WHO'S GOING HOME IN BODY BAGS?
I AM GROOT?
I THINK I'LL CHOOSE THE CHAMPION OPTION.
HEY, STARK...

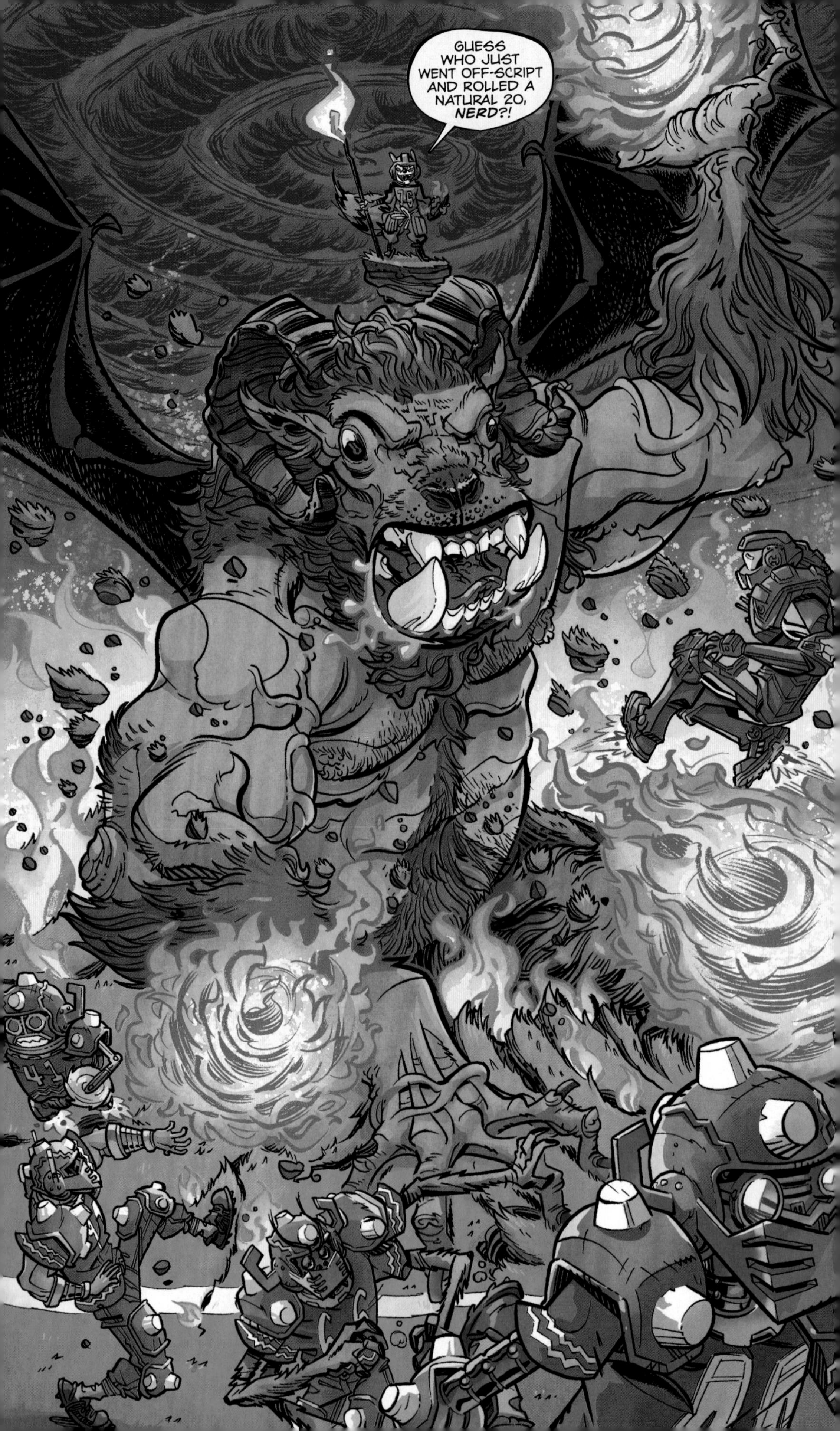
GUESS WHO JUST WENT OFF-SCRIPT AND ROLLED A NATURAL 20, *NERD*?!

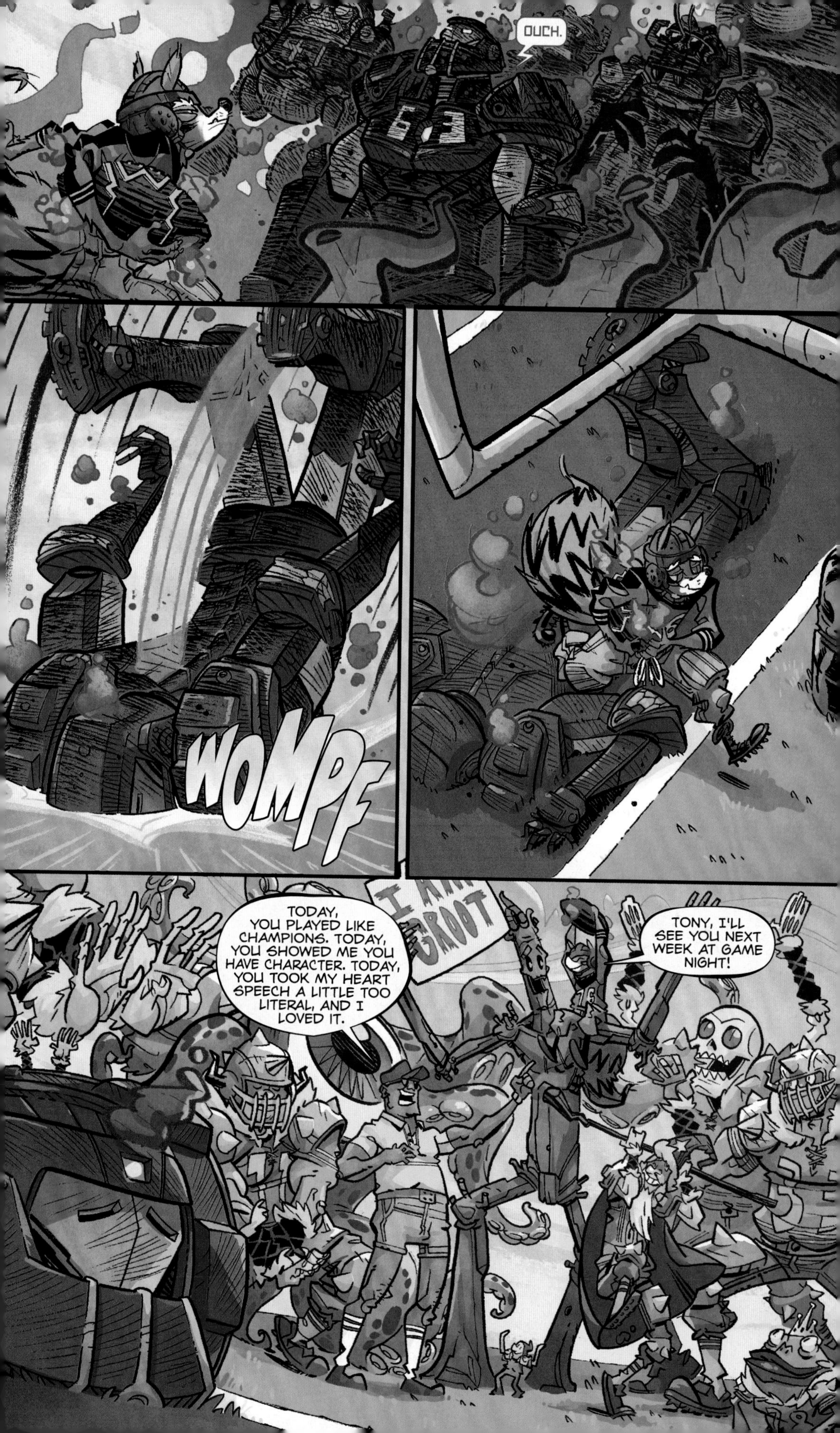
OUCH.
WOMPF
GROOT
TODAY, YOU PLAYED LIKE CHAMPIONS. TODAY, YOU SHOWED ME YOU HAVE CHARACTER. TODAY, YOU TOOK MY HEART SPEECH A LITTLE TOO LITERAL, AND I LOVED IT.
TONY, I'LL SEE YOU NEXT WEEK AT GAME NIGHT!

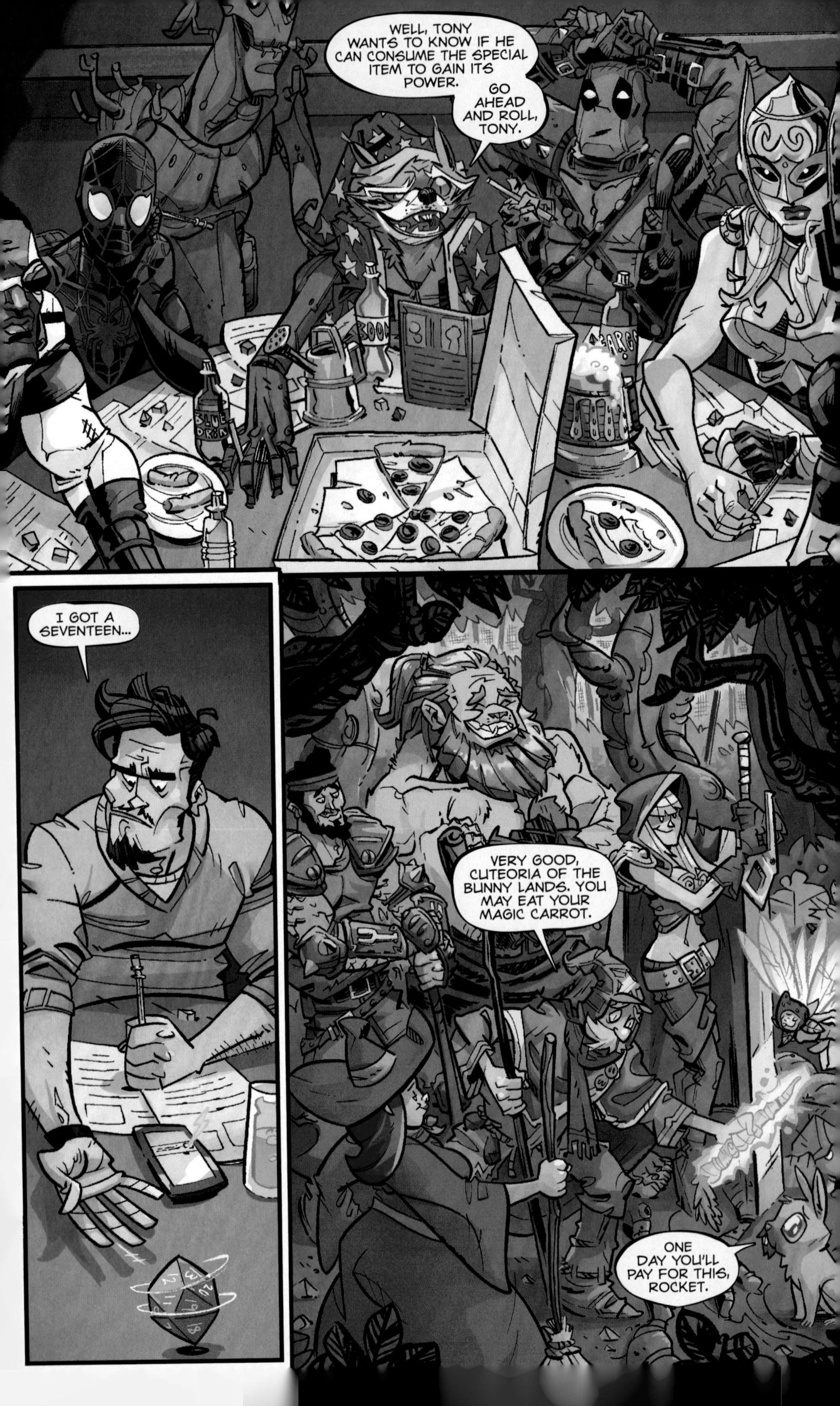
WELL, TONY WANTS TO KNOW IF HE CAN CONSUME THE SPECIAL ITEM TO GAIN ITS POWER.
GO AHEAD AND ROLL, TONY.
I GOT A SEVENTEEN...
VERY GOOD, CUTEORIA OF THE BUNNY LANDS. YOU MAY EAT YOUR MAGIC CARROT.
ONE DAY YOU'LL PAY FOR THIS, ROCKET.

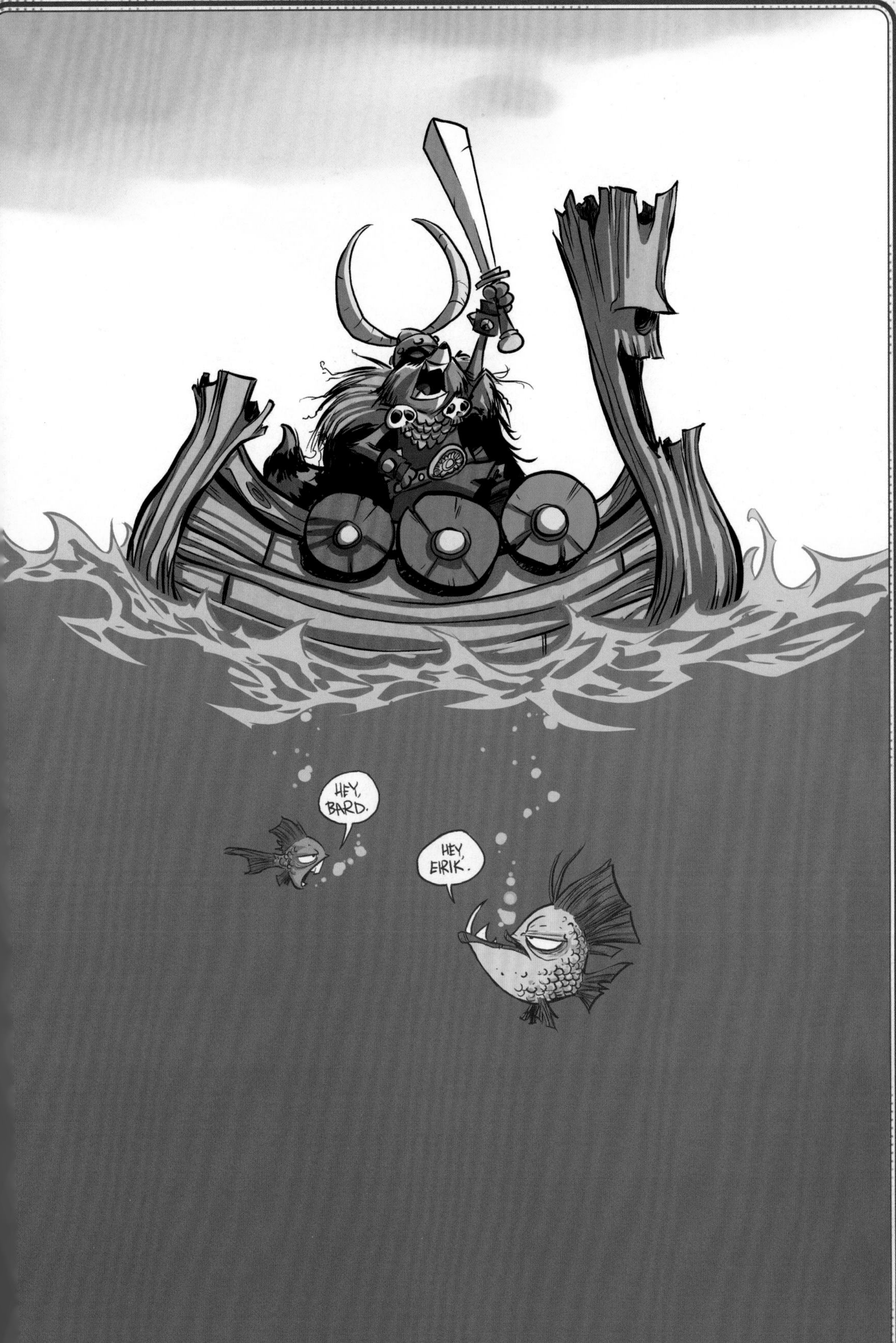
HEY, BARD.
HEY, EIRIK.

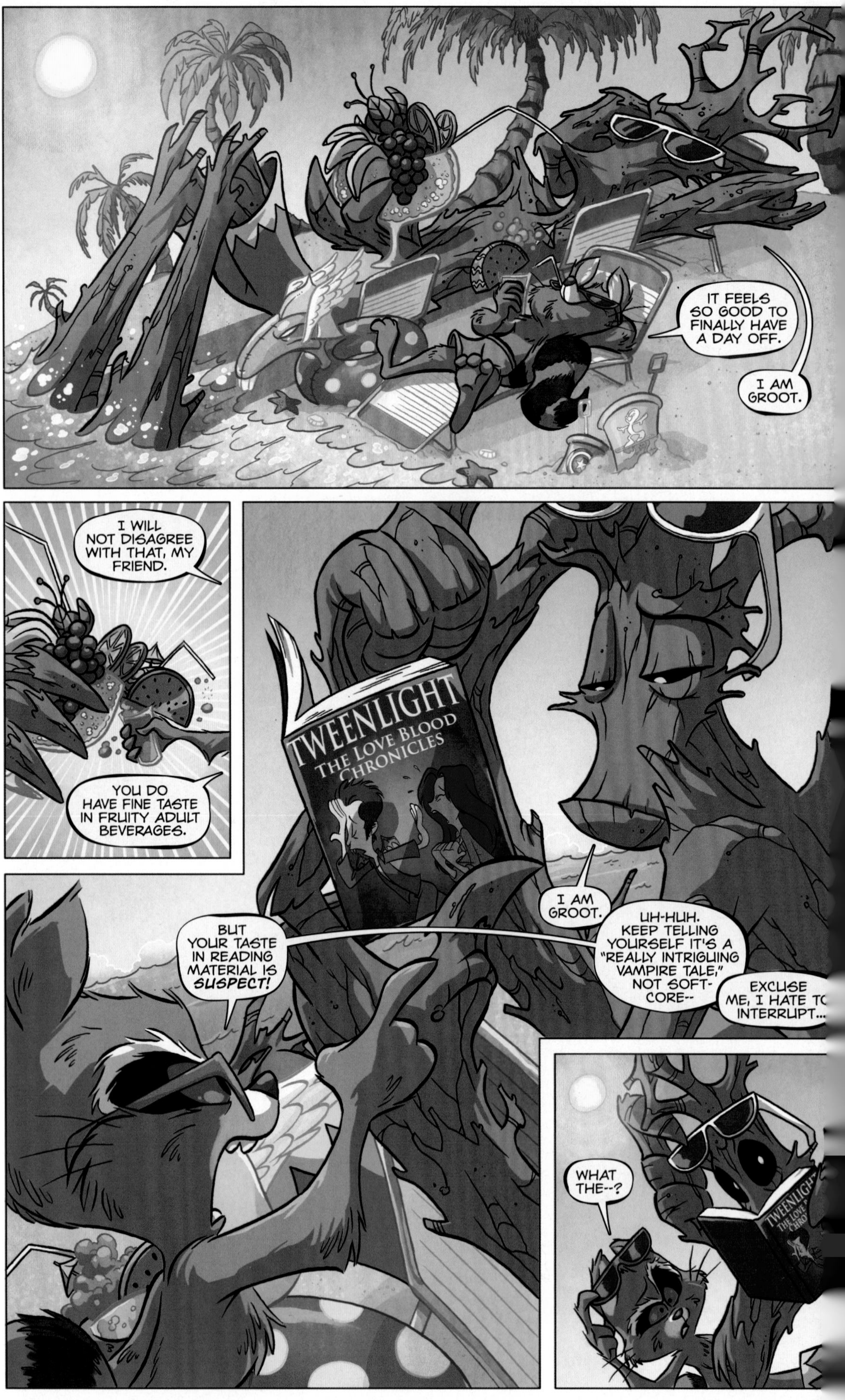
IT FEELS SO GOOD TO FINALLY HAVE A DAY OFF.
I AM GROOT.
I WILL NOT DISAGREE WITH THAT, MY FRIEND.
YOU DO HAVE FINE TASTE IN FRUITY ADULT BEVERAGES.
TWEENLIGHT THE LOVE BLOOD CHRONICLES
I AM GROOT.
BUT YOUR TASTE IN READING MATERIAL IS SUSPECT!
UH-HUH. KEEP TELLING YOURSELF IT'S A "REALLY INTRIGUING VAMPIRE TALE," NOT SOFT-CORE--
EXCUSE ME, I HATE TO INTERRUPT...
WHAT THE--?
TWEENLIGHT THE LOVE CHRON

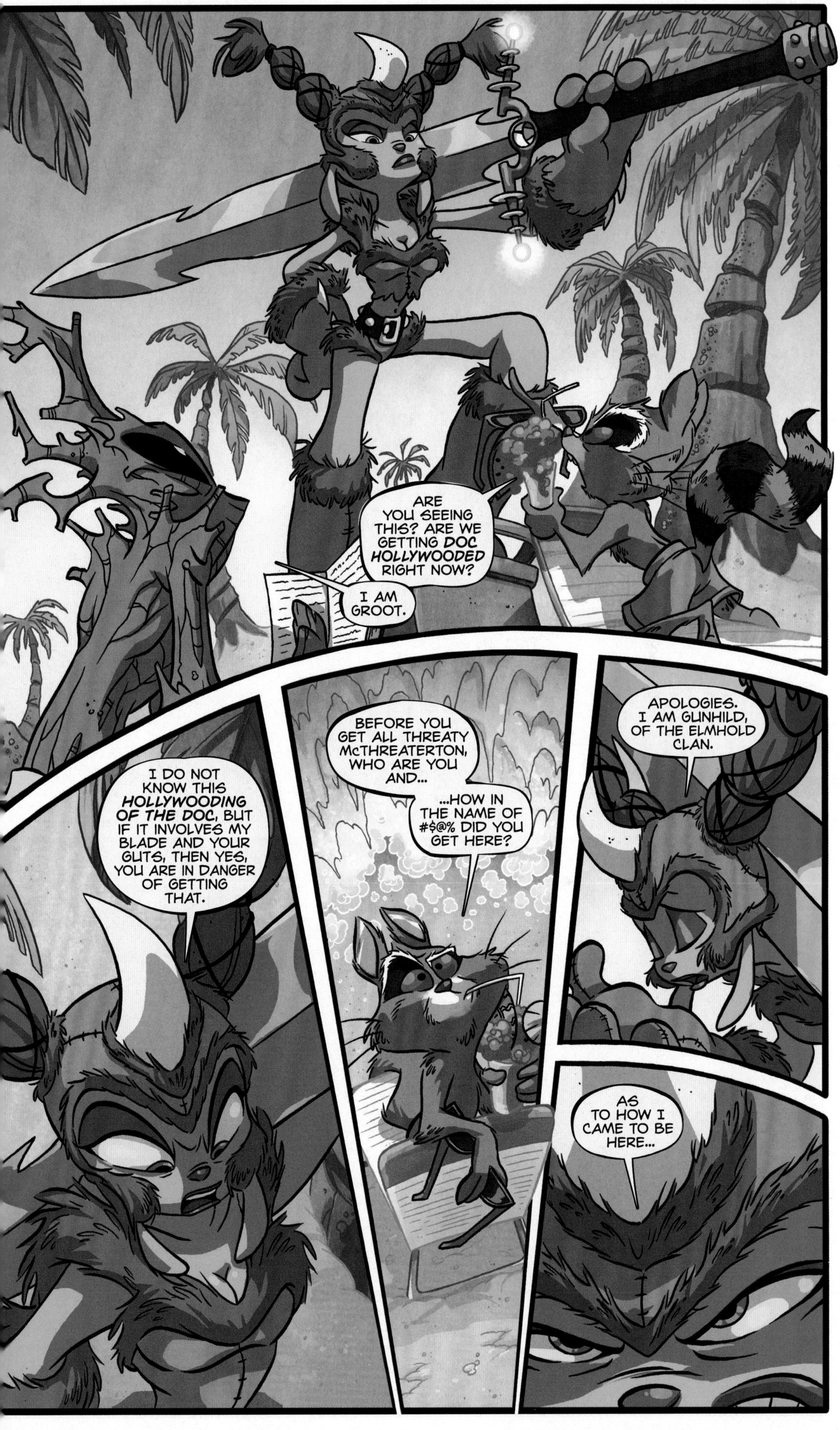

ARE YOU SEEING THIS? ARE WE GETTING DOC HOLLYWOODED RIGHT NOW?
I AM GROOT.
I DO NOT KNOW THIS HOLLYWOODING OF THE DOC, BUT IF IT INVOLVES MY BLADE AND YOUR GUTS, THEN YES, YOU ARE IN DANGER OF GETTING THAT.
BEFORE YOU GET ALL THREATY McTHREATERTON, WHO ARE YOU AND...
...HOW IN THE NAME OF #$@% DID YOU GET HERE?
APOLOGIES. I AM GUNHILD, OF THE ELMHOLD CLAN.
AS TO HOW I CAME TO BE HERE...

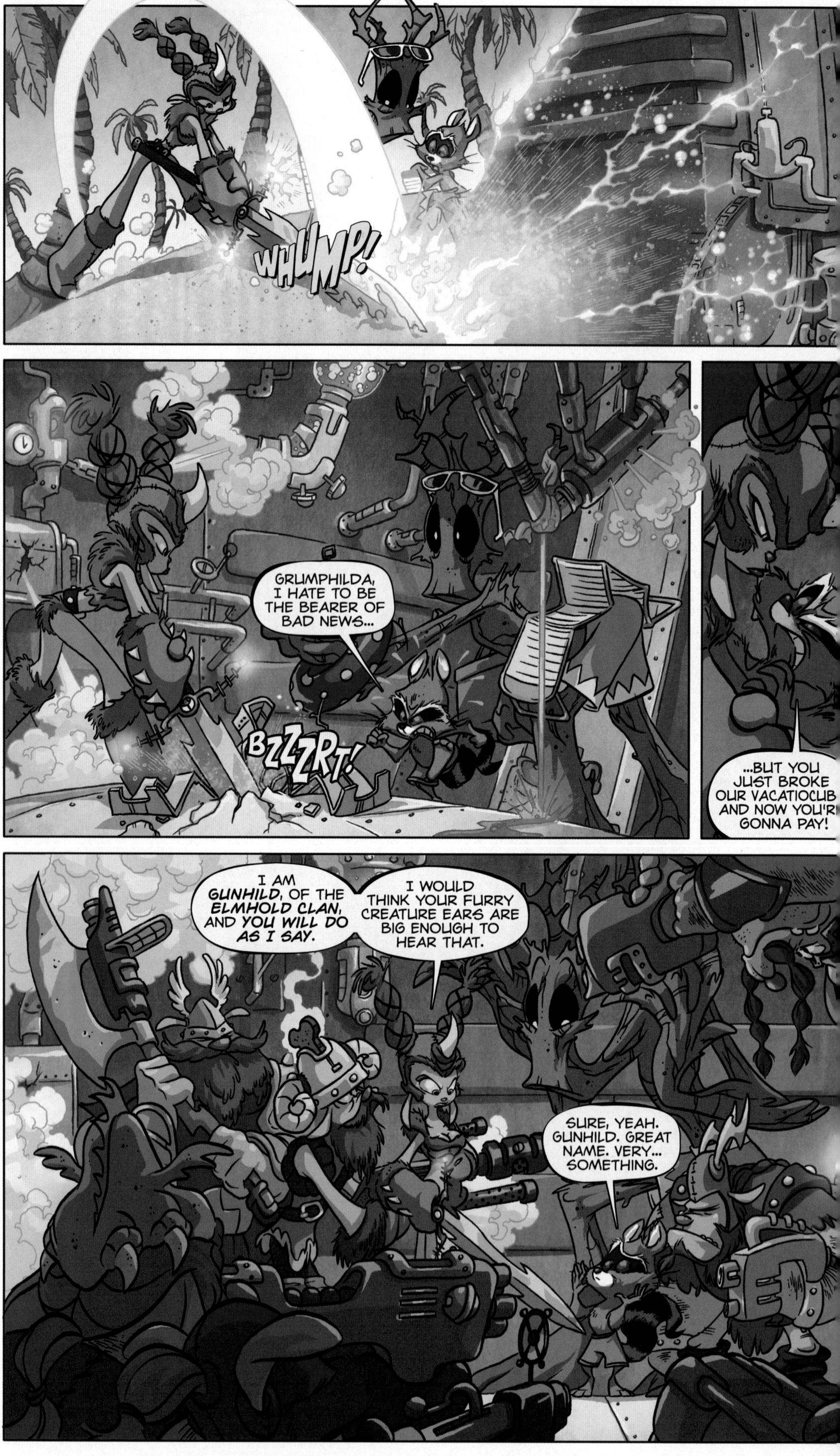
WHUMP!
GRUMPHILDA, I HATE TO BE THE BEARER OF BAD NEWS...
BZZZRT!
...BUT YOU JUST BROKE OUR VACATIOCLUB AND NOW YOU'R GONNA PAY!
I AM GUNHILD, OF THE ELMHOLD CLAN, AND YOU WILL DO AS I SAY.
I WOULD THINK YOUR FURRY CREATURE EARS ARE BIG ENOUGH TO HEAR THAT.
SURE, YEAH. GUNHILD. GREAT NAME. VERY... SOMETHING.

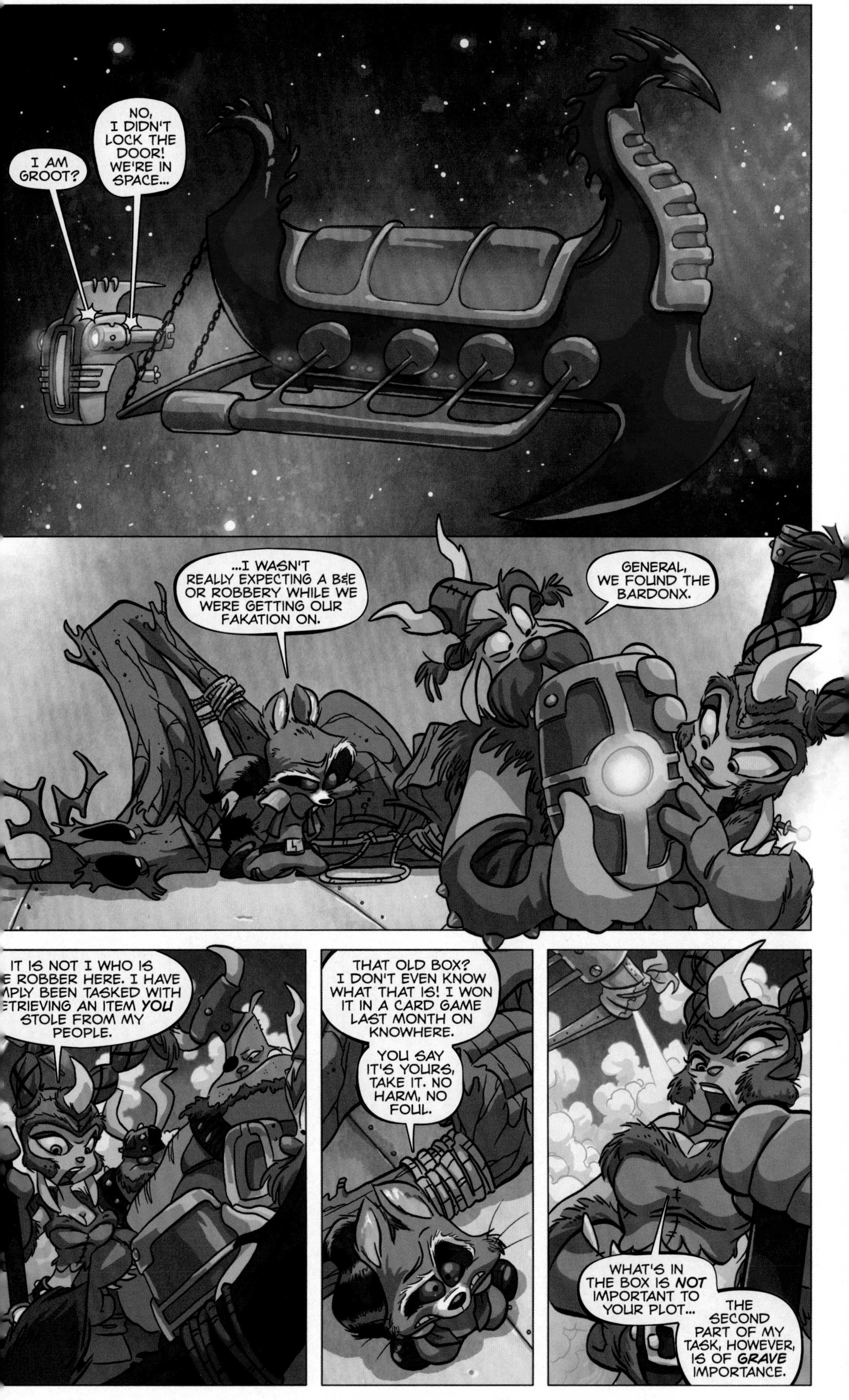
I AM GROOT?
NO, I DIDN'T LOCK THE DOOR! WE'RE IN SPACE...
...I WASN'T REALLY EXPECTING A B&E OR ROBBERY WHILE WE WERE GETTING OUR FAKATION ON.
GENERAL, WE FOUND THE BARDONX.
IT IS NOT I WHO IS E ROBBER HERE. I HAVE MPLY BEEN TASKED WITH ETRIEVING AN ITEM *YOU* STOLE FROM MY PEOPLE.
THAT OLD BOX? I DON'T EVEN KNOW WHAT THAT IS! I WON IT IN A CARD GAME LAST MONTH ON KNOWHERE.
YOU SAY IT'S YOURS, TAKE IT. NO HARM, NO FOUL.
WHAT'S IN THE BOX IS *NOT* IMPORTANT TO YOUR PLOT...
THE SECOND PART OF MY TASK, HOWEVER, IS OF *GRAVE* IMPORTANCE.

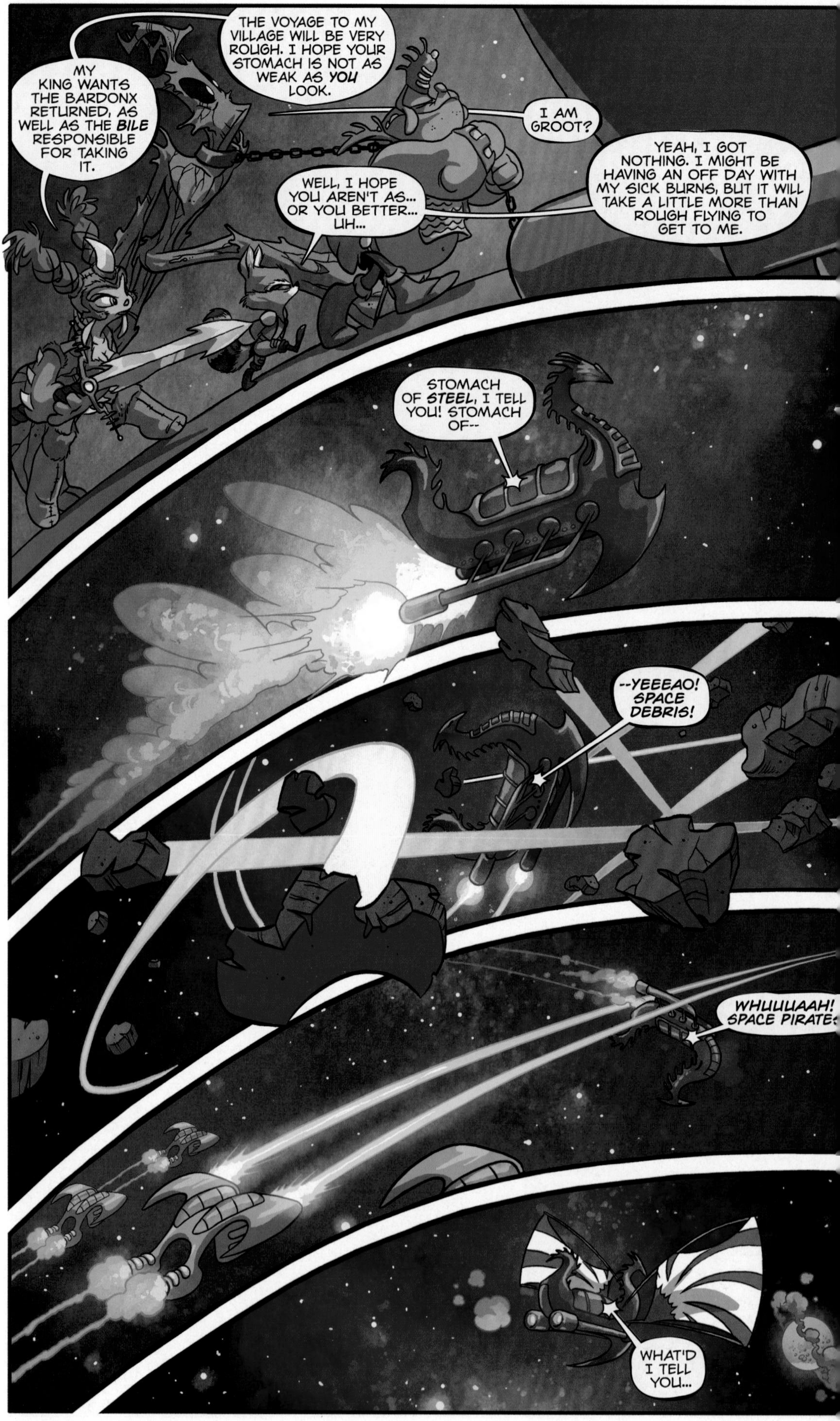
MY KING WANTS THE BARDONX RETURNED, AS WELL AS THE BILE RESPONSIBLE FOR TAKING IT.
THE VOYAGE TO MY VILLAGE WILL BE VERY ROUGH. I HOPE YOUR STOMACH IS NOT AS WEAK AS YOU LOOK.
I AM GROOT?
WELL, I HOPE YOU AREN'T AS... OR YOU BETTER... UH...
YEAH, I GOT NOTHING. I MIGHT BE HAVING AN OFF DAY WITH MY SICK BURNS, BUT IT WILL TAKE A LITTLE MORE THAN ROUGH FLYING TO GET TO ME.
STOMACH OF STEEL, I TELL YOU! STOMACH OF--
--YEEEAO! SPACE DEBRIS!
WHUUUAAH! SPACE PIRATE-
WHAT'D I TELL YOU...

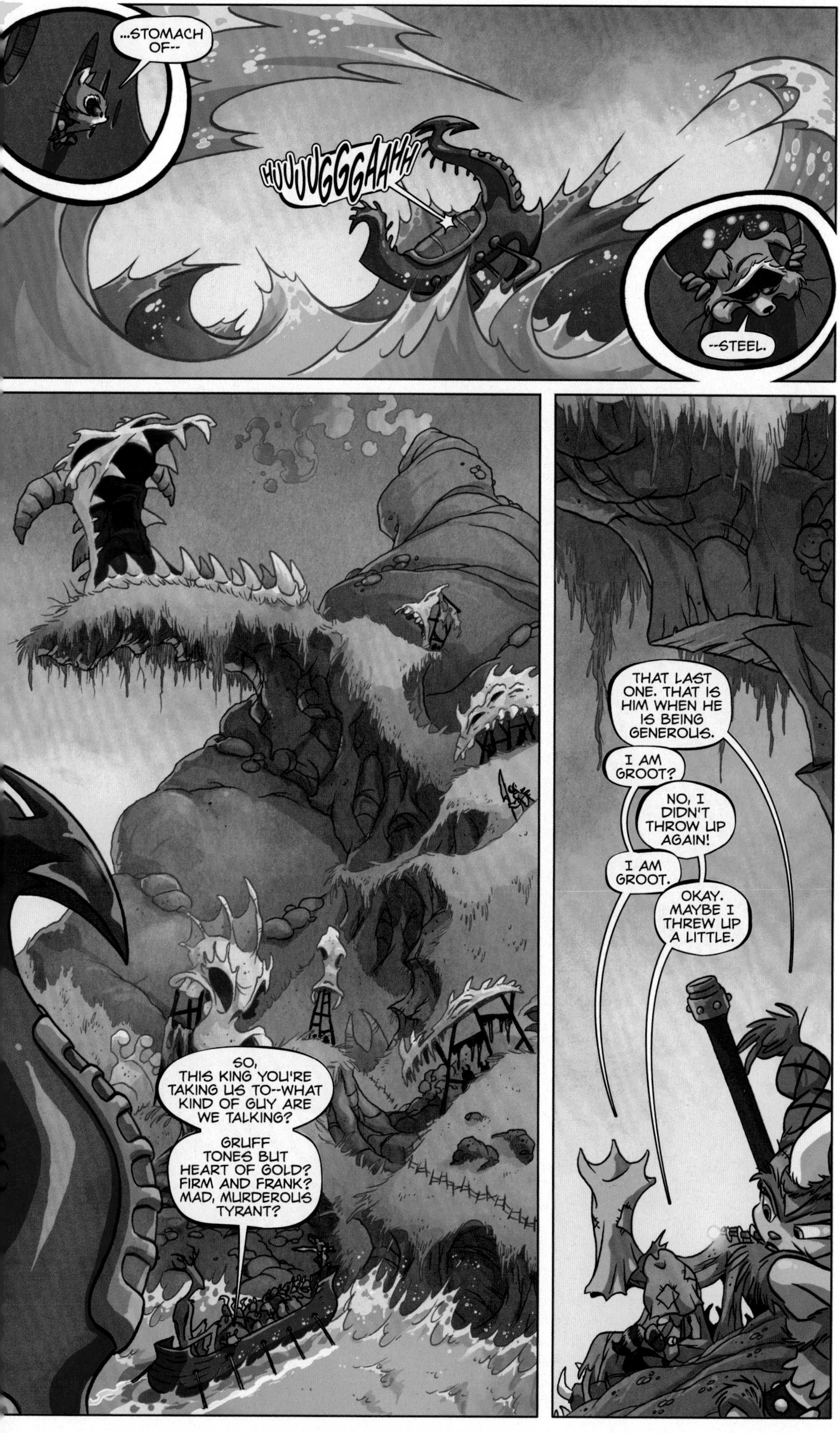
...STOMACH OF--
HUUUUGGGAAHH
--STEEL.
SO, THIS KING YOU'RE TAKING US TO--WHAT KIND OF GUY ARE WE TALKING?
GRUFF TONES BUT HEART OF GOLD? FIRM AND FRANK? MAD, MURDEROUS TYRANT?
THAT LAST ONE. THAT IS HIM WHEN HE IS BEING GENEROUS.
I AM GROOT?
NO, I DIDN'T THROW UP AGAIN!
I AM GROOT.
OKAY. MAYBE I THREW UP A LITTLE.

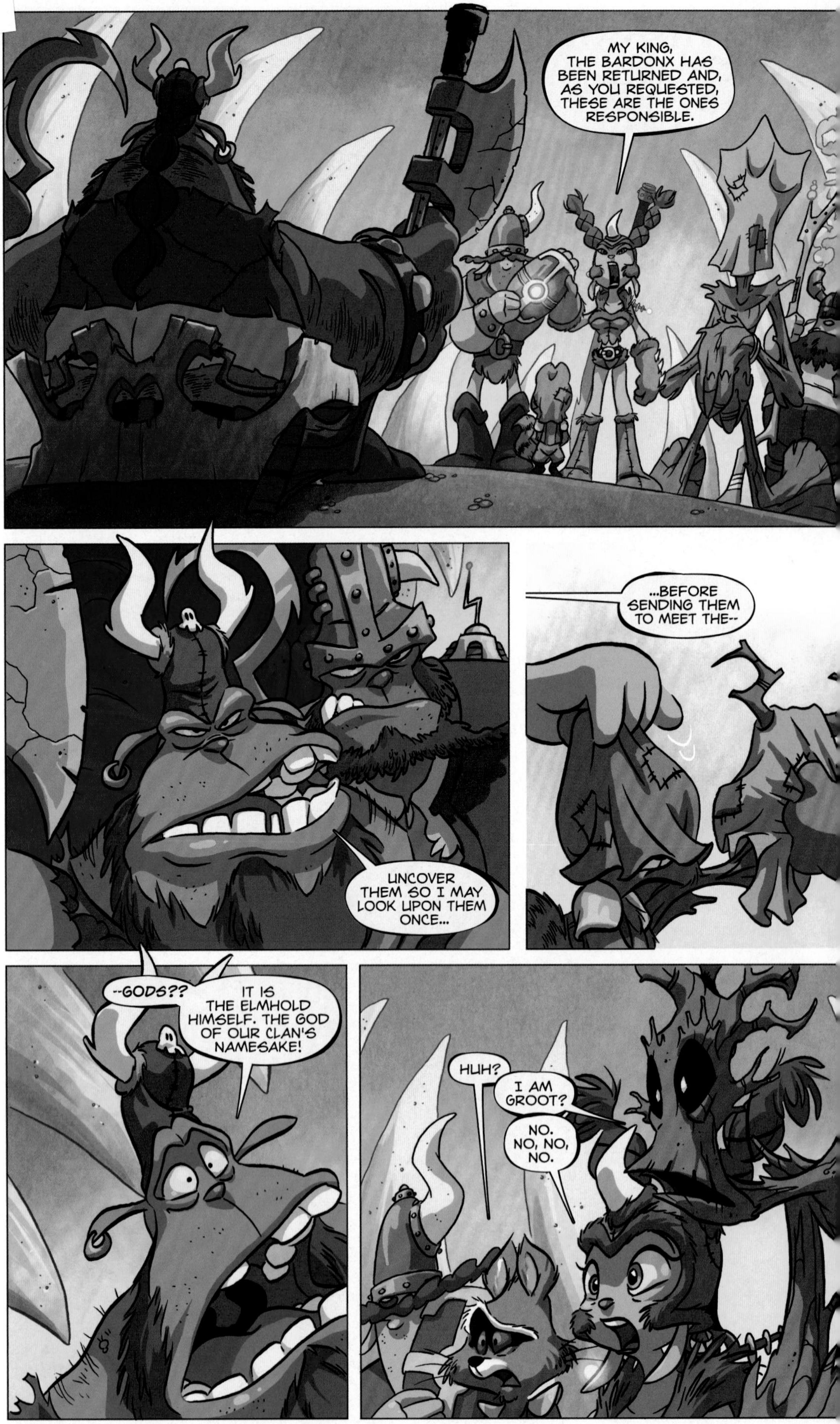
MY KING, THE BARDONX HAS BEEN RETURNED AND, AS YOU REQUESTED, THESE ARE THE ONES RESPONSIBLE.
UNCOVER THEM SO I MAY LOOK UPON THEM ONCE...
...BEFORE SENDING THEM TO MEET THE--
--GODS??
IT IS THE ELMHOLD HIMSELF. THE GOD OF OUR CLAN'S NAMESAKE!
HUH?
I AM GROOT?
NO. NO, NO, NO.

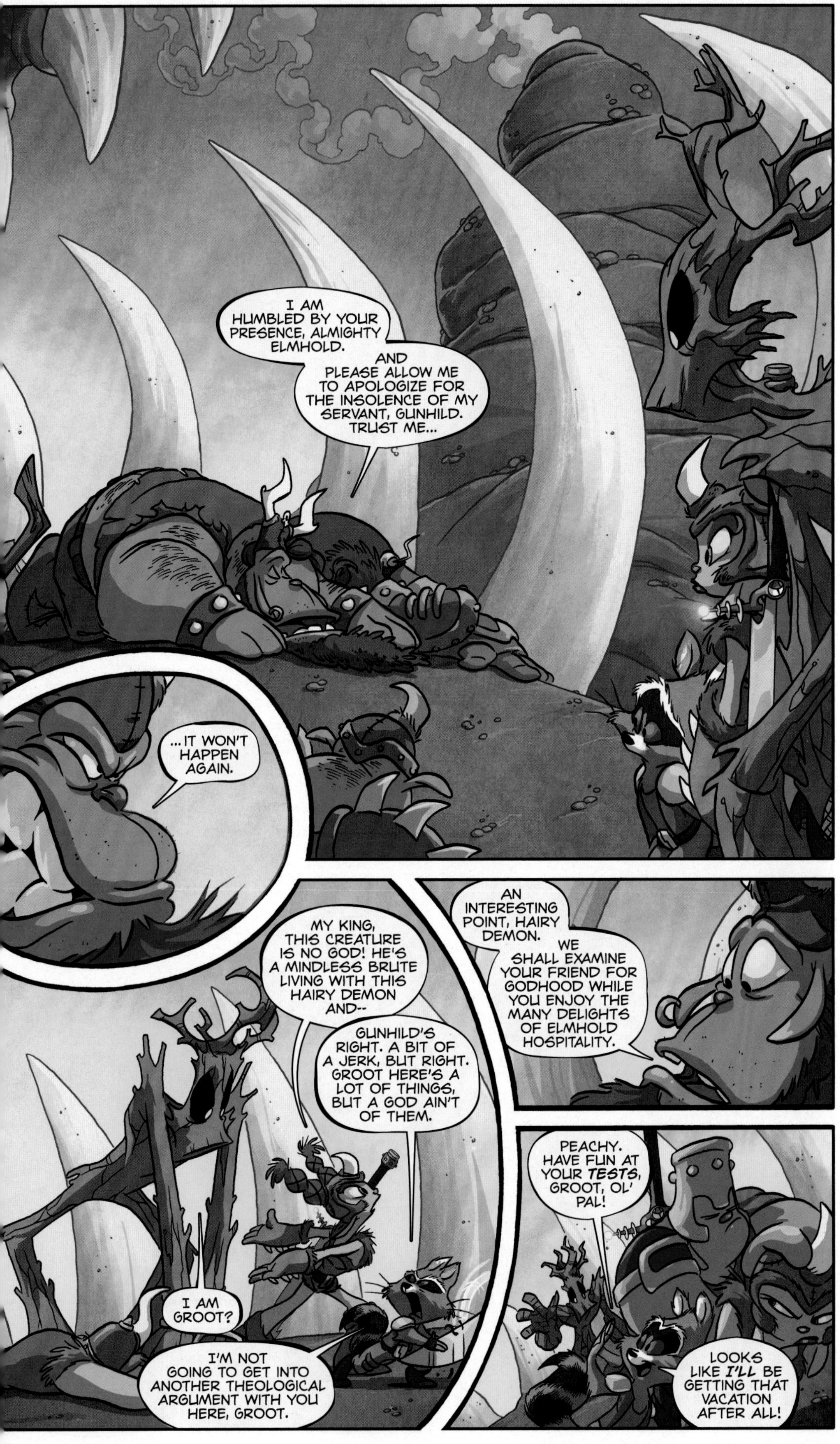
I AM HUMBLED BY YOUR PRESENCE, ALMIGHTY ELMHOLD.
AND PLEASE ALLOW ME TO APOLOGIZE FOR THE INSOLENCE OF MY SERVANT, GUNHILD. TRUST ME...
...IT WON'T HAPPEN AGAIN.
MY KING, THIS CREATURE IS NO GOD! HE'S A MINDLESS BRUTE LIVING WITH THIS HAIRY DEMON AND--
GUNHILD'S RIGHT. A BIT OF A JERK, BUT RIGHT. GROOT HERE'S A LOT OF THINGS, BUT A GOD AIN'T OF THEM.
I AM GROOT?
I'M NOT GOING TO GET INTO ANOTHER THEOLOGICAL ARGUMENT WITH YOU HERE, GROOT.
AN INTERESTING POINT, HAIRY DEMON.
WE SHALL EXAMINE YOUR FRIEND FOR GODHOOD WHILE YOU ENJOY THE MANY DELIGHTS OF ELMHOLD HOSPITALITY.
PEACHY. HAVE FUN AT YOUR *TESTS*, GROOT, OL' PAL!
LOOKS LIKE *I'LL* BE GETTING THAT VACATION AFTER ALL!

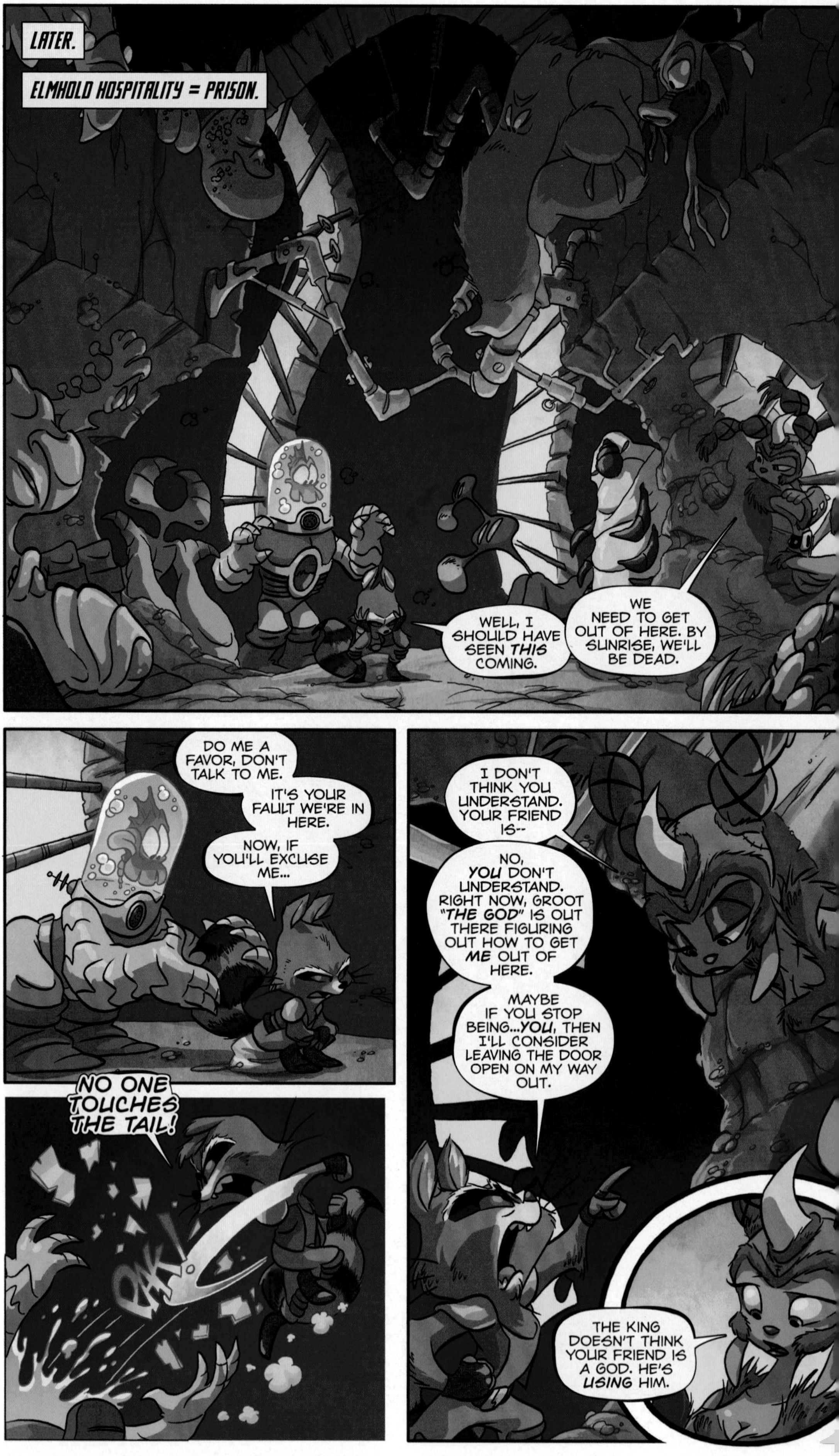
LATER.
ELMHOLD HOSPITALITY = PRISON.
WELL, I SHOULD HAVE SEEN THIS COMING.
WE NEED TO GET OUT OF HERE. BY SUNRISE, WE'LL BE DEAD.
DO ME A FAVOR, DON'T TALK TO ME.
IT'S YOUR FAULT WE'RE IN HERE.
NOW, IF YOU'LL EXCUSE ME...
I DON'T THINK YOU UNDERSTAND. YOUR FRIEND IS--
NO, YOU DON'T UNDERSTAND. RIGHT NOW, GROOT "THE GOD" IS OUT THERE FIGURING OUT HOW TO GET ME OUT OF HERE.
MAYBE IF YOU STOP BEING...YOU, THEN I'LL CONSIDER LEAVING THE DOOR OPEN ON MY WAY OUT.
NO ONE TOUCHES THE TAIL!
THE KING DOESN'T THINK YOUR FRIEND IS A GOD. HE'S USING HIM.

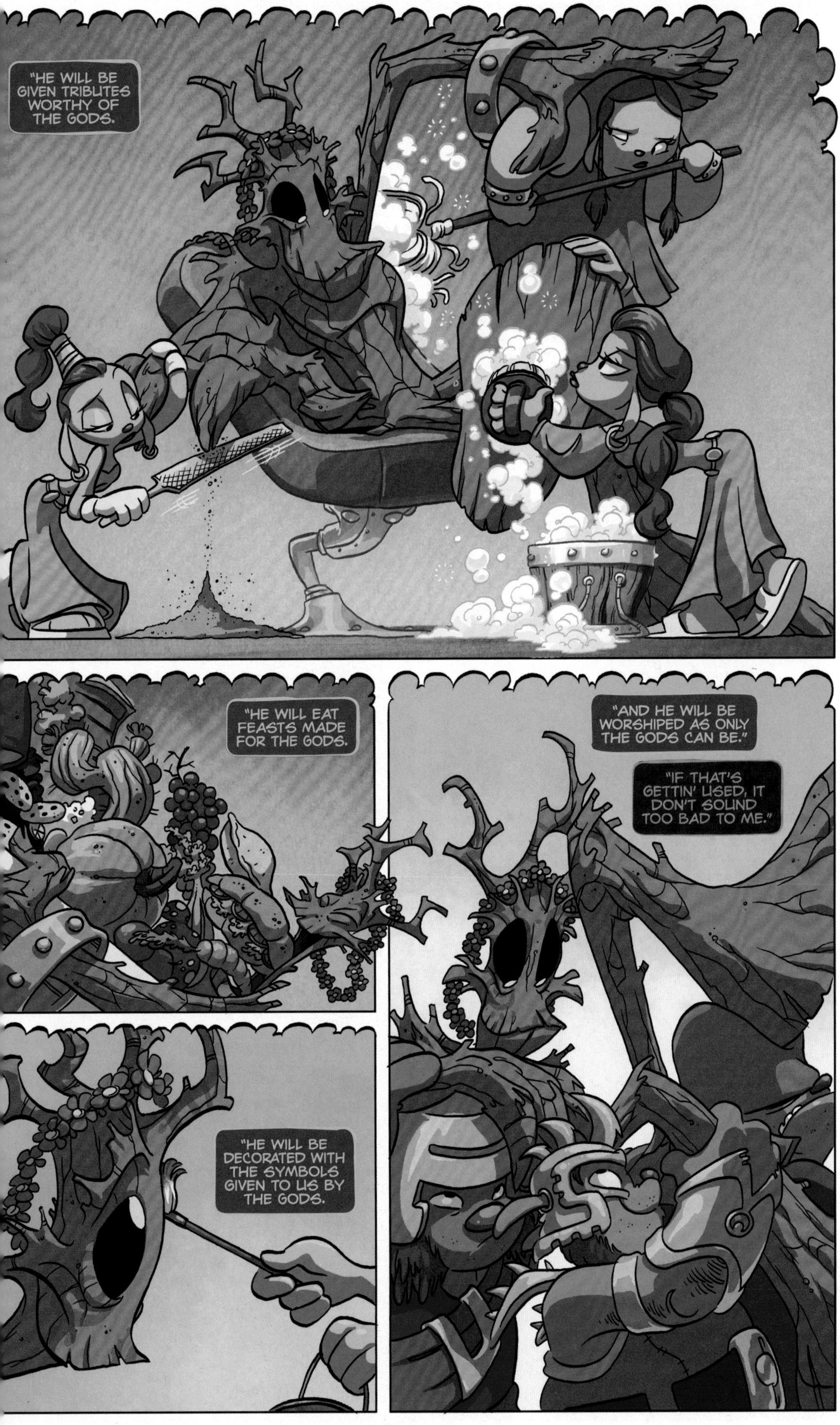
"HE WILL BE GIVEN TRIBUTES WORTHY OF THE GODS.
"HE WILL EAT FEASTS MADE FOR THE GODS.
"HE WILL BE DECORATED WITH THE SYMBOLS GIVEN TO US BY THE GODS.
"AND HE WILL BE WORSHIPED AS ONLY THE GODS CAN BE."
"IF THAT'S GETTIN' USED, IT DON'T SOUND TOO BAD TO ME."

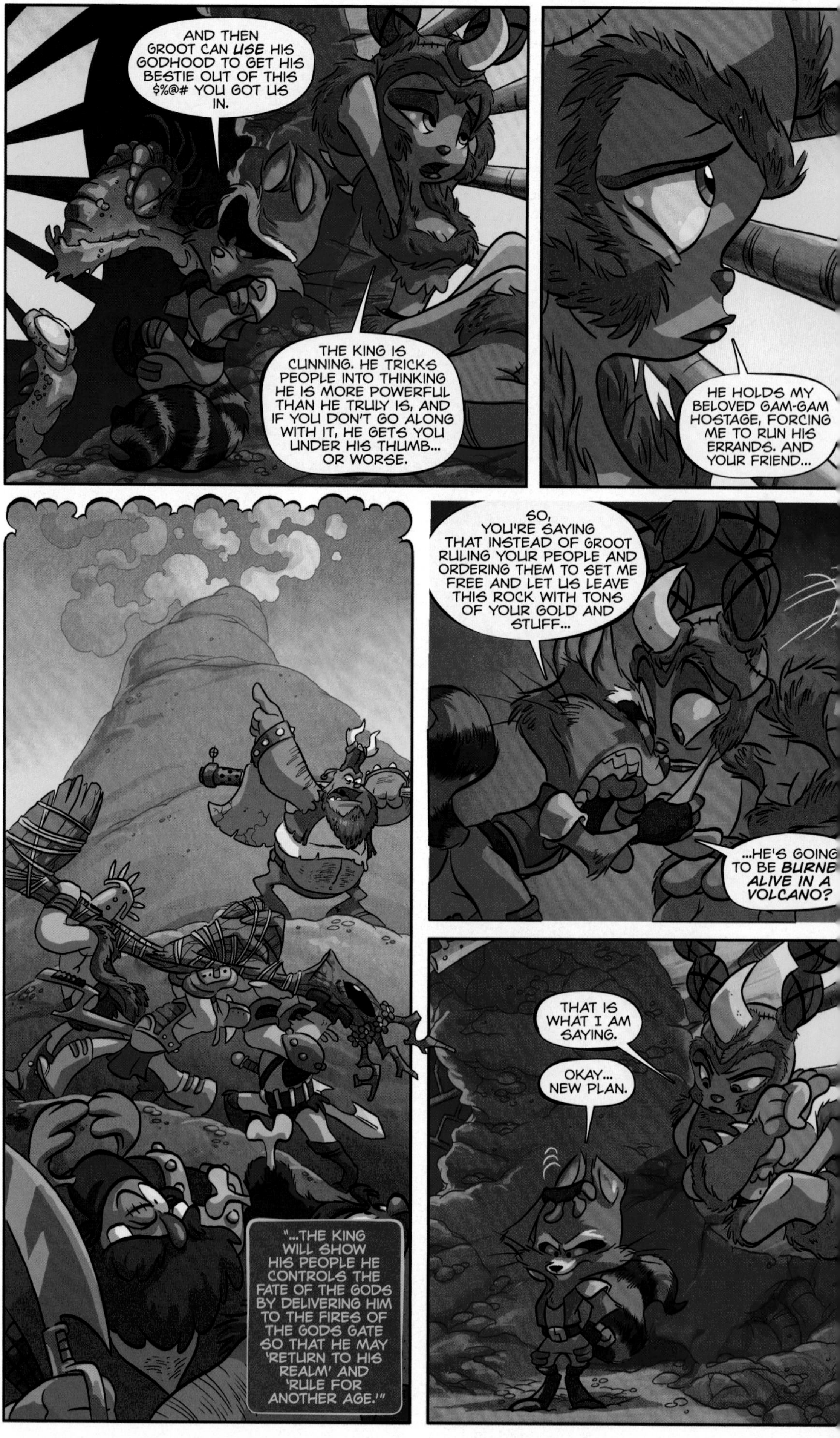
AND THEN GROOT CAN USE HIS GODHOOD TO GET HIS BESTIE OUT OF THIS $%@# YOU GOT US IN.
THE KING IS CUNNING. HE TRICKS PEOPLE INTO THINKING HE IS MORE POWERFUL THAN HE TRULY IS, AND IF YOU DON'T GO ALONG WITH IT, HE GETS YOU UNDER HIS THUMB... OR WORSE.
HE HOLDS MY BELOVED GAM-GAM HOSTAGE, FORCING ME TO RUN HIS ERRANDS. AND YOUR FRIEND...
"...THE KING WILL SHOW HIS PEOPLE HE CONTROLS THE FATE OF THE GODS BY DELIVERING HIM TO THE FIRES OF THE GODS GATE SO THAT HE MAY 'RETURN TO HIS REALM' AND 'RULE FOR ANOTHER AGE.'"
SO, YOU'RE SAYING THAT INSTEAD OF GROOT RULING YOUR PEOPLE AND ORDERING THEM TO SET ME FREE AND LET US LEAVE THIS ROCK WITH TONS OF YOUR GOLD AND STUFF...
...HE'S GOING TO BE BURNE ALIVE IN A VOLCANO?
THAT IS WHAT I AM SAYING.
OKAY... NEW PLAN.

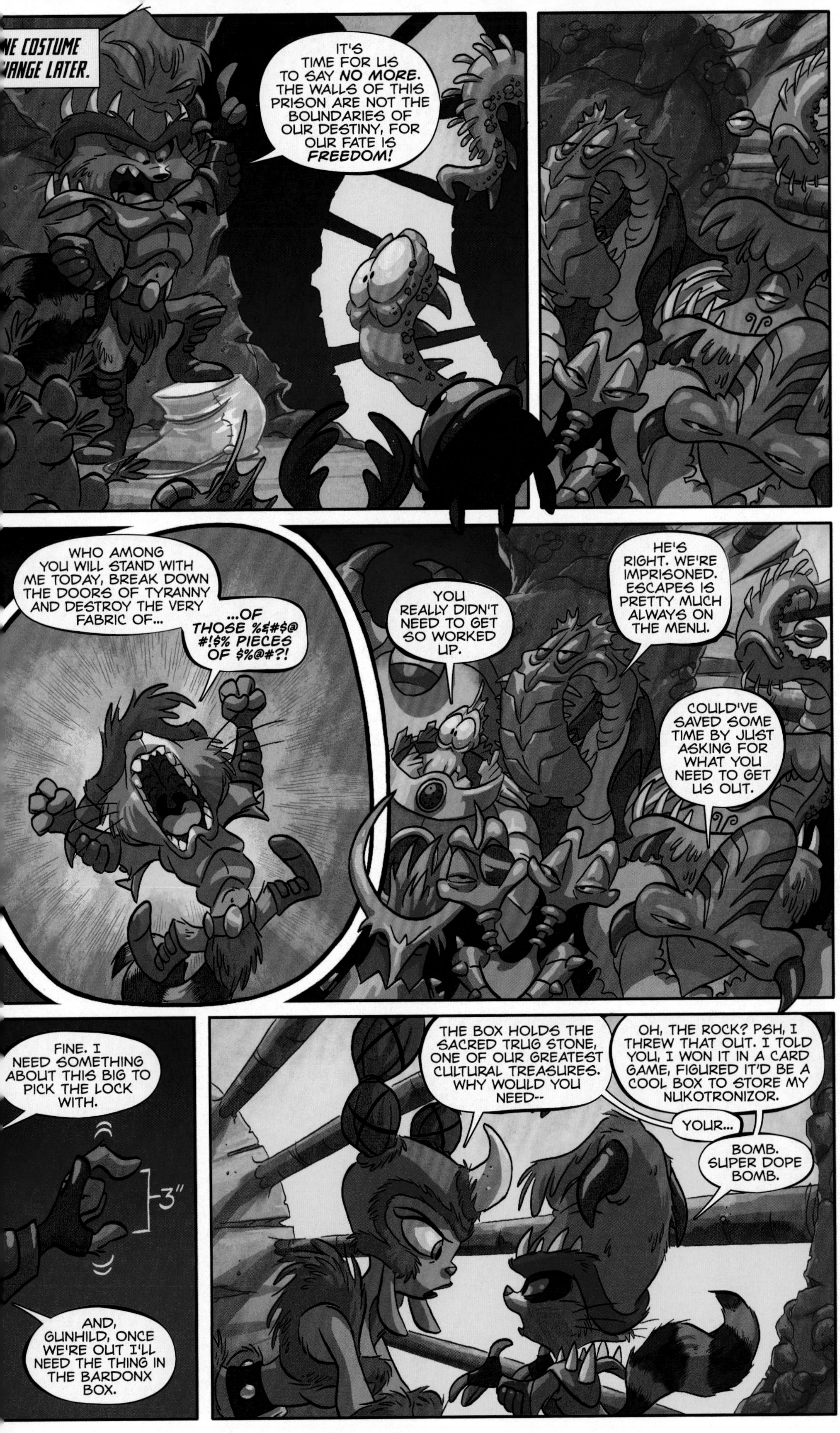
NE COSTUME
HANGE LATER.
IT'S TIME FOR US TO SAY NO MORE. THE WALLS OF THIS PRISON ARE NOT THE BOUNDARIES OF OUR DESTINY, FOR OUR FATE IS FREEDOM!
WHO AMONG YOU WILL STAND WITH ME TODAY, BREAK DOWN THE DOORS OF TYRANNY AND DESTROY THE VERY FABRIC OF...
...OF THOSE %&#$@ #!$% PIECES OF $%@#?!
YOU REALLY DIDN'T NEED TO GET SO WORKED UP.
HE'S RIGHT. WE'RE IMPRISONED. ESCAPES IS PRETTY MUCH ALWAYS ON THE MENU.
COULD'VE SAVED SOME TIME BY JUST ASKING FOR WHAT YOU NEED TO GET US OUT.
FINE. I NEED SOMETHING ABOUT THIS BIG TO PICK THE LOCK WITH.
3"
AND, GUNHILD, ONCE WE'RE OUT I'LL NEED THE THING IN THE BARDONX BOX.
THE BOX HOLDS THE SACRED TRUG STONE, ONE OF OUR GREATEST CULTURAL TREASURES. WHY WOULD YOU NEED--
OH, THE ROCK? PSH, I THREW THAT OUT. I TOLD YOU, I WON IT IN A CARD GAME, FIGURED IT'D BE A COOL BOX TO STORE MY NUKOTRONIZOR.
YOUR...
BOMB. SUPER DOPE BOMB.

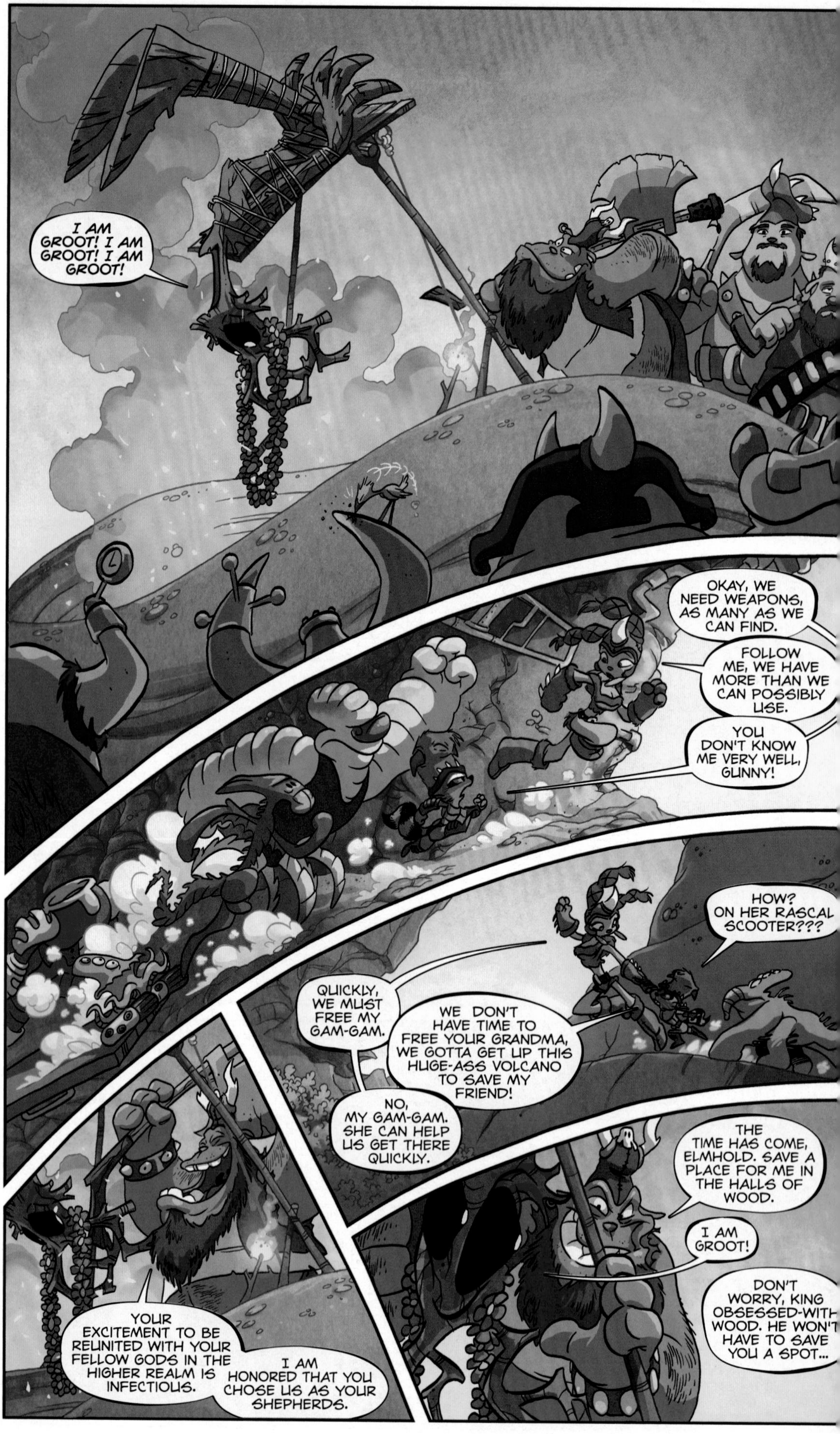
I AM GROOT! I AM GROOT! I AM GROOT!
OKAY, WE NEED WEAPONS, AS MANY AS WE CAN FIND.
FOLLOW ME, WE HAVE MORE THAN WE CAN POSSIBLY USE.
YOU DON'T KNOW ME VERY WELL, GUNNY!
QUICKLY, WE MUST FREE MY GAM-GAM.
WE DON'T HAVE TIME TO FREE YOUR GRANDMA, WE GOTTA GET UP THIS HUGE-ASS VOLCANO TO SAVE MY FRIEND!
NO, MY GAM-GAM. SHE CAN HELP US GET THERE QUICKLY.
HOW? ON HER RASCAL SCOOTER???
YOUR EXCITEMENT TO BE REUNITED WITH YOUR FELLOW GODS IN THE HIGHER REALM IS INFECTIOUS.
I AM HONORED THAT YOU CHOSE US AS YOUR SHEPHERDS.
THE TIME HAS COME, ELMHOLD. SAVE A PLACE FOR ME IN THE HALLS OF WOOD.
I AM GROOT!
DON'T WORRY, KING OBSESSED-WITH WOOD. HE WON'T HAVE TO SAVE YOU A SPOT...

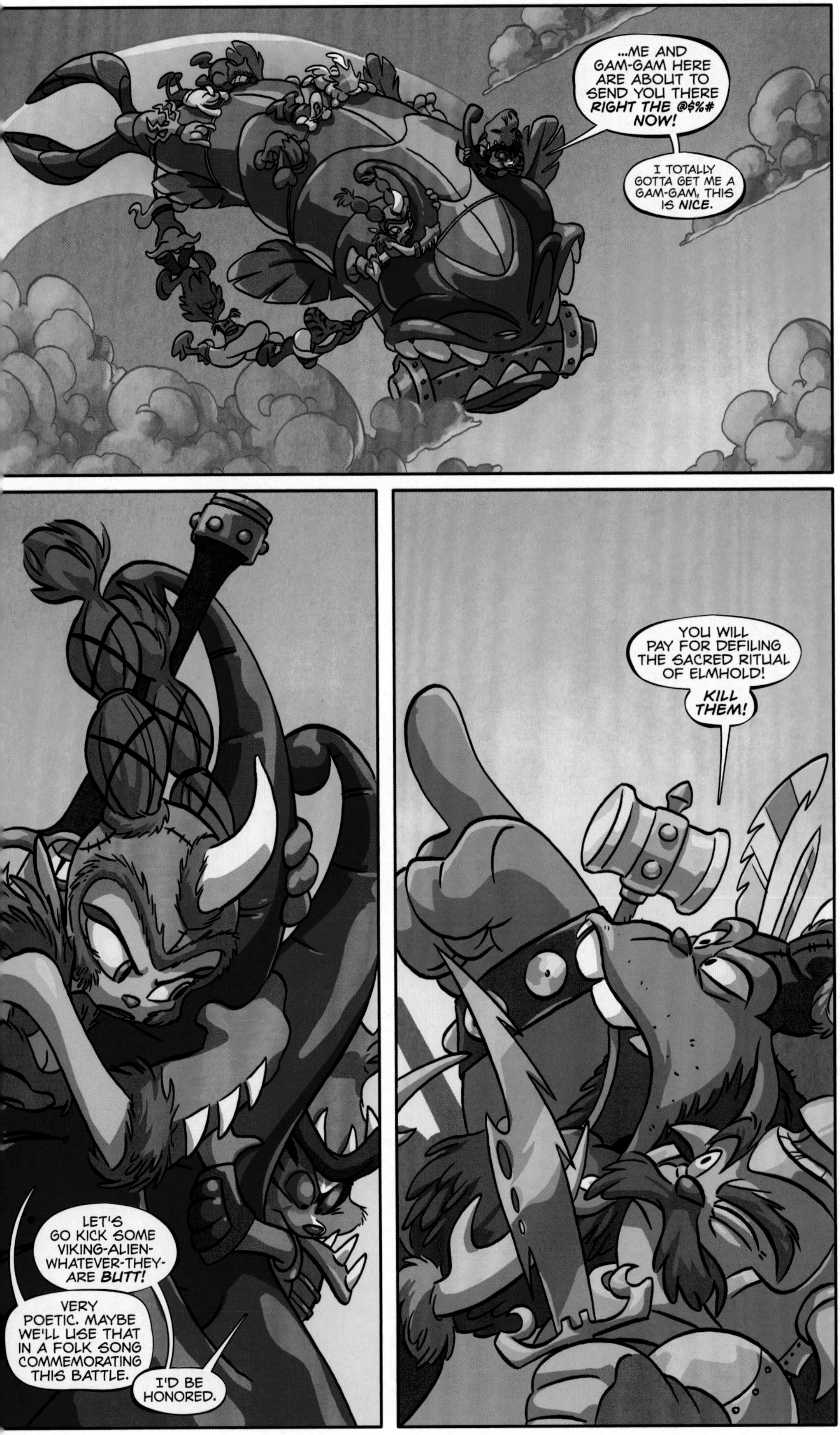
...ME AND GAM-GAM HERE ARE ABOUT TO SEND YOU THERE RIGHT THE @$%# NOW!
I TOTALLY GOTTA GET ME A GAM-GAM, THIS IS NICE.
LET'S GO KICK SOME VIKING-ALIEN-WHATEVER-THEY-ARE BUTT!
VERY POETIC. MAYBE WE'LL USE THAT IN A FOLK SONG COMMEMORATING THIS BATTLE.
I'D BE HONORED.
YOU WILL PAY FOR DEFILING THE SACRED RITUAL OF ELMHOLD!
KILL THEM!

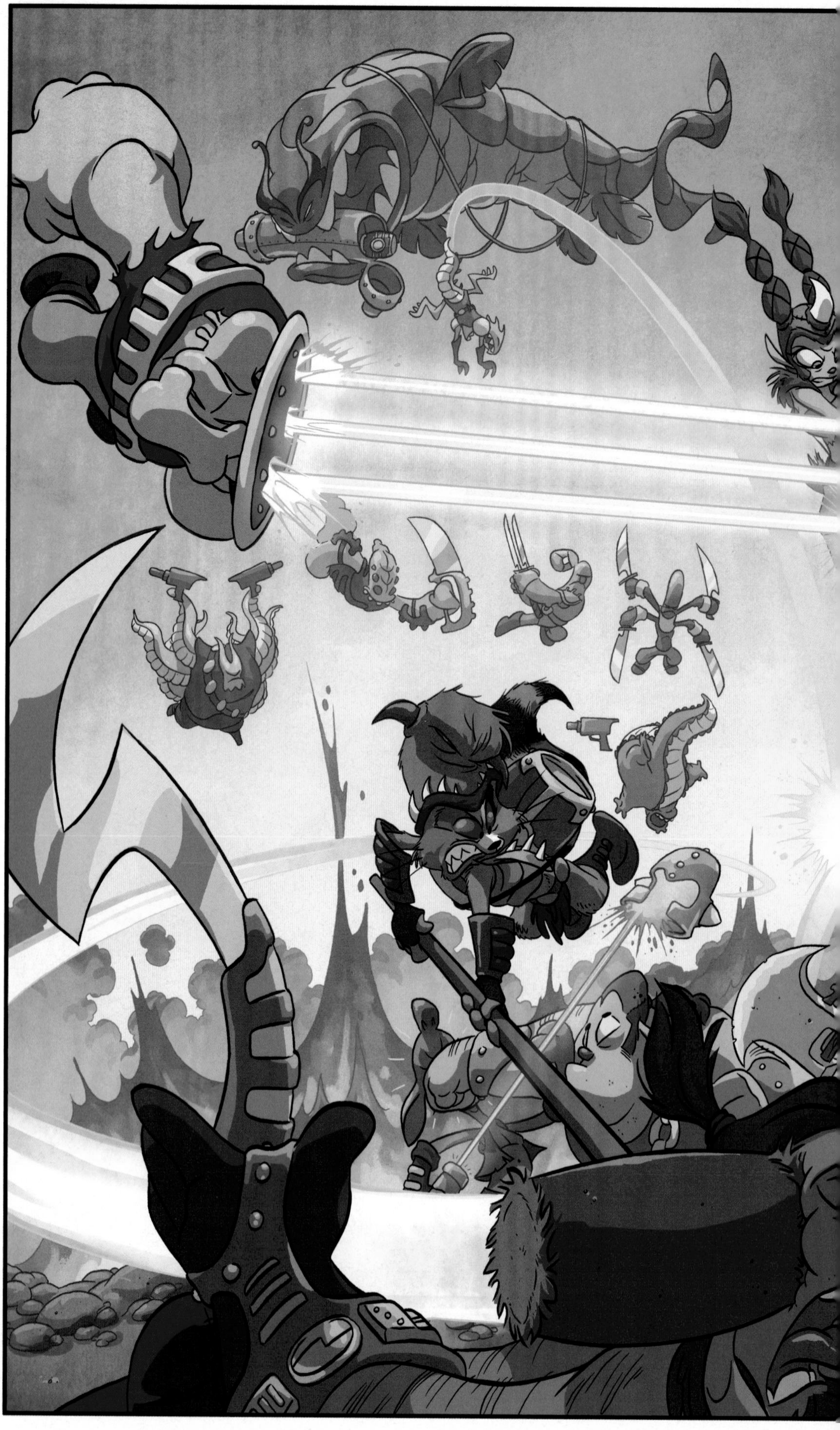

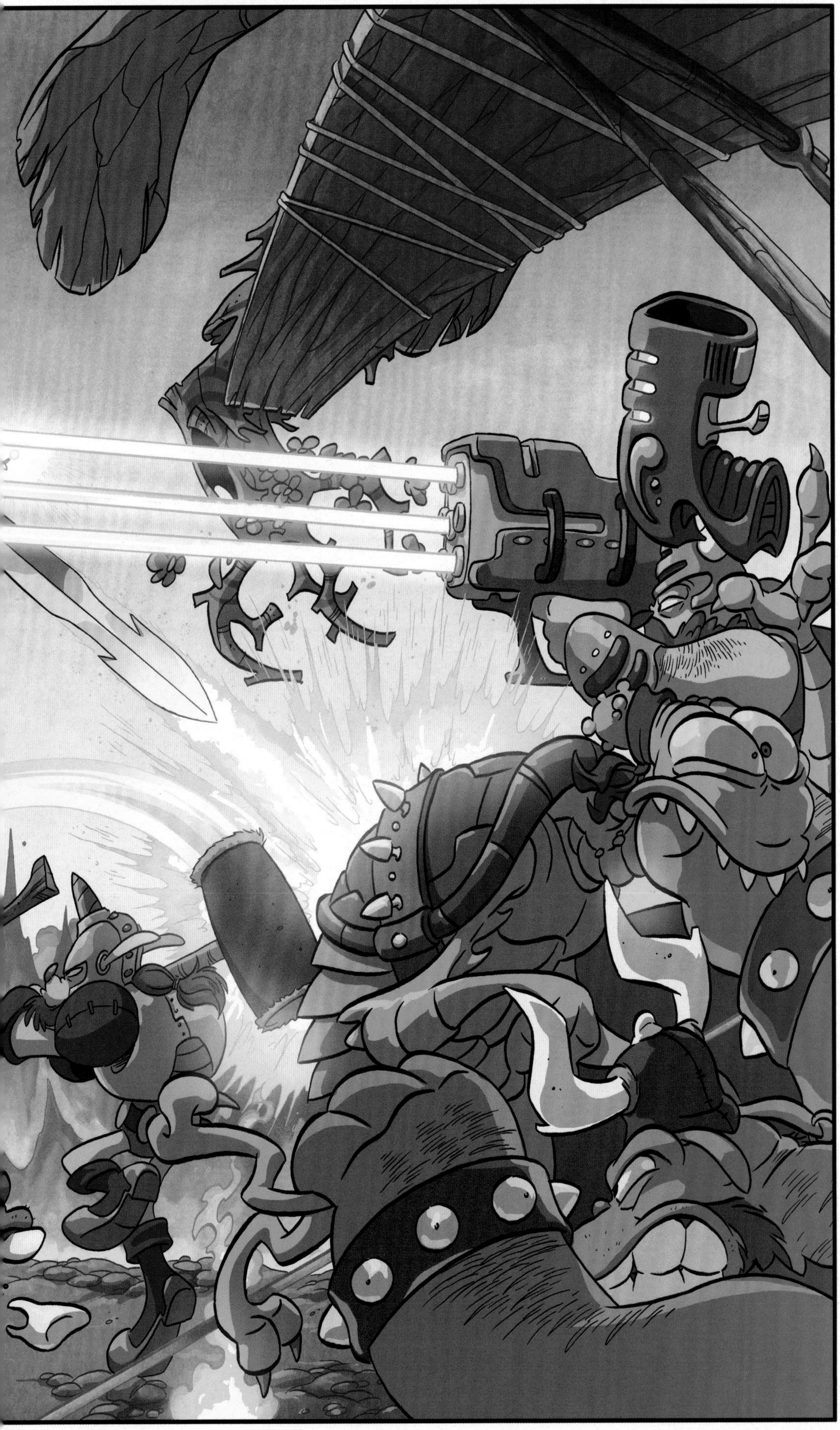

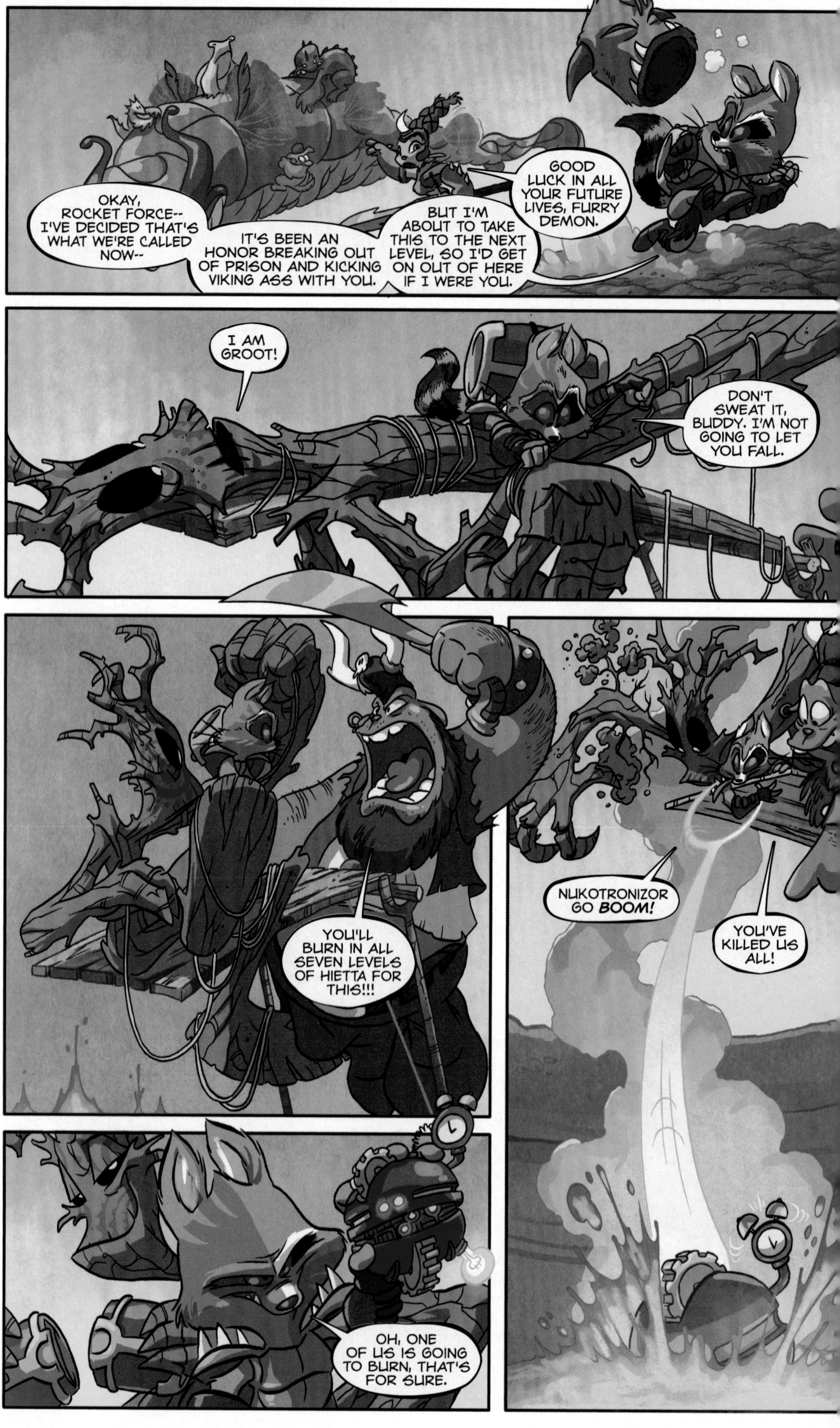
OKAY, ROCKET FORCE-- I'VE DECIDED THAT'S WHAT WE'RE CALLED NOW--
IT'S BEEN AN HONOR BREAKING OUT OF PRISON AND KICKING VIKING ASS WITH YOU.
BUT I'M ABOUT TO TAKE THIS TO THE NEXT LEVEL, SO I'D GET ON OUT OF HERE IF I WERE YOU.
GOOD LUCK IN ALL YOUR FUTURE LIVES, FURRY DEMON.
I AM GROOT!
DON'T SWEAT IT, BUDDY. I'M NOT GOING TO LET YOU FALL.
YOU'LL BURN IN ALL SEVEN LEVELS OF HIETTA FOR THIS!!!
OH, ONE OF US IS GOING TO BURN, THAT'S FOR SURE.
NUKOTRONIZOR GO **BOOM!**
YOU'VE KILLED US ALL!

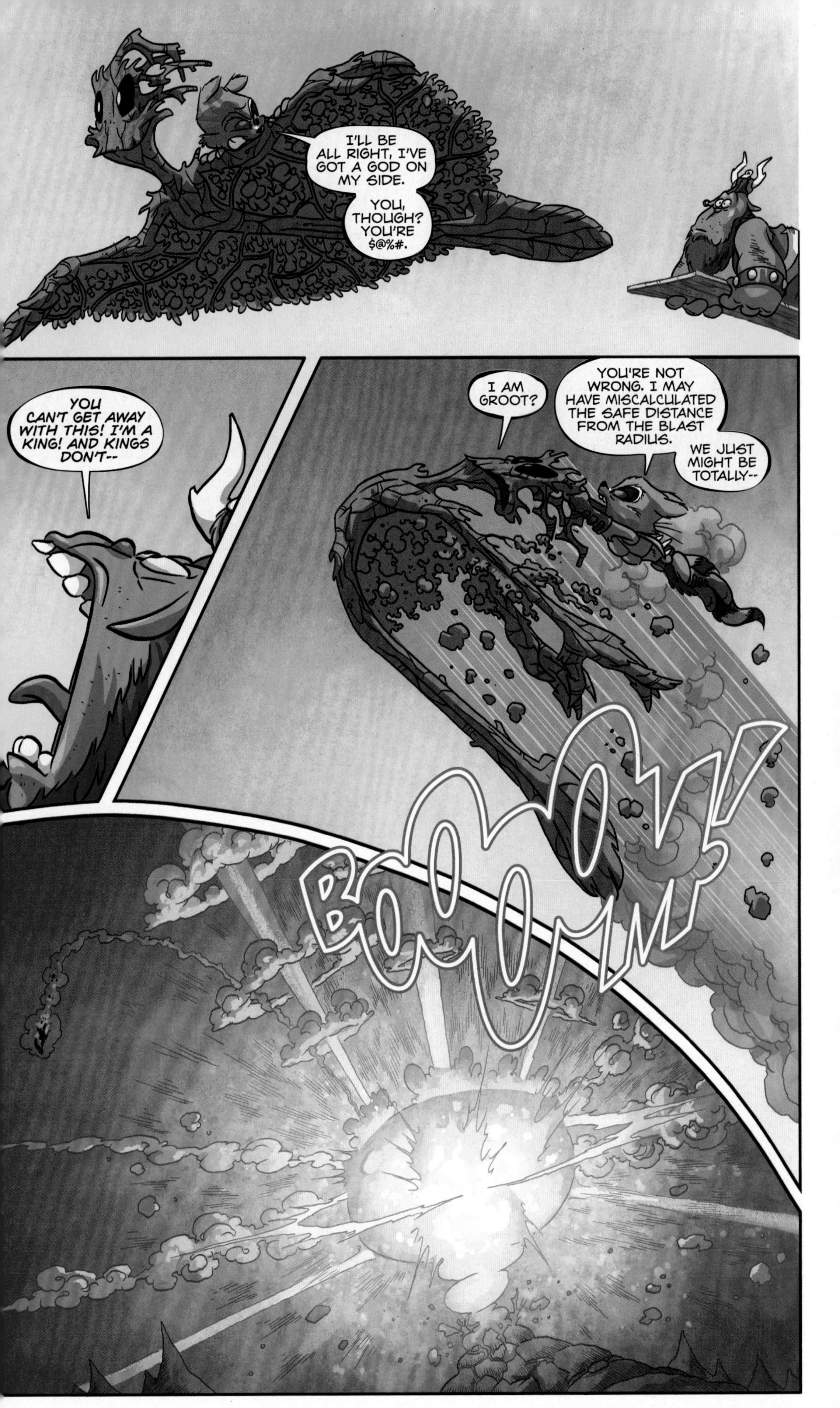
I'LL BE ALL RIGHT, I'VE GOT A GOD ON MY SIDE.
YOU, THOUGH? YOU'RE $@%#.
YOU CAN'T GET AWAY WITH THIS! I'M A KING! AND KINGS DON'T--
I AM GROOT?
YOU'RE NOT WRONG. I MAY HAVE MISCALCULATED THE SAFE DISTANCE FROM THE BLAST RADIUS.
WE JUST MIGHT BE TOTALLY--
BOOOOM!

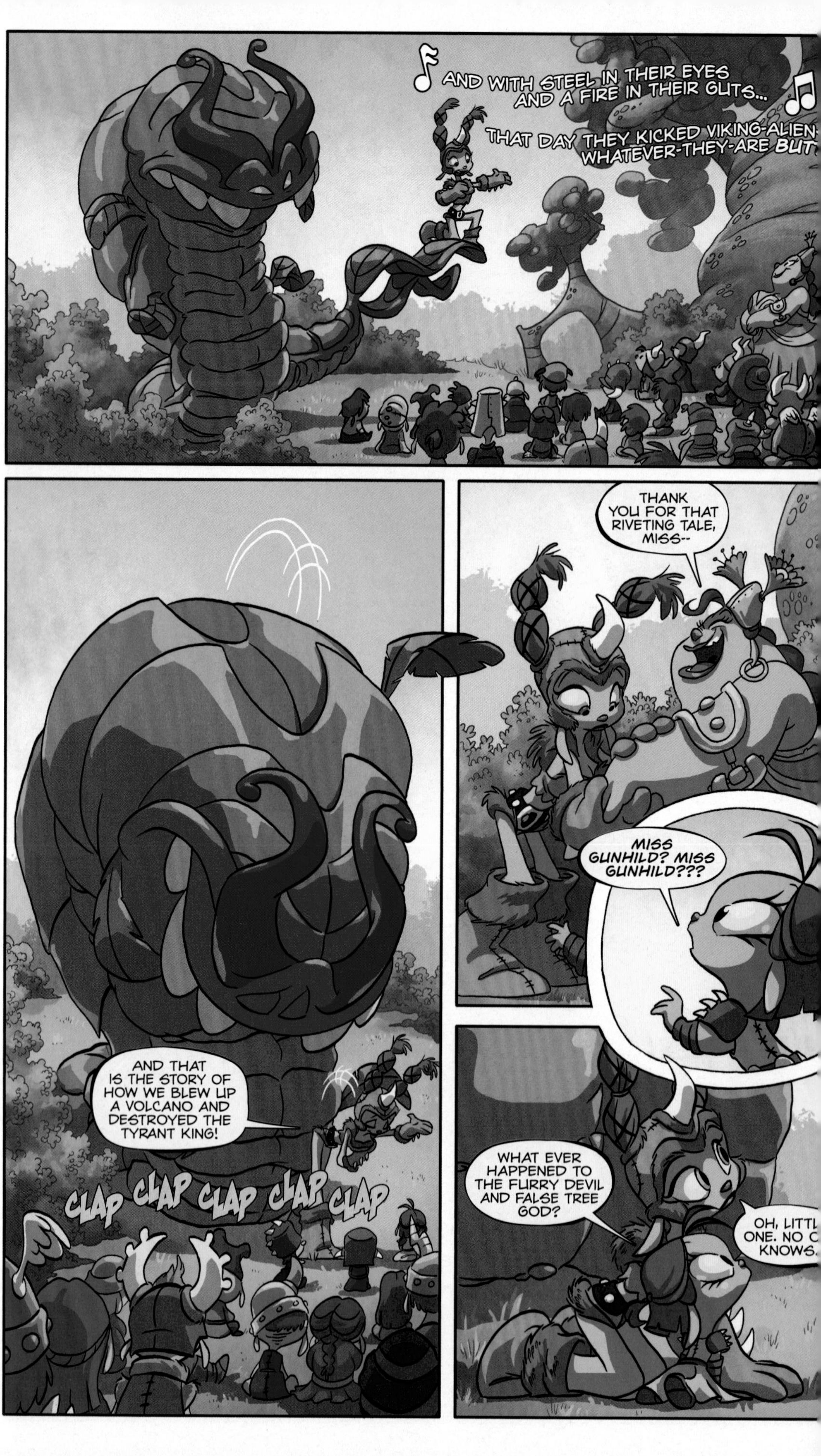
AND WITH STEEL IN THEIR EYES
AND A FIRE IN THEIR GUTS...
THAT DAY THEY KICKED VIKING-ALIEN-WHATEVER-THEY-ARE BUTT
AND THAT IS THE STORY OF HOW WE BLEW UP A VOLCANO AND DESTROYED THE TYRANT KING!
CLAP CLAP CLAP CLAP CLAP
THANK YOU FOR THAT RIVETING TALE, MISS--
MISS GUNHILD? MISS GUNHILD???
WHAT EVER HAPPENED TO THE FURRY DEVIL AND FALSE TREE GOD?
OH, LITTL ONE. NO C KNOWS.

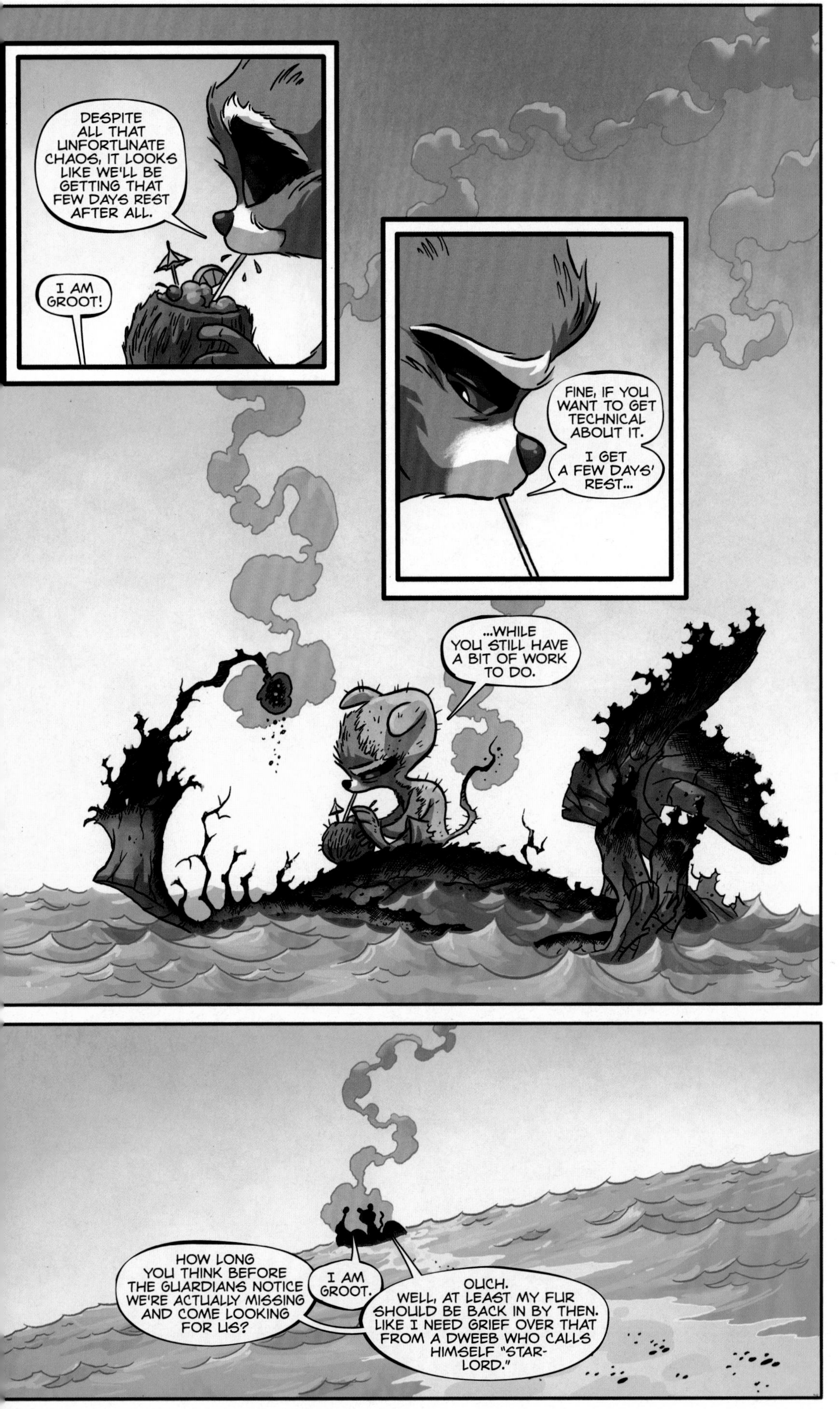
DESPITE ALL THAT UNFORTUNATE CHAOS, IT LOOKS LIKE WE'LL BE GETTING THAT FEW DAYS REST AFTER ALL.
I AM GROOT!
FINE, IF YOU WANT TO GET TECHNICAL ABOUT IT.
I GET A FEW DAYS' REST...
...WHILE YOU STILL HAVE A BIT OF WORK TO DO.
HOW LONG YOU THINK BEFORE THE GUARDIANS NOTICE WE'RE ACTUALLY MISSING AND COME LOOKING FOR US?
I AM GROOT.
OUCH. WELL, AT LEAST MY FUR SHOULD BE BACK IN BY THEN. LIKE I NEED GRIEF OVER THAT FROM A DWEEB WHO CALLS HIMSELF "STAR-LORD."

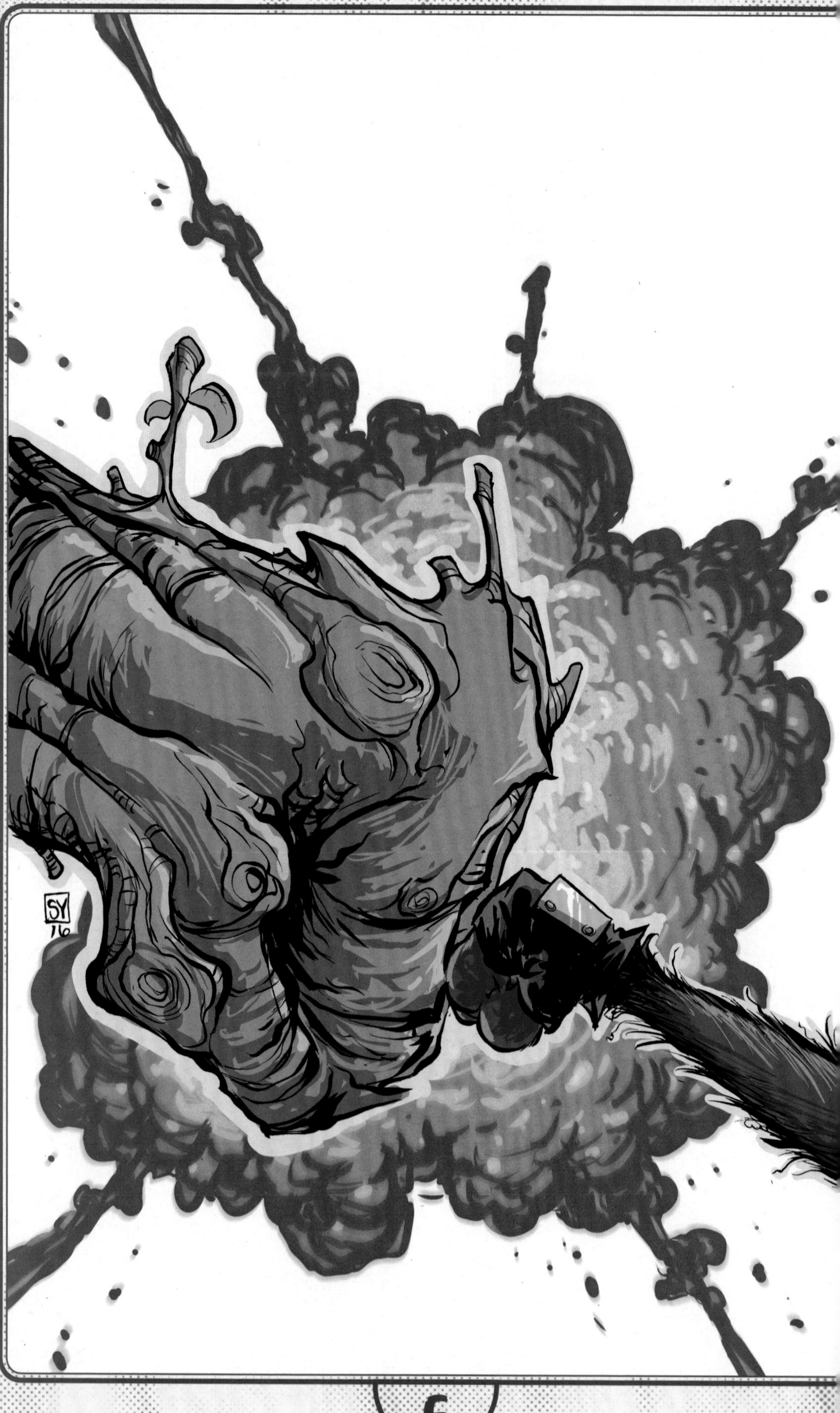

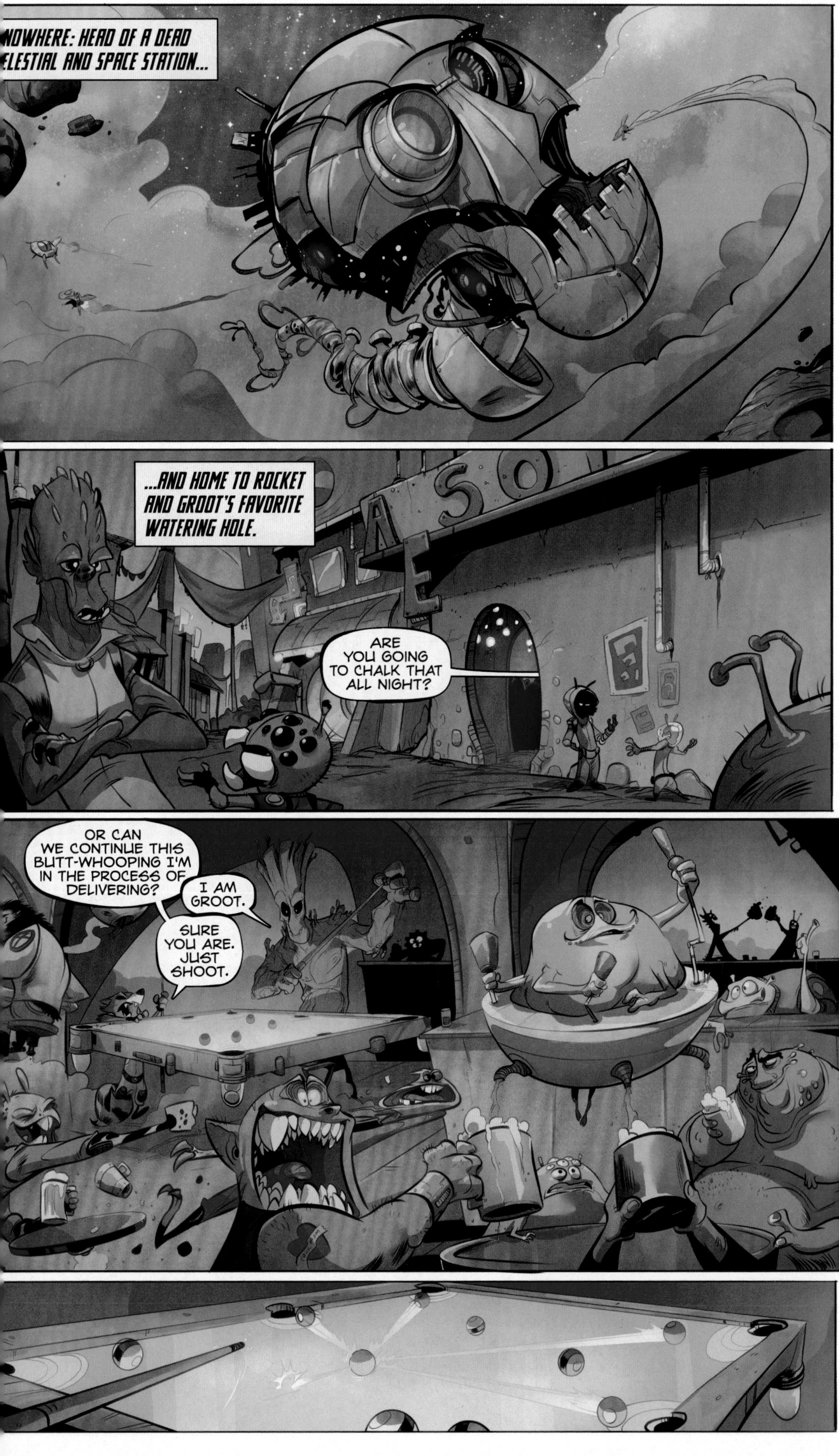
NOWHERE: HEAD OF A DEAD CELESTIAL AND SPACE STATION...
...AND HOME TO ROCKET AND GROOT'S FAVORITE WATERING HOLE.
ARE YOU GOING TO CHALK THAT ALL NIGHT?
OR CAN WE CONTINUE THIS BUTT-WHOOPING I'M IN THE PROCESS OF DELIVERING?
I AM GROOT.
SURE YOU ARE. JUST SHOOT.

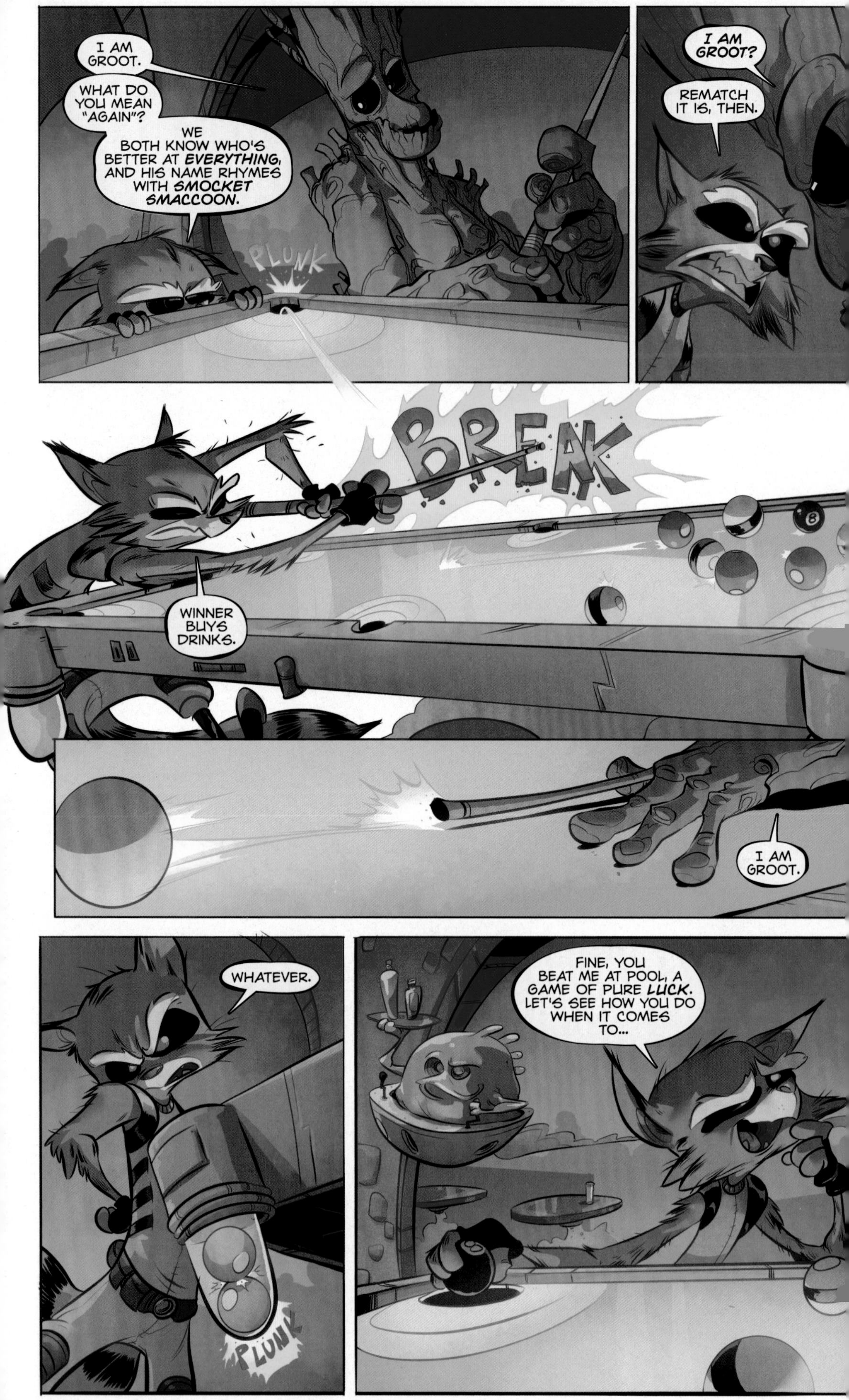

I AM GROOT.
WHAT DO YOU MEAN "AGAIN"?
WE BOTH KNOW WHO'S BETTER AT EVERYTHING, AND HIS NAME RHYMES WITH SMOCKET SMACCOON.
PLUNK
I AM GROOT?
REMATCH IT IS, THEN.
BREAK
WINNER BUYS DRINKS.
I AM GROOT.
WHATEVER.
PLUNK
FINE, YOU BEAT ME AT POOL, A GAME OF PURE LUCK. LET'S SEE HOW YOU DO WHEN IT COMES TO...

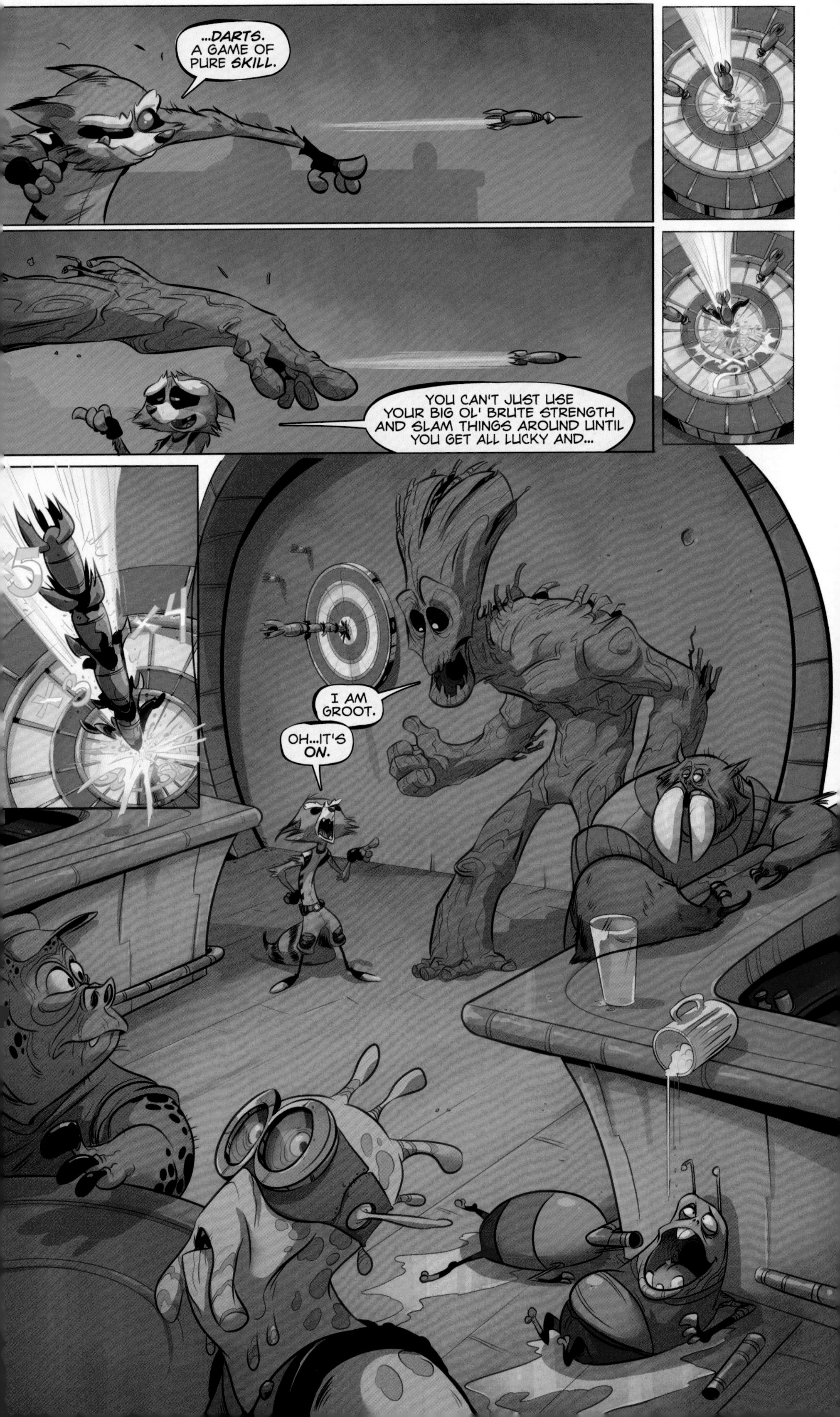
...DARTS. A GAME OF PURE SKILL.
YOU CAN'T JUST USE YOUR BIG OL' BRUTE STRENGTH AND SLAM THINGS AROUND UNTIL YOU GET ALL LUCKY AND...
I AM GROOT.
OH...IT'S ON.

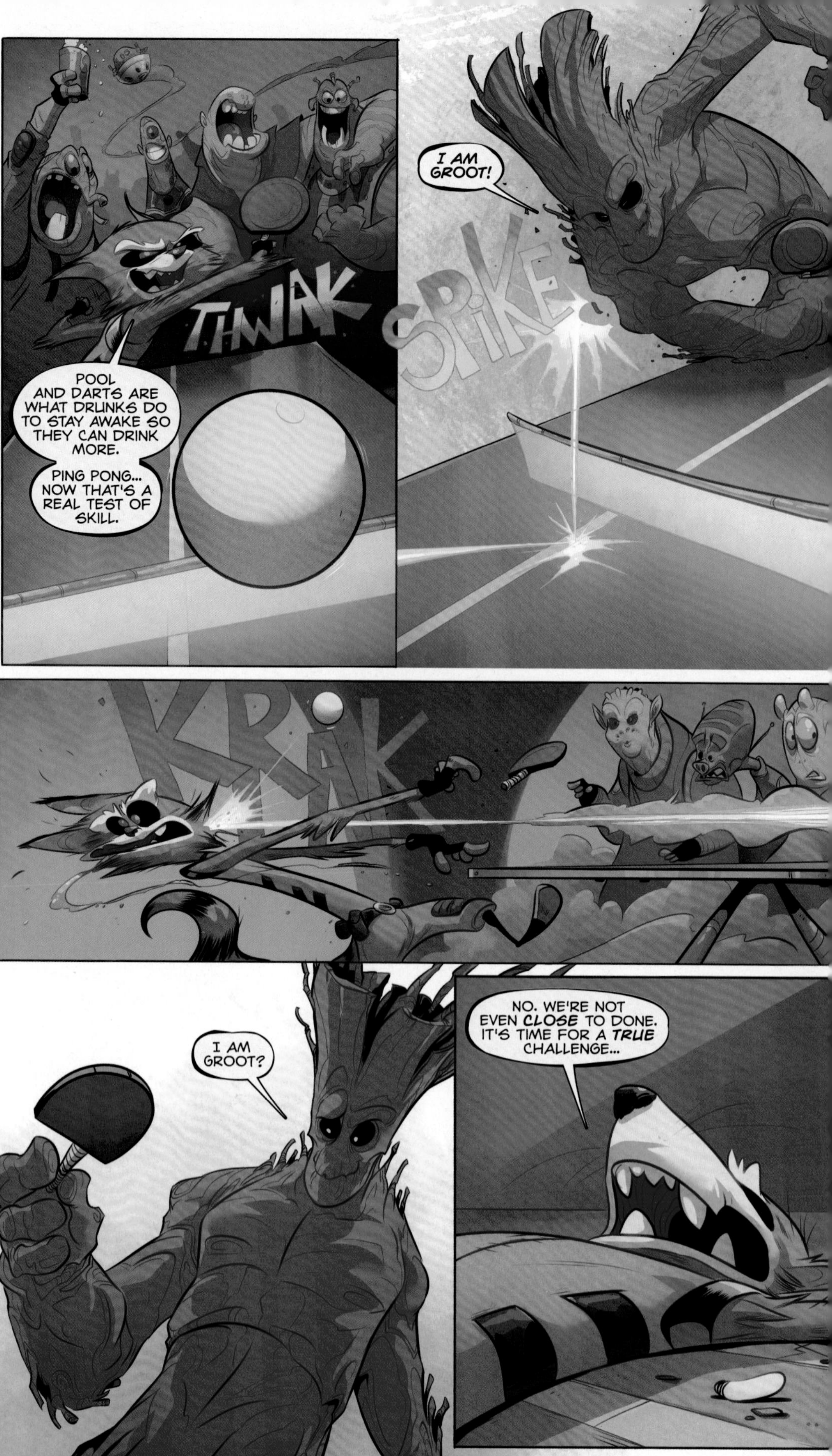
THWAK
POOL AND DARTS ARE WHAT DRUNKS DO TO STAY AWAKE SO THEY CAN DRINK MORE.
PING PONG... NOW THAT'S A REAL TEST OF SKILL.
I AM GROOT!
SPIKE
KRAK
I AM GROOT?
NO. WE'RE NOT EVEN CLOSE TO DONE. IT'S TIME FOR A TRUE CHALLENGE...

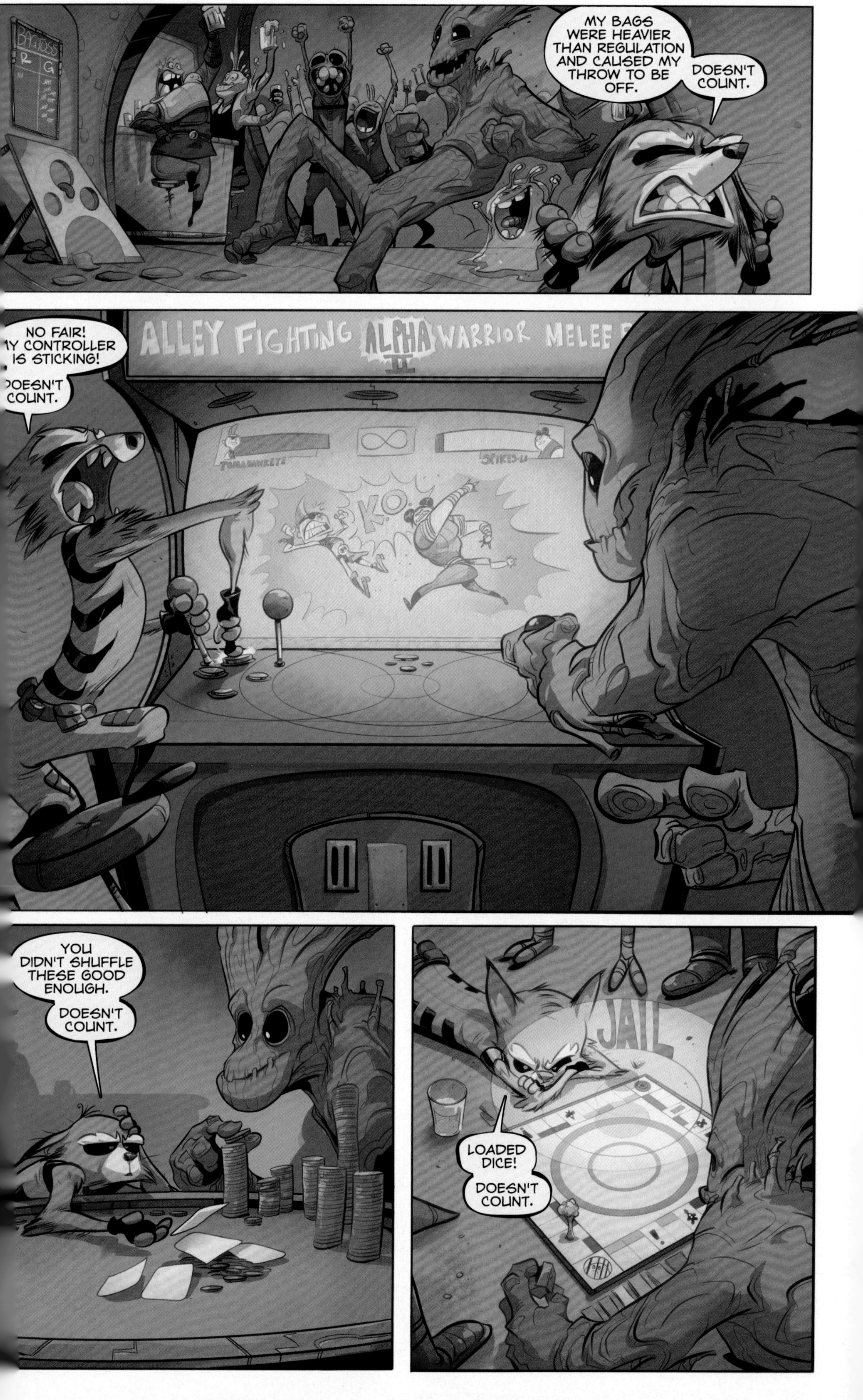
BAG TOSS
R G
MY BAGS WERE HEAVIER THAN REGULATION AND CAUSED MY THROW TO BE OFF.
DOESN'T COUNT.
ALLEY FIGHTING ALPHA II WARRIOR MELEE
K.O.
NO FAIR! MY CONTROLLER IS STICKING!
DOESN'T COUNT.
YOU DIDN'T SHUFFLE THESE GOOD ENOUGH.
DOESN'T COUNT.
JAIL
LOADED DICE!
DOESN'T COUNT.

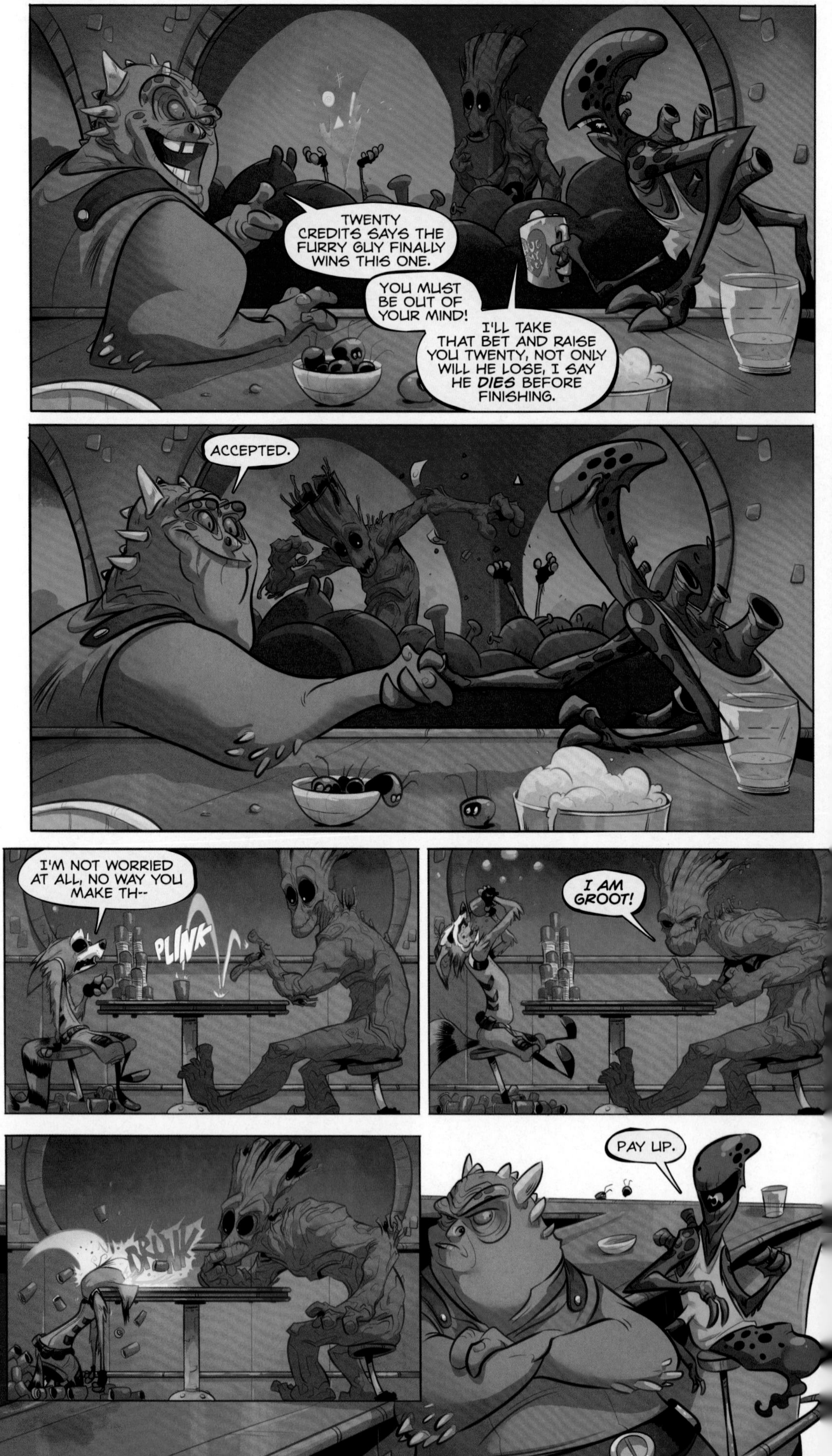
TWENTY CREDITS SAYS THE FURRY GUY FINALLY WINS THIS ONE.
YOU MUST BE OUT OF YOUR MIND!
I'LL TAKE THAT BET AND RAISE YOU TWENTY, NOT ONLY WILL HE LOSE, I SAY HE DIES BEFORE FINISHING.
ACCEPTED.
I'M NOT WORRIED AT ALL, NO WAY YOU MAKE TH--
PLINK
I AM GROOT!
PAY UP.

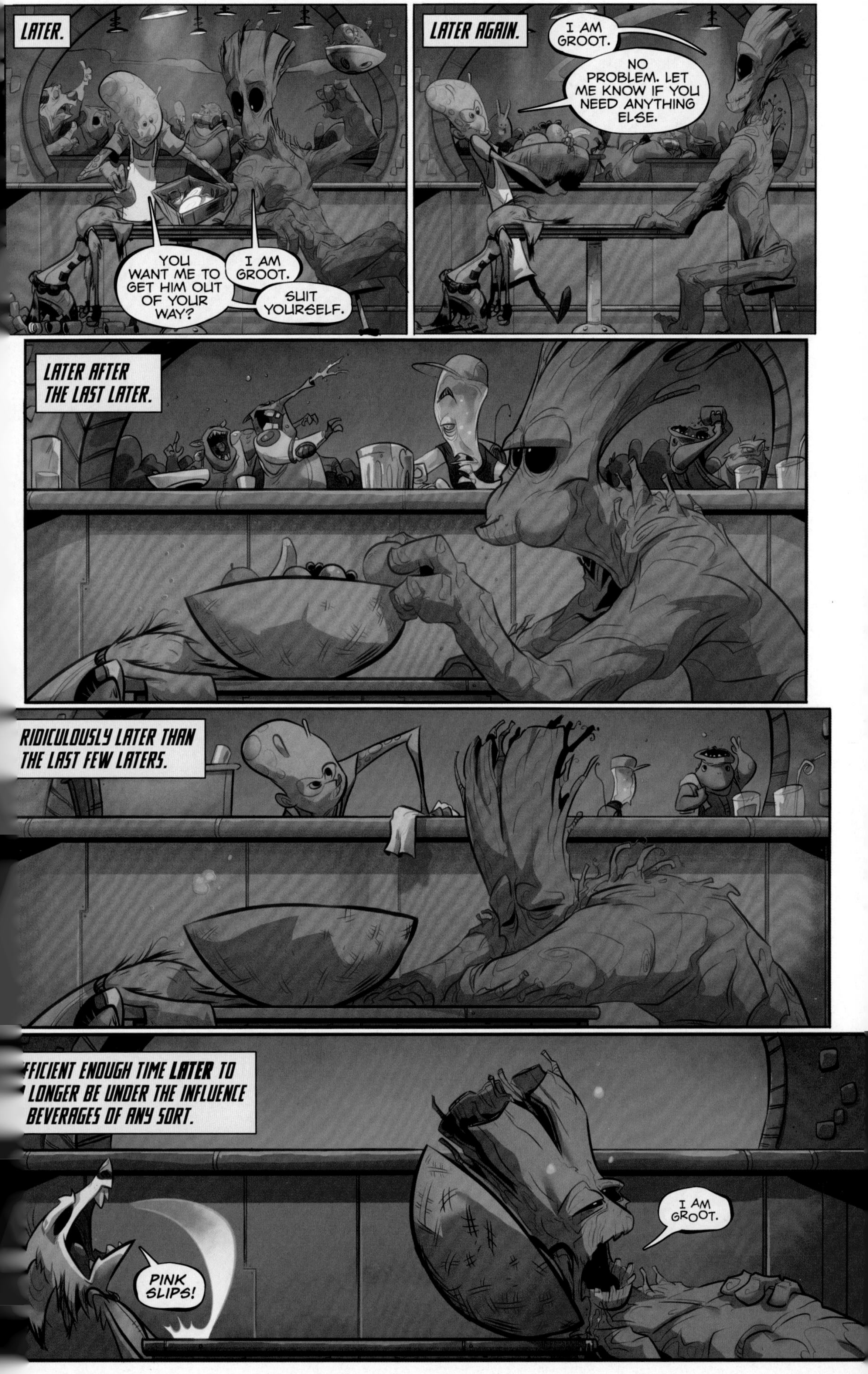
LATER.
YOU WANT ME TO GET HIM OUT OF YOUR WAY?
I AM GROOT.
SUIT YOURSELF.
LATER AGAIN.
I AM GROOT.
NO PROBLEM. LET ME KNOW IF YOU NEED ANYTHING ELSE.
LATER AFTER THE LAST LATER.
RIDICULOUSLY LATER THAN THE LAST FEW LATERS.
FFICIENT ENOUGH TIME LATER TO
LONGER BE UNDER THE INFLUENCE
BEVERAGES OF ANY SORT.
PINK SLIPS!
I AM GROOT.

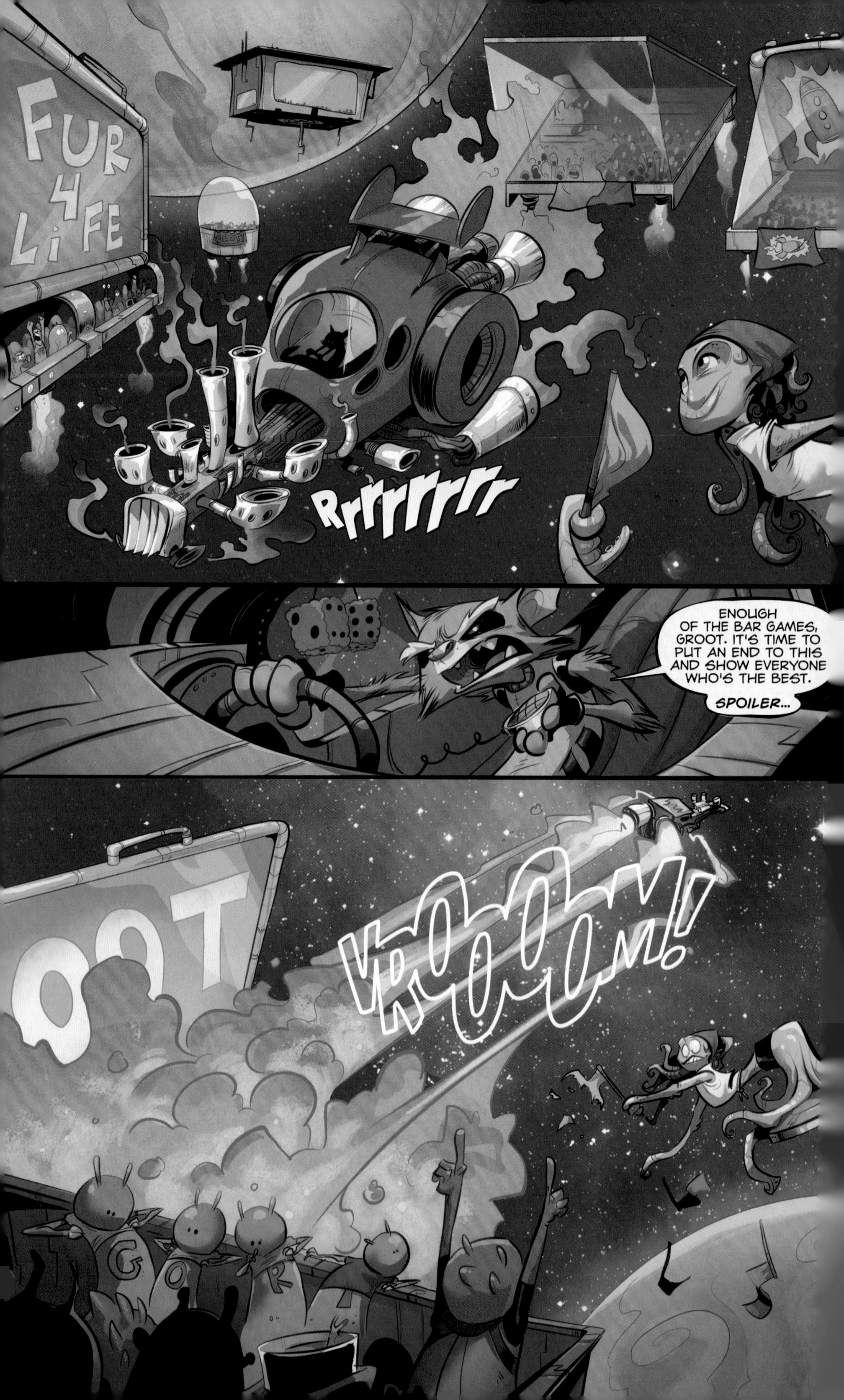
FUR 4 LiFE
Rrrrrrrr
ENOUGH OF THE BAR GAMES, GROOT. IT'S TIME TO PUT AN END TO THIS AND SHOW EVERYONE WHO'S THE BEST.
SPOILER...
OOT
VROOOOM!
G
O
R

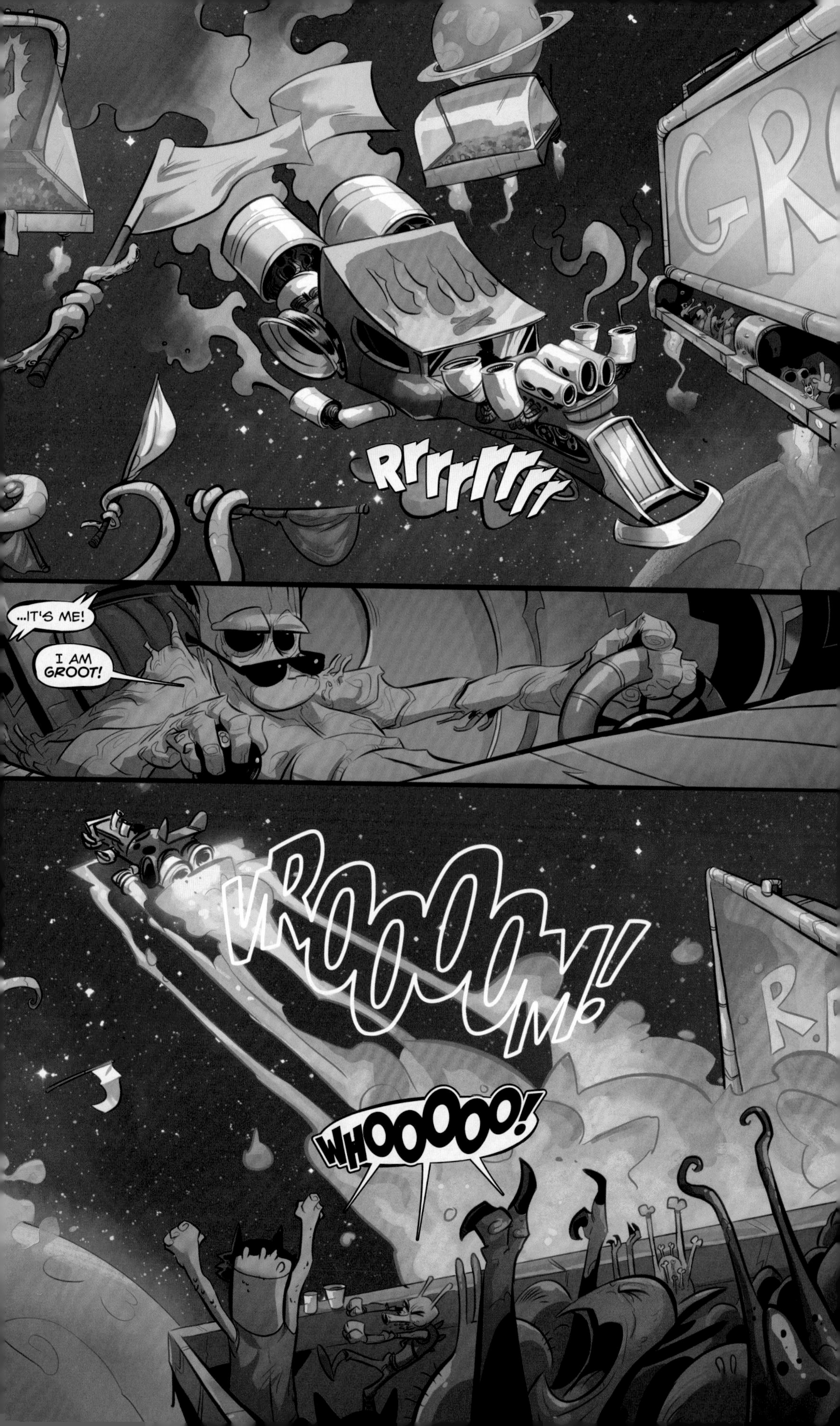
GRO
RRRRRRR
...IT'S ME!
I AM GROOT!
VROOOOM!
WHOOOOOO!

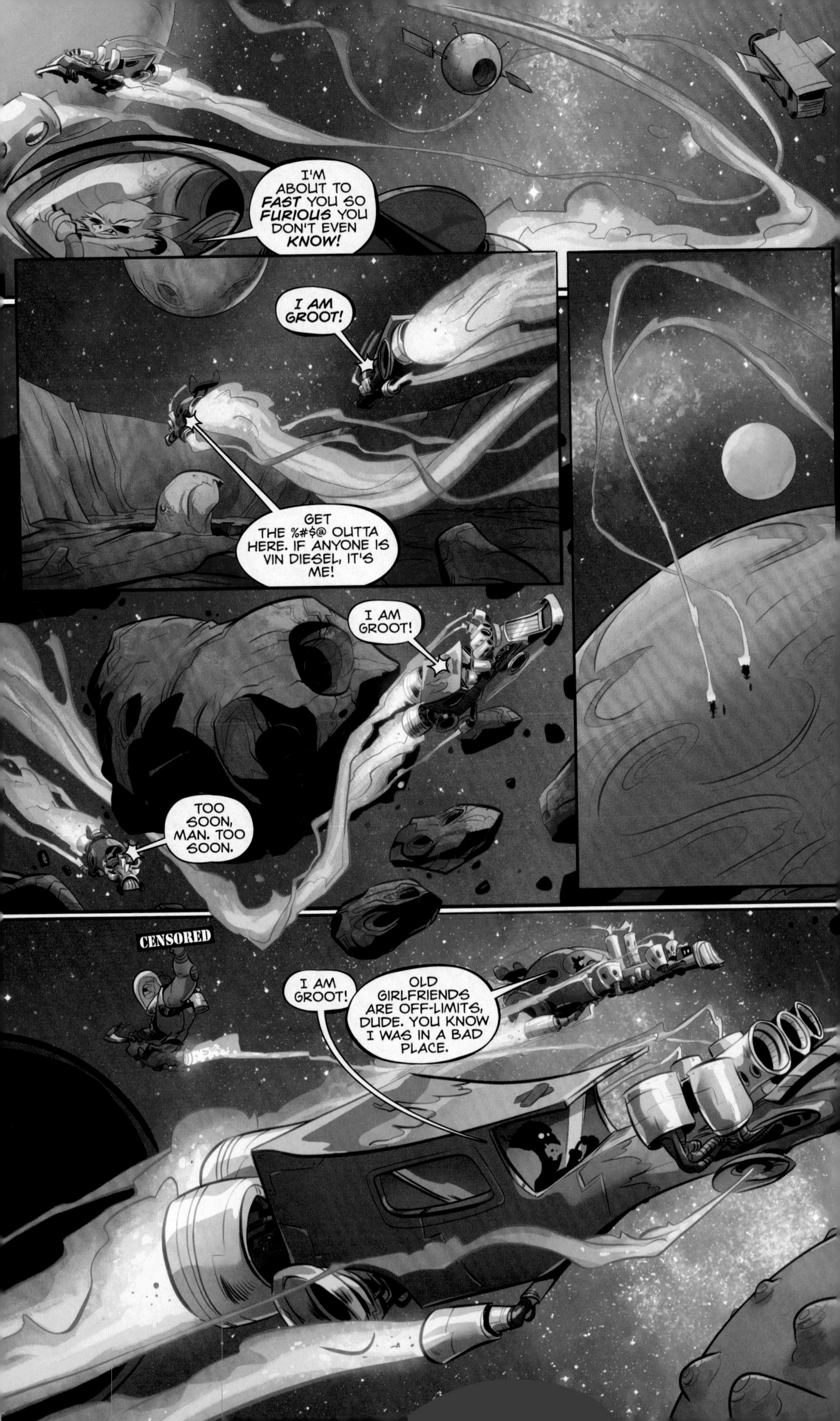

I'M ABOUT TO FAST YOU SO FURIOUS YOU DON'T EVEN KNOW!
I AM GROOT!
GET THE %#$@ OUTTA HERE. IF ANYONE IS VIN DIESEL, IT'S ME!
I AM GROOT!
TOO SOON, MAN. TOO SOON.
CENSORED
I AM GROOT!
OLD GIRLFRIENDS ARE OFF-LIMITS, DUDE. YOU KNOW I WAS IN A BAD PLACE.

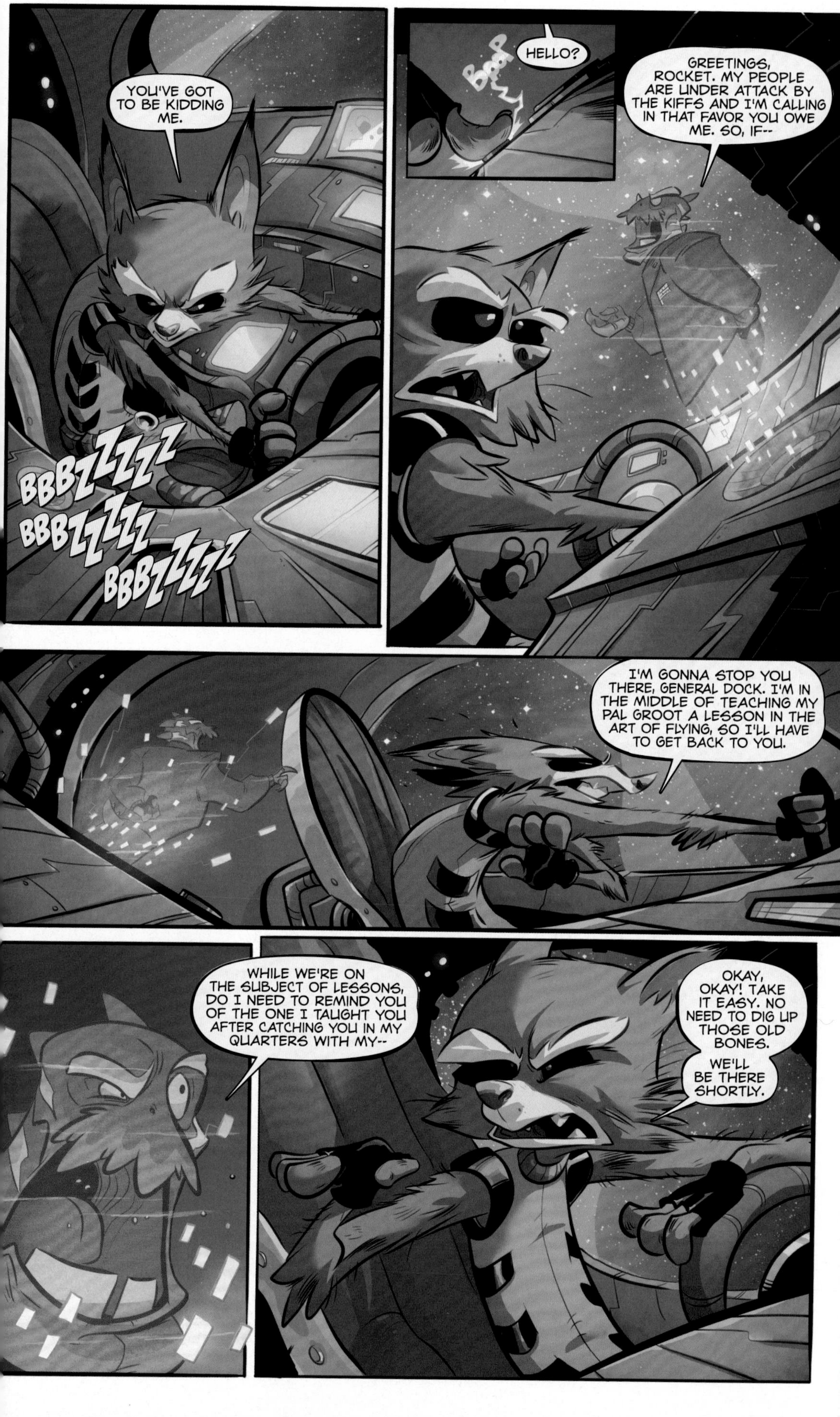
YOU'VE GOT TO BE KIDDING ME.
BBBZZZZZZ
BBBZZZZZZ
BBBZZZZZZ
BOOP
HELLO?
GREETINGS, ROCKET. MY PEOPLE ARE UNDER ATTACK BY THE KIFFS AND I'M CALLING IN THAT FAVOR YOU OWE ME. SO, IF--
I'M GONNA STOP YOU THERE, GENERAL DOCK. I'M IN THE MIDDLE OF TEACHING MY PAL GROOT A LESSON IN THE ART OF FLYING, SO I'LL HAVE TO GET BACK TO YOU.
WHILE WE'RE ON THE SUBJECT OF LESSONS, DO I NEED TO REMIND YOU OF THE ONE I TAUGHT YOU AFTER CATCHING YOU IN MY QUARTERS WITH MY--
OKAY, OKAY! TAKE IT EASY. NO NEED TO DIG UP THOSE OLD BONES.
WE'LL BE THERE SHORTLY.

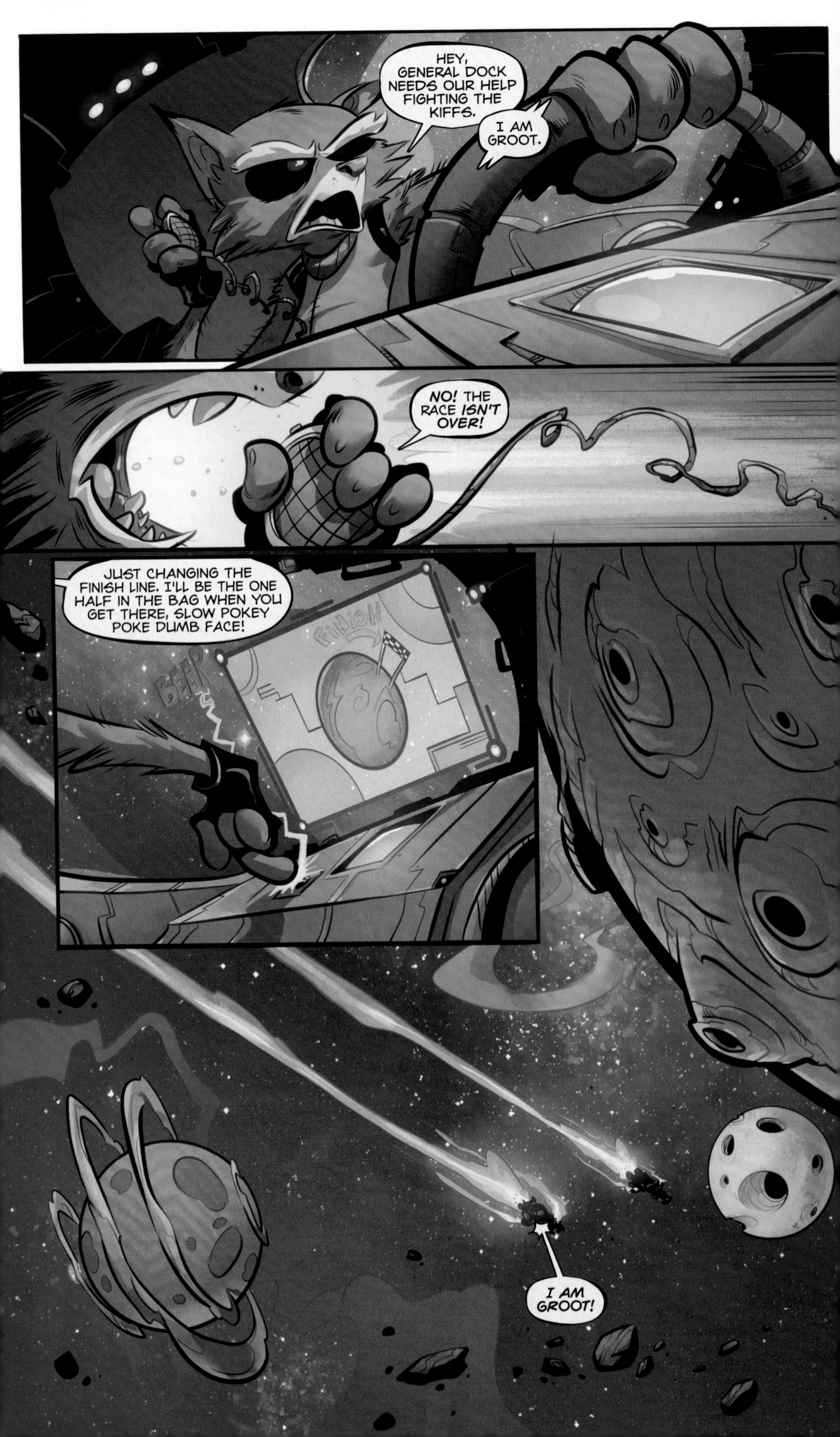
HEY, GENERAL DOCK NEEDS OUR HELP FIGHTING THE KIFFS.
I AM GROOT.
NO! THE RACE ISN'T OVER!
JUST CHANGING THE FINISH LINE. I'LL BE THE ONE HALF IN THE BAG WHEN YOU GET THERE, SLOW POKEY POKE DUMB FACE!
BEEP
FINISH
I AM GROOT!

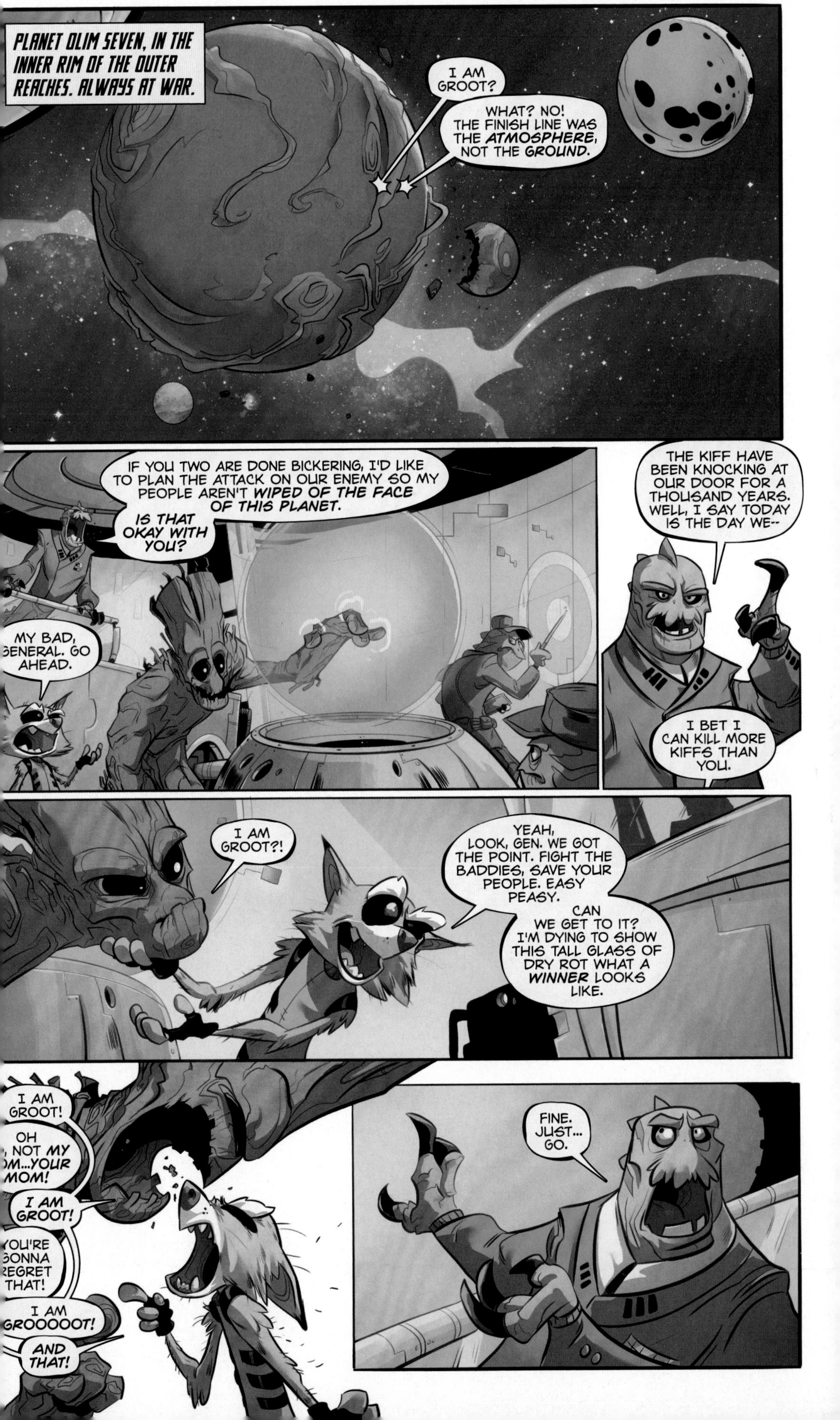
PLANET OLIM SEVEN, IN THE INNER RIM OF THE OUTER REACHES. ALWAYS AT WAR.
I AM GROOT?
WHAT? NO! THE FINISH LINE WAS THE ATMOSPHERE, NOT THE GROUND.
IF YOU TWO ARE DONE BICKERING, I'D LIKE TO PLAN THE ATTACK ON OUR ENEMY SO MY PEOPLE AREN'T WIPED OF THE FACE OF THIS PLANET.
IS THAT OKAY WITH YOU?
MY BAD, ENERAL. GO AHEAD.
THE KIFF HAVE BEEN KNOCKING AT OUR DOOR FOR A THOUSAND YEARS. WELL, I SAY TODAY IS THE DAY WE--
I BET I CAN KILL MORE KIFFS THAN YOU.
I AM GROOT?!
YEAH, LOOK, GEN. WE GOT THE POINT. FIGHT THE BADDIES, SAVE YOUR PEOPLE. EASY PEASY.
CAN WE GET TO IT? I'M DYING TO SHOW THIS TALL GLASS OF DRY ROT WHAT A WINNER LOOKS LIKE.
I AM GROOT!
I AM GROOT!
I AM GROOOOOT!
AND THAT!
FINE. JUST... GO.

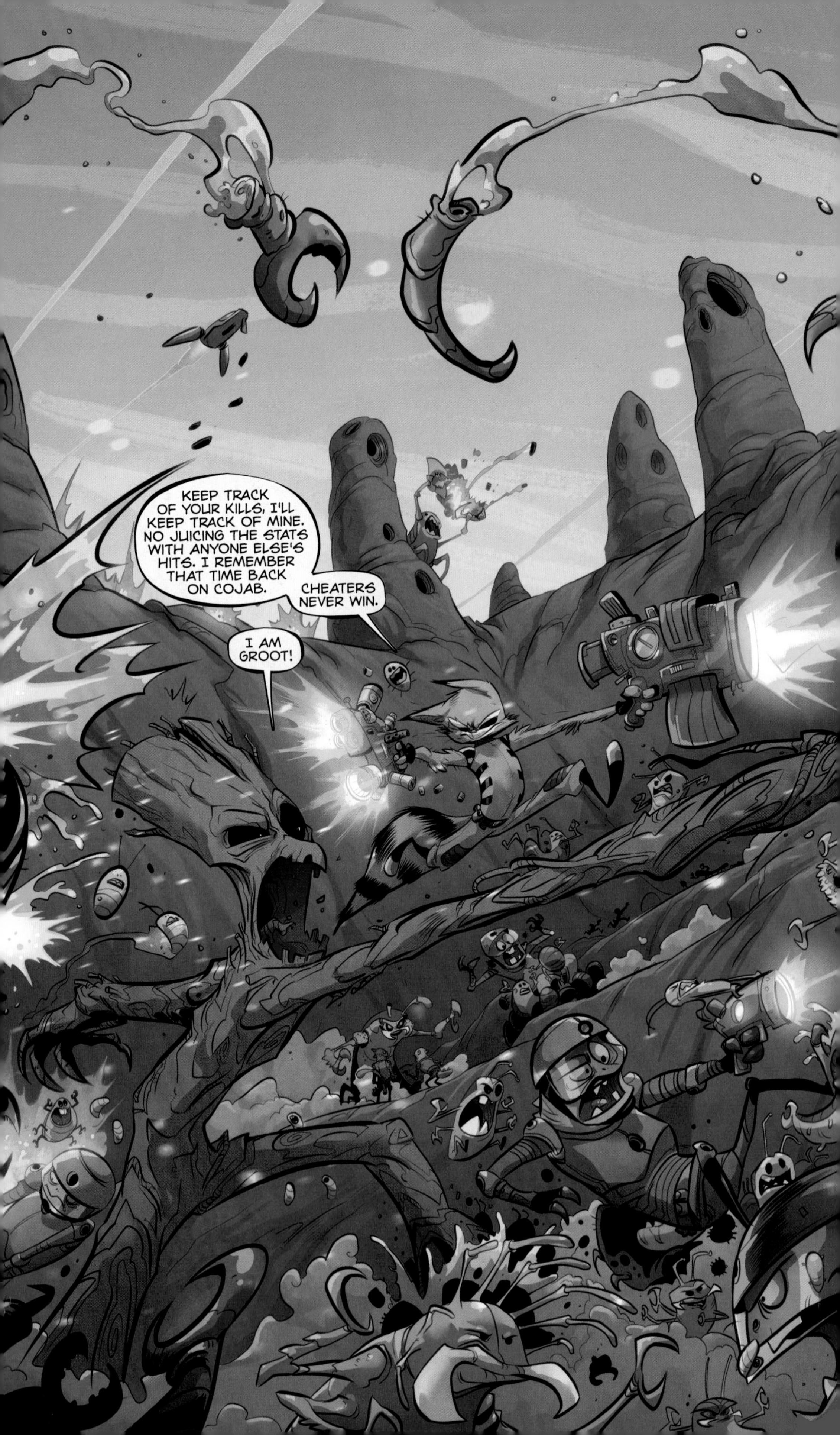
KEEP TRACK OF YOUR KILLS, I'LL KEEP TRACK OF MINE. NO JUICING THE STATS WITH ANYONE ELSE'S HITS. I REMEMBER THAT TIME BACK ON COJAB.
CHEATERS NEVER WIN.
I AM GROOT!

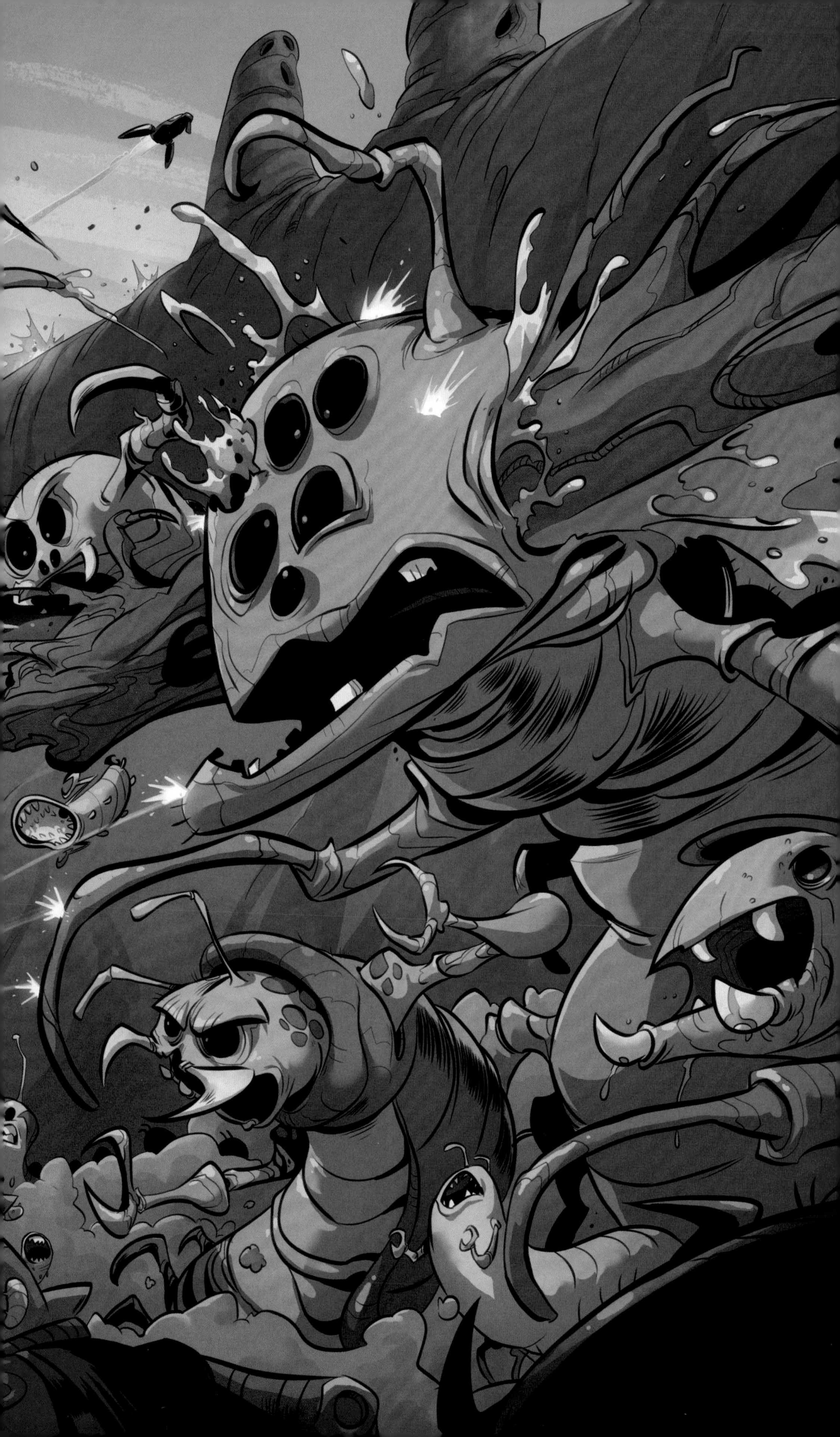

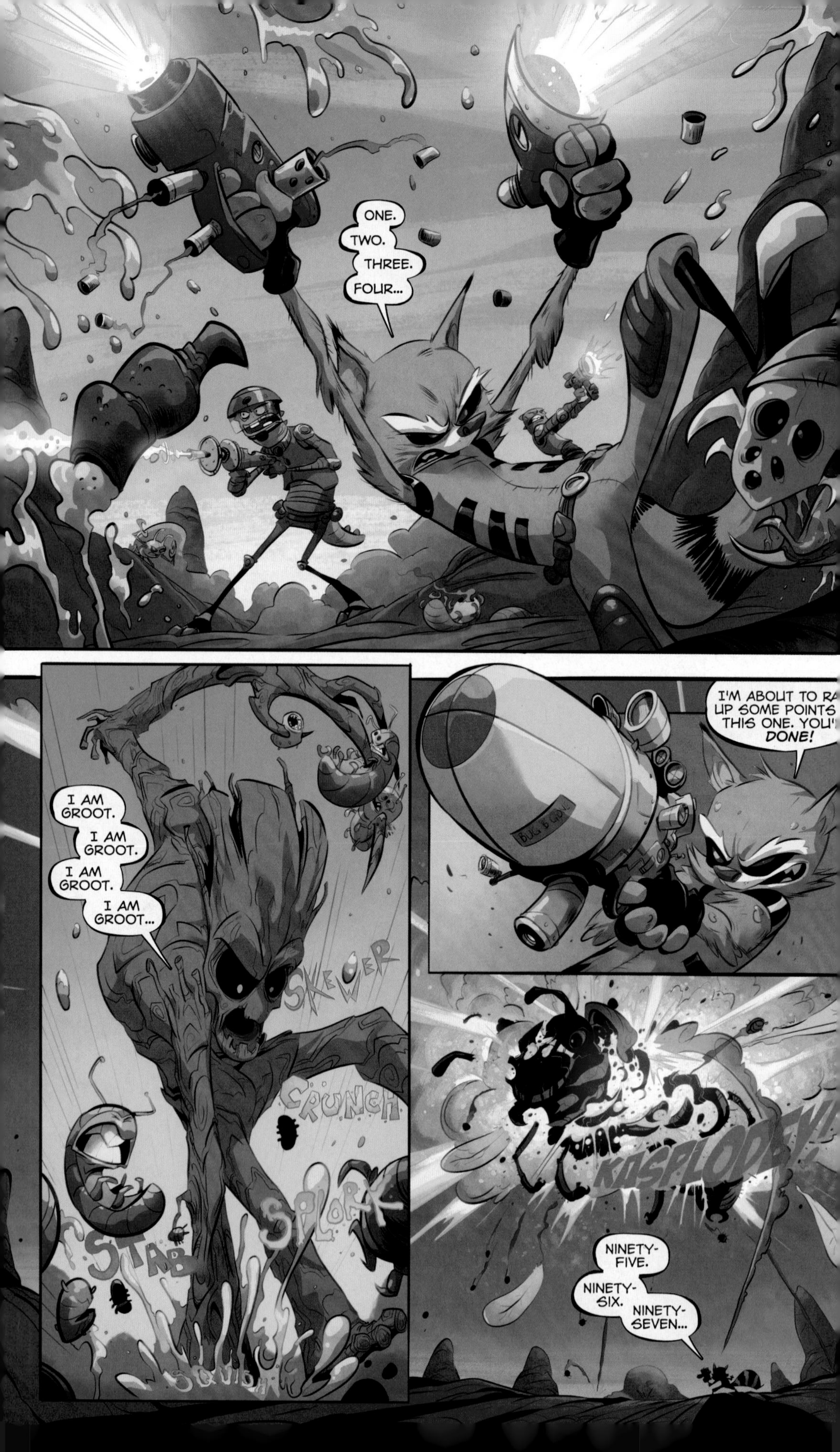
ONE. TWO. THREE. FOUR...
I AM GROOT. I AM GROOT. I AM GROOT. I AM GROOT...
SKEWER
CRUNCH
SPLORK
STAB
SQUISH
I'M ABOUT TO RA UP SOME POINTS THIS ONE. YOU' DONE!
KASPLODEY!
NINETY-FIVE. NINETY-SIX. NINETY-SEVEN...

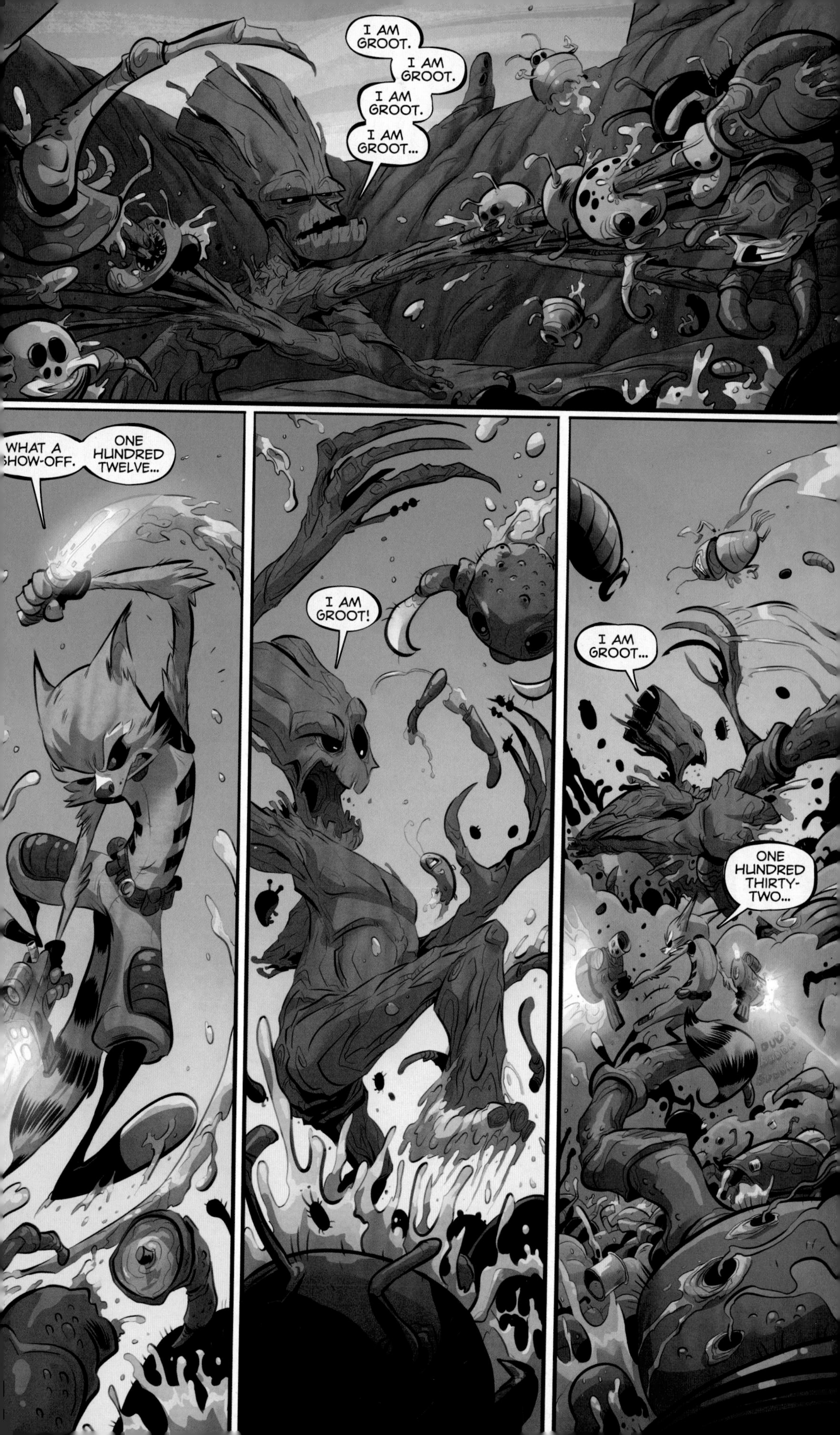
I AM GROOT.
I AM GROOT.
I AM GROOT.
I AM GROOT...
WHAT A SHOW-OFF.
ONE HUNDRED TWELVE...
I AM GROOT!
I AM GROOT...
ONE HUNDRED THIRTY-TWO...

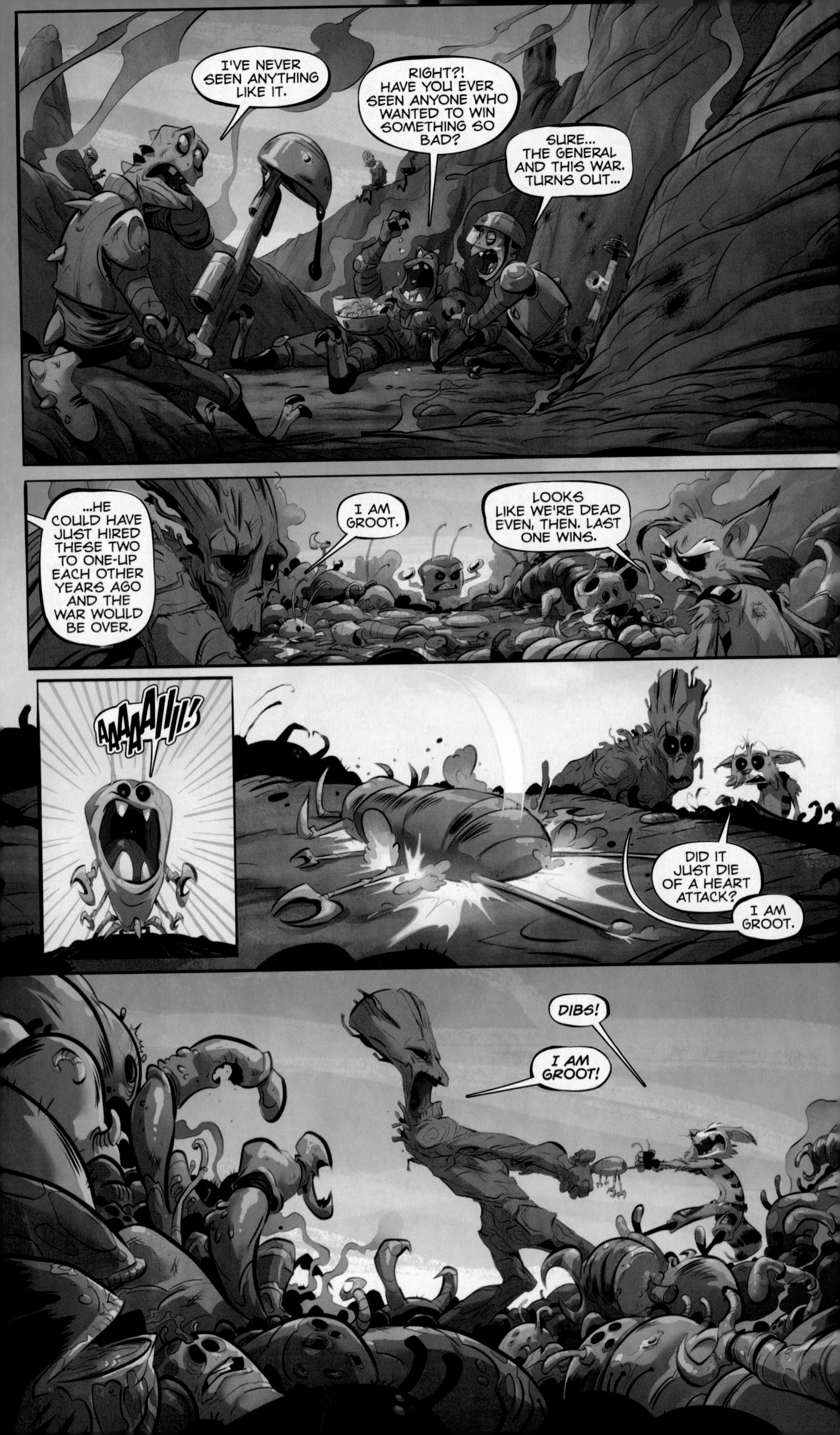
I'VE NEVER SEEN ANYTHING LIKE IT.
RIGHT?! HAVE YOU EVER SEEN ANYONE WHO WANTED TO WIN SOMETHING SO BAD?
SURE... THE GENERAL AND THIS WAR. TURNS OUT...
...HE COULD HAVE JUST HIRED THESE TWO TO ONE-UP EACH OTHER YEARS AGO AND THE WAR WOULD BE OVER.
I AM GROOT.
LOOKS LIKE WE'RE DEAD EVEN, THEN. LAST ONE WINS.
AAAAAIIIII!
DID IT JUST DIE OF A HEART ATTACK?
I AM GROOT.
DIBS!
I AM GROOT!

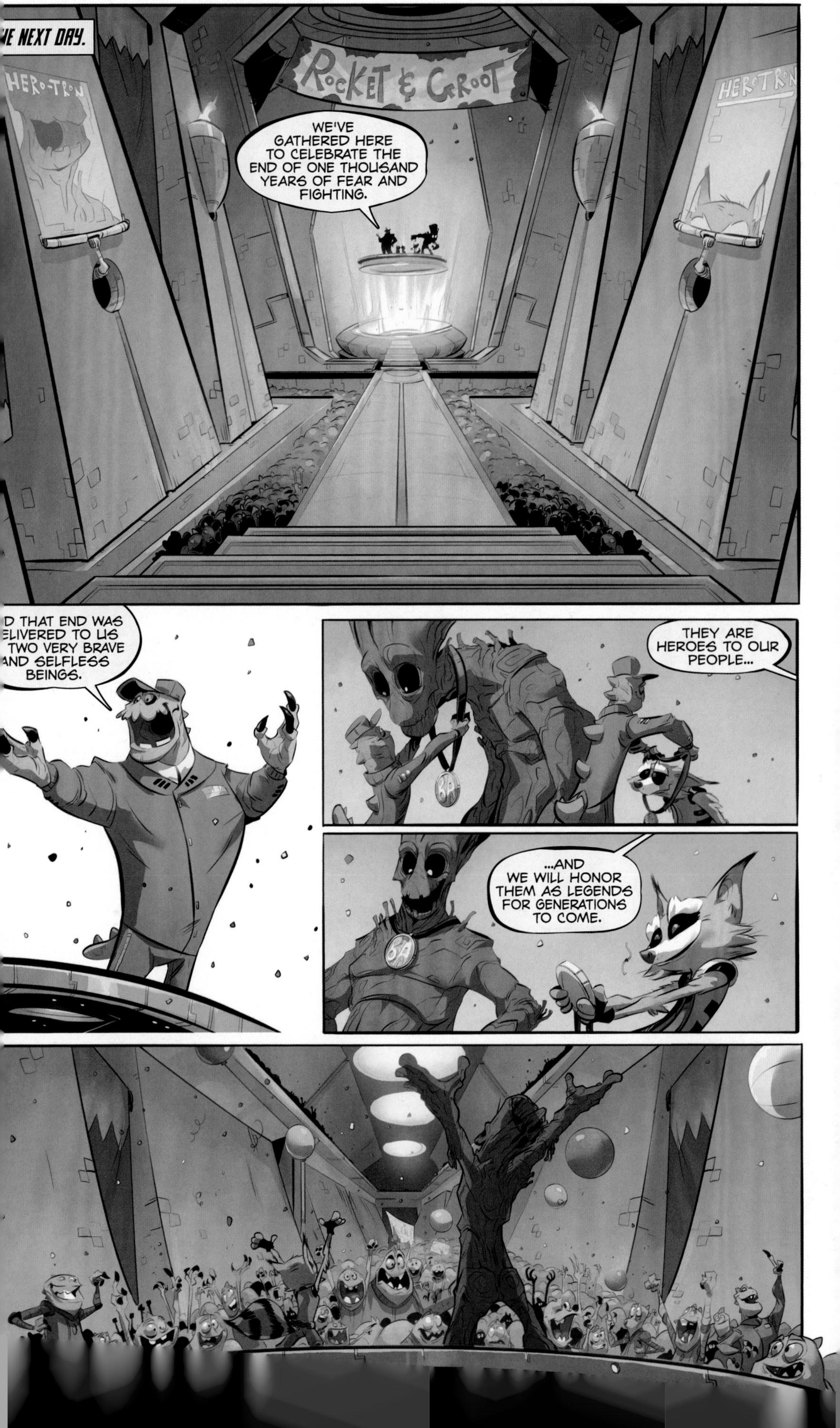
E NEXT DAY.
ROCKET & GROOT
HERO-TRON
HERO-TRON
WE'VE GATHERED HERE TO CELEBRATE THE END OF ONE THOUSAND YEARS OF FEAR AND FIGHTING.
D THAT END WAS ELIVERED TO US TWO VERY BRAVE AND SELFLESS BEINGS.
THEY ARE HEROES TO OUR PEOPLE...
...AND WE WILL HONOR THEM AS LEGENDS FOR GENERATIONS TO COME.

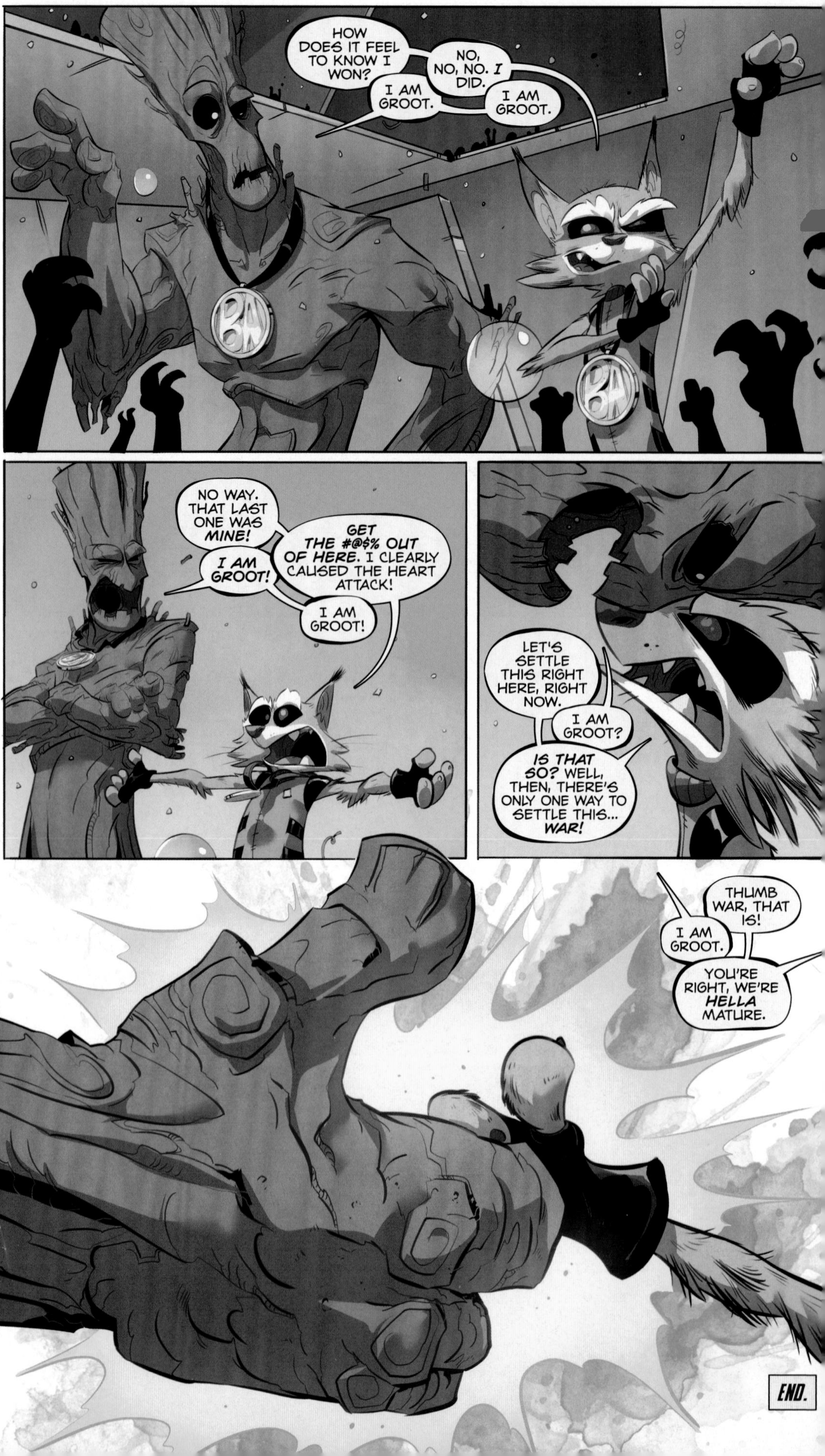
HOW DOES IT FEEL TO KNOW I WON?
NO, NO, NO. I DID.
I AM GROOT.
I AM GROOT.
NO WAY. THAT LAST ONE WAS MINE!
I AM GROOT!
GET THE #@$% OUT OF HERE. I CLEARLY CAUSED THE HEART ATTACK!
I AM GROOT!
LET'S SETTLE THIS RIGHT HERE, RIGHT NOW.
I AM GROOT?
IS THAT SO? WELL, THEN, THERE'S ONLY ONE WAY TO SETTLE THIS... WAR!
THUMB WAR, THAT IS!
I AM GROOT.
YOU'RE RIGHT, WE'RE HELLA MATURE.
END.

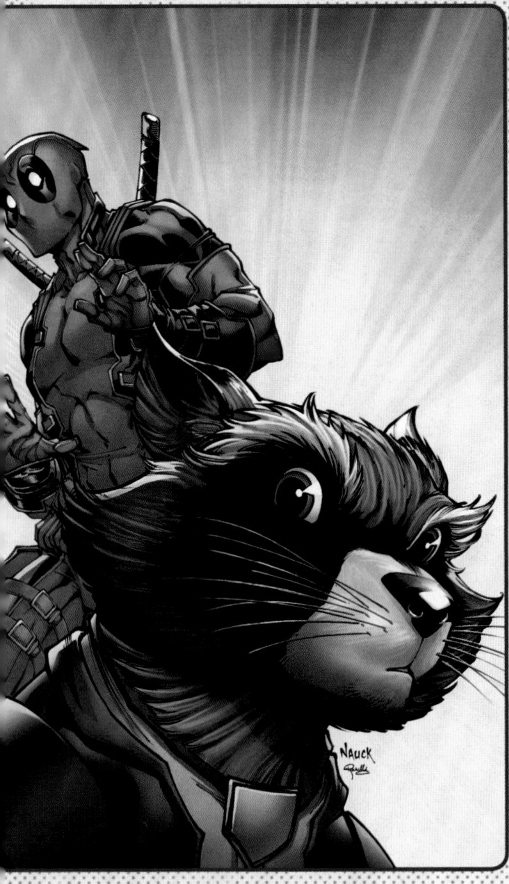

TODD NAUCK & RACHELLE ROSENBERG
1 DEADPOOL VARIANT

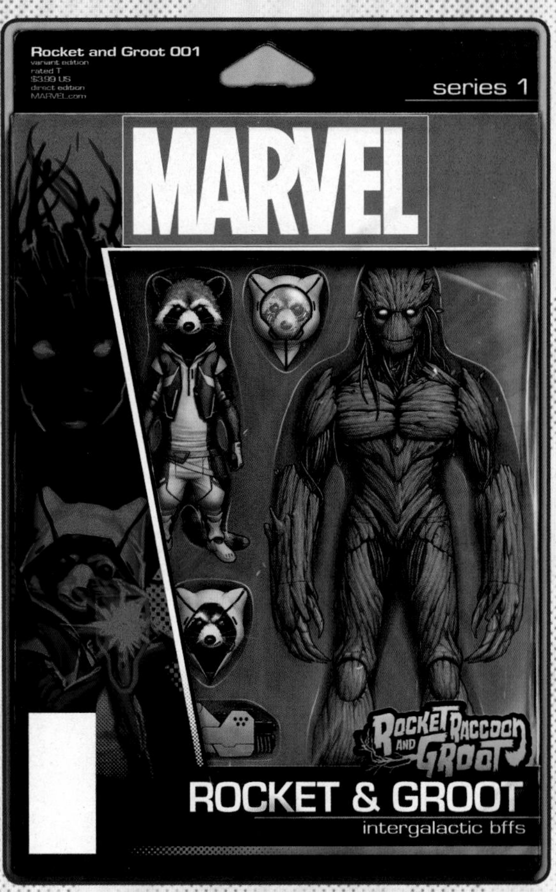

Rocket and Groot 001
variant edition
rated T
$3.99 US
direct edition
MARVEL.com
series 1
MARVEL
Rocket Raccoon and Groot
ROCKET & GROOT
intergalactic bffs

JOHN TYLER CHRISTOPHER
1 ACTION FIGURE VARIANT

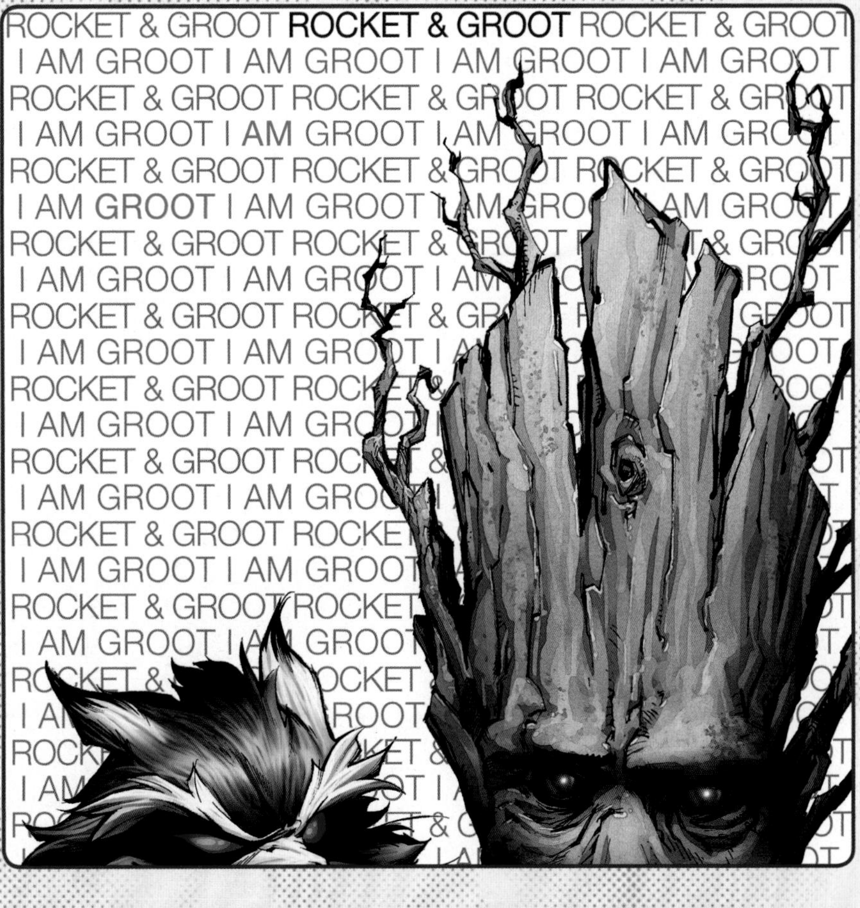

ROCKET & GROOT ROCKET & GROOT ROCKET & GROOT
I AM GROOT I AM GROOT I AM GROOT I AM GROOT

KHARY RANDOLPH
1 HIP-HOP VARIANT

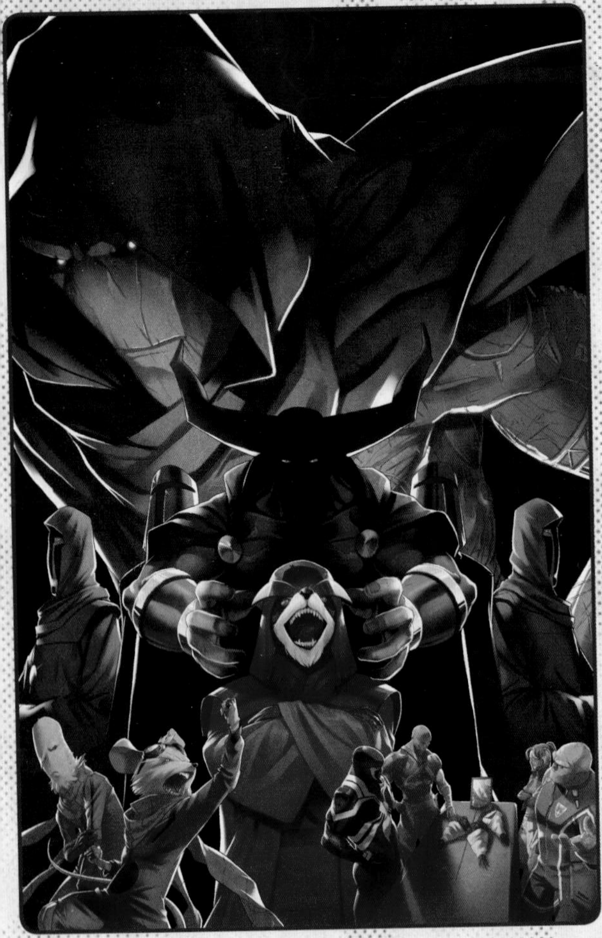

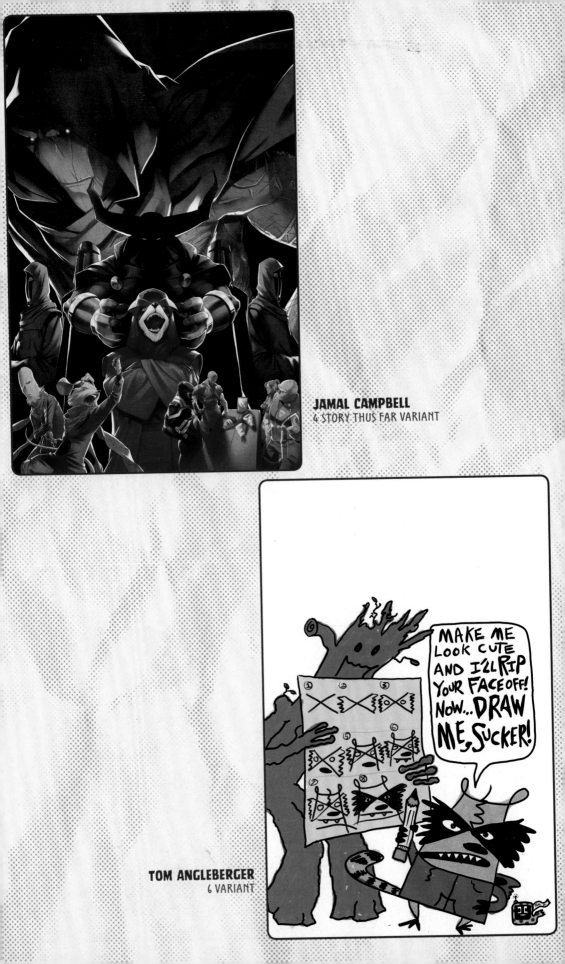

JAMAL CAMPBELL
4 STORY THUS FAR VARIANT

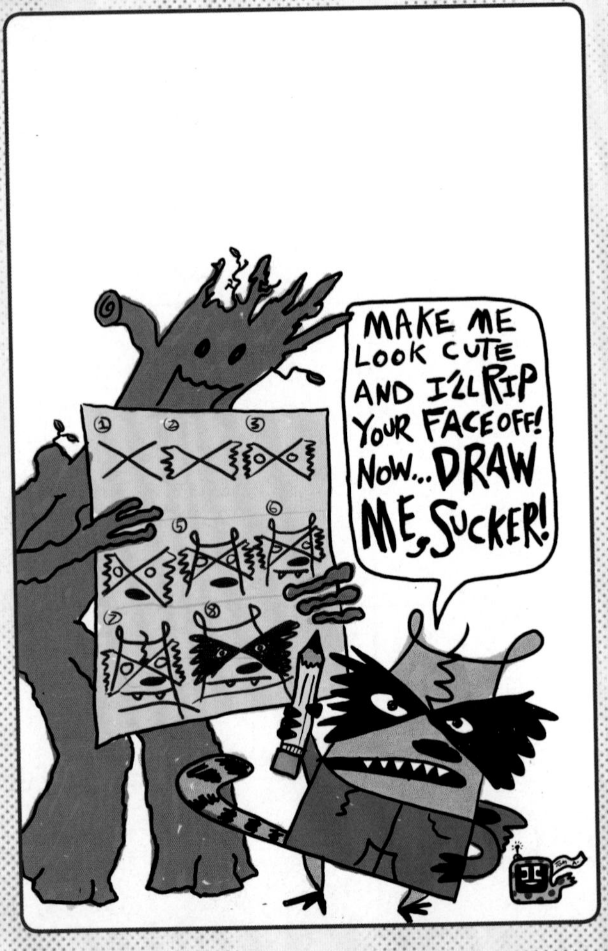
MAKE ME LOOK CUTE AND I'LL RIP YOUR FACE OFF! NOW... DRAW ME, SUCKER!

TOM ANGLEBERGER
6 VARIANT